Management Accounting
Making it world class

Ralph William Adler

BUTTERWORTH
HEINEMANN

OXFORD   AUCKLAND   BOSTON   JOHANNESBURG   MELBOURNE   NEW DELHI

Butterworth-Heinemann
Linacre House, Jordan Hill, Oxford OX2 8DP
225 Wildwood Avenue, Woburn, MA 01801-2041
A division of Reed Educational and Professional Publishing Ltd

A member of the Reed Elsevier plc group

First published 1999

British Library Cataloguing in Publication Data
Adler, Ralph
    Management accounting: making it world class
    1. Managerial accounting
    I. Title
    658.1′511

ISBN 0 7506 4144 4

Printed and bound in Great Britain by
Biddles Ltd, Guildford and King's Lynn

Contents

List of figures   ix
List of tables   x
Preface   xi
Acknowledgements   xiii

1 Introduction   **1**
Plan of the book   3
References   4

Part One Becoming a World Class Organization

2 World class organizations: conventional wisdom   **7**
Discovering the secret of excellent organizations   8
Working definitions of JIT and TQM   10
JIT as a business philosophy   11
TQM as a business philosophy   13
Attempts to include advanced manufacturing technology as a
   component of a WCO   14
Summary   15
References   15

3 World class organizations: the missing link   **16**
What is VAA?   17
How JIT, TQM, and VAA reinforce one another and support an
   organization's quest to become a WCO   19
Inventory planning   20
Pull inventory systems   22
Advanced manufacturing technology   23
Employee empowerment   23
Quality monitoring   24
Advanced accounting approaches   25

Summary   26
References   26

Part Two Advanced Costing Methods

4 Activity-based costing   **29**
The problems with traditional cost accounting systems   30
Symptoms of an obsolete cost system   32
Developing a better costing system   33
Illuminating the 'hidden factory'   34
What is ABC?   35
The mechanics of ABC   37
Using ABC to cost more than just products   39
Situations most likely to benefit from ABC implementation   42
Summary   45
References   45

5 Cost of quality   **46**
Tracing the roots of the quality movement   47
What is quality?   48
Accounting for cost of quality   55
What are cost of quality reporting systems?   56
The Honda approach to quality costing   57
Juran's cost of quality approach   59
Taguchi's quadratic loss function   60
Summary   60
References   61

6 Target costing activity-based   **62**
The history of target cost management   64
The five stages of target cost management   66
Further target cost management issues   75
Summary   76
References   76

Part Three Advanced Performance Measures

7 Financial performance measures   **81**
Return-on-investment (ROI)   82
Residual income (RI)   83
Shareholder value analysis (SVA)   86
Economic value added (EVA)   89
A comparison of the four corporate performance measures   94
Summary   96
References   96

8 Non-financial performance measures   **98**
  Impediments to the adoption of non-financial performance measures   99
  Catalysts of non-financial performance measures   99
  How strategy precedes the development of non-financial performance
    measures   101
  Examples of non-financial performance measures   101
  Striking the right balance   109
  Summary   110
  References   111

9 Benchmarking   **112**
  Benchmarking: what it is and where it came from   113
  Why is benchmarking important?   116
  Types of benchmarking   118
  The stages of benchmarking   121
  The limitations of benchmarking   125
  Summary   127
  References   127

Part Four Strategic Management Issues

10 Strategic cost management   **131**
  What is wrong with the traditional cost accounting paradigm?   132
  What is strategic cost management?   135
  Executing SCM   141
  Summary   143
  References   144

11 Strategic investment decisions   **145**
  A classic case of cost-benefit analysis?   146
  The shortcomings of traditional, financially focused approaches
    to strategic investment decisions   148
  Alternative approaches to evaluating and selecting strategic
    investment proposals   153
  Summary   160
  References   160

12 Strategic dimensions to transfer pricing and outsourcing   **162**
  The importance of transfer pricing   163
  Strategic dimensions of transfer pricing   164
  Selecting transfer prices that support organizational strategy   166
  Using organizational strategy to determine preferred transfer pricing
    methods   168
  Implications of the transfer pricing model for managers   172
  Summary   173
  References   173

13 A destiny for management accounting   **175**
   The evolving nature of management accounting   176
   Where to from here?   178
   References   180

List of abbreviations   181
Glossary   183
Name index   188
Company index   191
Subject index   193

Figures

2.1 Traditional conception of a WCO   9
2.2 Illustration of how inventory serves to conceal organizational problems   11
3.1 Revised conception of a WCO   19
3.2 The interconnected nature of JIT, TQM, and VAA   21
4.1 Activity and cost hierarchy   36
4.2 Primary applications of ABC information   39
4.3 Situational determinants of ABC usefulness   43
5.1 Taguchi's loss function   53
5.2 Juran's economic conformance level approach   59
6.1 New products: commitment of costs versus cost expenditures   65
8.1 The performance pyramid   108
9.1 Benchmarking customer retention rates   115
9.2 Benchmarking employee retention rates   115
9.3 A customer service staircase showing the interrelationships between
benchmarking and TQM   117
9.4 Flow diagram of steps to benchmarking   122
10.1 An illustration of a resource grid   138
10.2 Steps to the implementation of SCM   142
12.1 A strategic transfer pricing model   167
13.1 Evolution of the management accounting role   177

Tables

5.1 A comparison of Deming, Juran, Crosby, and Taguchi's
approaches to quality   54
5.2 Cost of quality categorizations   57
7.1 Palo Alto Software's five-year cash flow projections   89
7.2 SVA calculation for Palo Alto Software   89
7.3 EVA adjustments needed to capital and NOPAT   91
7.4 Calculating NOPAT for 1997 and 1998   93
7.5 Calculation of economic capital for 1997 and 1998   94
7.6 EVA for 1997 (assuming a 12% cost of capital)   94
7.7 EVA for 1998 (assuming a 12% cost of capital)   94
9.1 An illustrative example of organizational support processes and
associated activities to benchmark   119
9.2 Xerox's approach to benchmarking   121
9.3 AT&T's approach to benchmarking   121
9.4 Alcoa's approach to benchmarking   122
10.1 Porter's list of cost drivers   141
11.1 AMT benefits and factors that serve to make these benefits possible   147
11.2 Strategic investment decision making using MADM   156
11.3 Strategic investment decision making using the uncertainty method   159
12.1 A glossary of transfer pricing terms   168
13.1 Management accounting responsibilities and evolutionary stages   177

Preface

Throughout my years as a practising accountant and now as an educator, I have constantly found myself rebelling against what I see as a flabby, often times out-of-shape and out-of-tune, management accounting discipline. Like many of the critics, I am especially critical of the distorted and irrelevant management accounting information that is produced. When I worked as a practising accountant I could more easily point the finger at the failure of academics to push forward the frontiers of management accounting. But now, in my role as one of these educators, such a strategy is untenable. This book represents my attempt to influence the direction of management accounting.

Today's management accountant, just like the rest of his/her corporate brethren, is increasingly finding that either you add value to the firm or you seek employment elsewhere. While the management accountant's power has historically come from his/her indispensable double entry wizardry, accountants must begin asking themselves how much longer they can legitimize an organizational function that is increasingly being debunked as decision irrelevant and organizationally wasteful.

For some people it might appear that the management accountant's role is nearing its end. There are, for example, management consultants and gurus who urge organizations to become world class by adopting total quality management (TQM) and just-in-time (JIT). Coupled with the adoption of these practices is a growing role for, and increased importance awarded to, the functions of operations and human resources. Meanwhile, the management accounting function atrophies and loses importance.

But if becoming a successful, world class organization is simply about adopting TQM and JIT, one might ask why General Motors and IBM were the recipients of the highly prestigious Baldrige Award for quality at the very time that their economic and competitive performances were plummeting? Or one might ask why Peter Keen and Ellen Knapp, in their book *Every Manager's Guide to Business Process*, have found that 50–70 per cent of all reengineering projects are widely acknowledged to have failed? Obviously there must be some additional factor needed if even the best exemplars of TQM and JIT can't achieve world class status.

Far from suggesting that management accounting is approaching its deathbed, this book argues that management accounting is the overlooked ingredient in becoming a world class organization. While some organizations, and in particular those that have radically altered the nature and operation of their management accounting function, have successfully harnessed the synergistic effects of combining JIT, TQM, and a newly invigorated management accounting function, other organizations have yet to understand the benefits that such an alliance can achieve. Most importantly, these underachieving organizations have yet to realize that JIT and TQM are hollow without a comprehensive information system to support their use.

Historically the management accountant has been the provider of information enabling senior managers to map strategies and deploy organizational resources. Of course, the decision of whether or not the management accountant should continue in this capacity must be based on existing skills and abilities and not historical anachronisms. To do otherwise is untenable and completely counter to modern management practices. As John Escover argues in a 1994 *Business Horizons* article, 'Worth (value) to the organization is measured in two ways: the ability to provide services that enhance the value-added process, and the ability of a group to justify its existence. As long as justification is allowed, organizations will struggle to be competitive' (July–August, pp. 47–50).

As this book argues, a resurrected and revitalized management accounting is still the logical organizational function to supply the organization's information needs. The management accountant possesses a wide range of business, corporate governance, and analytical skills that are matched by few, if any other, organizational members.

This book represents a radical departure from existing management accounting textbooks. Two main elements underlie its uniqueness. First, instead of starting with management accounting topics and trying to relate them to real-world phenomena, this book reverses the chronology. Second, the book is intended to engage readers in an interdisciplinary discourse of what today's organizations must do to remain competitive.

While this book is primarily geared toward MBA students, and seeks to help them interrelate topics they once viewed as separate and discreet, it is also intended to serve as an 'Every Manager's Guide' to understanding and learning if and how best to adopt such newly emerging advanced management accounting techniques as target costing, activity-based costing, economic value added, and strategic cost management, just to name a few. Today's, as well as tomorrow's, managers will find a working knowledge of these techniques essential in helping them to better understand what needs to be accomplished in order to survive in an increasingly global and highly competitive business environment. The journey to become a world class organization is an enormous undertaking, and like the horseman in Robert Frost's poem 'Stopping by Woods on a Snowy Evening', it is important to recognize that there are so many 'miles to go before I sleep'.

Ralph W. Adler
Dunedin, New Zealand
28 February 1998

Acknowledgements

This book has benefited greatly from the input of many business people, experts, and academics. The amount of time and counsel offered by these individuals has been immense. As one of my audit clients wryly noted soon after I began my career with KPMG, 'We should bill your firm for the CPE [continuing professional education] we provide you.' He was right. The learning I took with me from these audit engagements was unparalleled to any in-house training I ever received. I witnessed first hand the strengths and failings of management accounting practice. Looking back in time, I now understand that it was these early 'CPE experiences' that formed the genesis of this book. I am grateful to the many individuals who contributed to my 'CPE'.

During the research for this book, there have been a number of US- and New Zealand-based companies that have hosted my many and repeated visits. I am indebted to their kindness and the unreserved manner in which they made staff available for interviews.

I am additionally indebted to university colleagues and students who commented on earlier drafts of this book. I have appreciated and greatly benefited from their many insightful suggestions for improving the book.

I also wish to thank my university for its support. My ability to complete this book was greatly facilitated by two research grants and a study leave.

And finally, but by no means least, I wish to thank my parents and my wife's parents. The majority of this book was written during my study leave in the US. Whenever my family and I stayed at either set of parents, I was always given a quiet place to work and a lighter share of the chores. I don't know if I deserved the latter, but I certainly recognized it. Thank you.

Ralph Adler

1

Introduction

The management accounting function, and in particular the information it produces, has often been criticized for lacking timeliness, accuracy and relevance. Prominent among the critics have been Thomas Johnson and Robert Kaplan. Their criticisms, contained in two highly influential books, *Relevance Lost* and *Relevance Regained*, reveal the tremendous disarray and great need for change that faces management accounting today.

The reasons why management accounting has fallen into such a state of disarray are well captured by Johnson and Kaplan. In particular, they suggest that the management accounting function has been shunted aside by what has become an increasingly bigger and more dominant organizational brother: the financial accounting function. The rise of the multinational behemoth requires complex internal systems for planning, controlling and co-ordinating its globe-spanning activities. Additionally, the company is required to maintain a substantial network of internal and administrative control systems to ensure it meets the multiple and often non-complementary regulatory reporting requirements of the various countries within which it operates. Not surprisingly, and as is the case with most squeaky wheel situations, the rigid and unbending deadlines that are imposed by banks, stock markets, and taxing authorities means that financial accounting issues are generally deemed more urgent than management accounting issues. Alas, financial accounting is given the lion's share of the resources, and management accounting dries into an insignificant tributary.

While some people might interpret today's imbalance in the resources devoted to financial and management accounting as a case in which the tail (i.e. the relatively few but very powerful external parties) is wagging the dog, the decline in management accounting can also be attributed to senior managers themselves. This situation is most ironic in light of the fact that management accounting's aim has always been to provide information that is relevant and useful to the operational and strategic decisions that senior managers make. Nevertheless, focused as they are on the stock options for which they have become increasingly dependent, these individuals are often more interested in the financial accounting information, with its predominantly external decision-maker focus, than they are with the strategic and operational insights that the management accounting function is meant to provide. As a consequence, instead of decisions being based on forward- and outward-looking information, decisions are increasingly made on information that is backward and inward looking. The folly of such an approach should be obvious. Senior managers who rely on financial accounting information to direct and guide their company are similar to the ship's captain who navigates his course by looking at the wake his vessel makes.

At this point the reader might be wondering, 'How, if firms are making decisions on such misguided information, can they be as successful as they are?' The answer to this question lies partly in the universal and ubiquitous nature of failed accounting systems and partly in what is still a relatively munificent and forgiving environment.

Very few firms have yet awoken to the outdated and outmoded state of their accounting systems. As a result, there is a general lack of awareness that appropriately devised and operated management accounting systems can endow a firm with a competitive advantage. Until a sufficient number of firms grasp this important point, firms will be allowed to operate their management accounting systems within a wide range of tolerance and not jeopardize the firm's survival.

Of course, this range of tolerance is continually narrowing. As trade and language barriers decrease, the idea of a fully integrated competitive environment, where all organizations operate on a level playing field, becomes more of a reality. Being unable to hide behind tariffs, import duties and quota systems, firms will face an increasingly competitive and unforgiving economic environment. While some people may rightfully note that today's firms have already entered this new economic order, it should be recognized that what we are now seeing and experiencing is but the tip of the iceberg. We are presently perched at the verge of the much heralded information revolution. Aided by this revolution, firms will be able to produce and market products and services in an increasingly customized and flexible manner anywhere throughout the world. As a result, such conventional ideas as operating as a generalist producer/provider or being a specialist who occupies a niche market will be overthrown. If managers believe that today's world is highly competitive, they should remember one fact: tomorrow's will be even more.

Far from taking a doomsday or apocalyptic perspective, this book is meant to help managers (and the students who will assume managerial roles) to anticipate and relish the forthcoming opportunities that will accompany these economic changes. Before managers will be able to reach this plateau, however, they will need to have some minimum understanding of the various management and accounting philosophies, practices and techniques that have recently been developed under the mantra of world class organizations. While many of these management approaches have featured prominently in the management literature, for example, total quality management, readers will be shortly introduced to the fact that these management approaches alone are not sufficient. Today's advanced management techniques need to be incorporated *and* integrated with the advanced management accounting practices.

Plan of the book

The book is divided into four main parts. The first part, consisting of Chapters 2 and 3, discusses the traditional definitions of world class organizations and proposes why such definitions insufficiently capture the concept. A revised conceptualization is proposed and serves as the book's pedagogical road map.

The second part of the book is devoted to a discussion of the advanced costing techniques that have been promoted over the past 15 years. Activity-based costing is discussed in Chapter 4. The ideas of Robin Cooper and Robert Kaplan, two of the more notable proponents of this technique, are examined at length. Also included, however, is a discussion of some of the concept's recent refinements and enhancements, including the innovative ideas of Mike Walker.

Chapter 5 discusses the concept of cost of quality. The chapter begins with a summary of the various quality gurus' approaches to total quality management. The ideas of Deming, Juran, Crosby and Taguchi are discussed in detail. The chapter then proceeds to explore past and present attempts to account for quality.

Target costing is discussed in Chapter 6. The chapter highlights the distinguishing features of target costing and, in the process, reveals how it is such an all-pervasive technique for Japanese manufacturers. The two-phase process of *genka kikaku and genka kaizen* is used to structure much of the discussion. Also, the interrelationships between life-cycle costing, cost of modelling, and target costing are unveiled.

Part Three of the book explores the various performance measures that are typically relied upon, as well as those that have only most recently appeared in the business and academic literature. Chapter 7 discusses financial performance measures. It begins by examining the problems of using such traditional financial measures of performance as return on investment (ROI) and residual income (RI). Next the chapter focuses on two of the newer financial performance measures: shareholder value analysis (SVA) and economic value added (EVA).

Chapter 8 explores the use of non-financial measures. This chapter starts by highlighting the increased popularity and use of non-financial measures. The chapter then shows how this upsurge in the use of non-financial measures parallels the evolution of firms from being cost efficient to becoming quality conscious, then capable of meeting customers' demands for variety, and now capable of meeting customers' demands for product novelty.

The topic of benchmarking is discussed in Chapter 9. This chapter seeks to inform the reader of both the virtues and pitfalls of benchmarking. The chapter begins by linking benchmarking with a firm's TQM initiative. The discussion then moves to a more detailed description of benchmarking, including examples of various firms' benchmarking practices. The chapter concludes with a discussion of the situational determinants that are most conducive to the use of benchmarking. The hope is for the reader to develop an appreciation for the types of environments in which benchmarking is both well and ill suited.

The fourth part of the book examines what are (or at least what should be) the strategic dimensions of management accounting. Chapter 10 discusses the issue of strategic cost management. Particular attention is paid to such topics as value chain analysis, cost driver analysis, and competitive advantage analysis.

The evaluation of strategic investment decisions is discussed in Chapter 11. The chapter begins by examining some of the difficulties and problems with using traditional analytical methods as the basis for choosing between strategic investment decisions. Because the basis of competition has changed from being cost efficient to being cost efficient *and* quality conscious *and* flexible *and* innovative, many of the traditional methods are ill suited for today's environment. The chapter will discuss some of the alternatives that can be used.

Chapter 12 examines how transfer pricing can (and should) be used to promote the firm's strategic objectives. Surprisingly, while many firms have begun adopting various management practices to achieve world-class status, few of these firms understand the important role that transfer pricing plays. Too often firms base sourcing decisions on narrowly framed cost/benefit analyses. The purpose of this chapter is to help the reader understand how a firm's chosen transfer pricing method can add to or detract from its strategic initiative.

The book's conclusion is presented in Chapter 13. This chapter is entitled 'A destiny for management accounting'. The chapter begins by exploring the past and present role of the management accounting function, noting how the accountant has evolved from being a rather passive historian of events to assuming a more active role in daily operating decisions. The chapter then proceeds to discuss how the role of the accountant must evolve further to the point where he or she assumes a proactive role and strategic focus. The purpose of this chapter is to provoke and stimulate debate on the role and future direction of management accounting.

References

Cooper, R. (1995). *When Lean Organizations Collide: Competing Through Confrontation*. Cambridge, MA: Harvard Business School Press.

Johnson, T. and Kaplan, R. (1987). *Relevance Lost: The Rise and Fall of Management Accounting*. Boston, MA: Harvard Business School Press.

Johnson, T. (1992). *Relevance Regained: From Top-Down Control to Bottom-Up Empowerment*. The Free Press.

Kaplan, R. (1984). The Evolution of Management Accounting. *Accounting Review*, **59**(3), 390–418.

Kaplan, R. (1994). Management Accounting Practice (1984–1994): Development of New Practice and Theory. *Management Accounting Research*, **5**, 247–260.

Laverty, K. (1996). Economic 'Short-Termism': The Debate, the Unresolved Issues, and the Implications for Management Practice and Research. *Academy of Management Review*, **21**(3), 825–860.

Simons, R. (1990). The Role of Management Accounting Systems in Creating Competitive Advantage. *Accounting, Organizations and Society*, **15**(1/2), 127–143.

Part One

Becoming a World Class Organization

World class organizations: conventional wisdom

Chapter objectives

■ Discuss how today's organizations must compete across a wide range of business activities.

■ Identify various exemplary organizations and the approaches they are taking to maintain their competitiveness.

■ Define and describe the term world class organization (WCO).

■ Explore the concepts of JIT and TQM.

■ Examine recent attempts to include advanced manufacturing technology as a further WCO component.

Today's organizations face ever-rising customer demands and expectations. Over the past four decades the performance that separates successful from unsuccessful firms has risen dramatically. To be successful in today's economic environment, organizations must excel on a wide range of business activities, including cost, quality, delivery, flexibility, and innovation.

The challenge of excelling across such a wide array of business activities, *and* sustaining this excellence, is substantial. Only a small number of organizations, even on a world-wide basis, have accomplished this feat. A handful of examples that spring to mind are Vanguard (the American mutual fund company), IKEA (the Swedish furniture retailer), Motorola (the American communications equipment manufacturer), Harley-Davidson (the American motorcycle manufacturer), and Bic (the ubiquitous pen maker). These firms have been able to successfully design their structures, systems, and processes in a way that ultimately endows their end customers with a set of advantages that competitors are unable to replicate.

IKEA, for example, has found a way to sell low-priced furniture without skimping on various other product attributes that customers typically value. For instance, by maintaining a warehouse adjacent to its furniture showrooms IKEA is able to achieve same-day-as-purchase deliveries. IKEA's competitors, by contrast, generally require six to eight weeks to make their deliveries. In addition to its fast deliveries, IKEA provides extended shopping hours and in-store childcare facilities. These latter two features help IKEA to meet the needs of its customer base – many of whom are juggling professional work lives with raising children – and to further differentiate itself as an innovative furniture retailer.

Vanguard represents a second example of a firm that excels across a variety of customer-cherished service attributes. Vanguard is a low-cost, high-performing stock and bond investment brokerage house. Its customers pay no entry or exit fees upon the purchase or sale of funds (i.e. funds are no-loads) and its management expense to assets managed ratio is one of the lowest in

> **Consider this ...**
>
> The world of manufacturing has changed dramatically over the past 20 years. In the post-war period until the late 1960s, most Australian industries were profitable, with stable demand for products, high utilization of factory capacity and high returns on investment for manufacturers. A senior executive of a large electrical products group said, 'We used to be able to sell everything we could make. It wasn't hard to be good back then. Being competitive now means being much better than we ever were before.'
>
> *Source*: Samson, D., Langfield-Smith, K. and McBride, P. (1993). In *Issues on Strategic Management Accounting* (J. Ratnatunga, J. Miller, N. Mudalige and A. Sohal, eds), London: Harcourt Brace Jovanovich.

the industry at three per cent. Vanguard's low-cost nature has not, however, prevented it from excelling on a variety of other service dimensions that investors generally seek. In fact, its low-cost structure has actually *contributed* to making Vanguard a high-quality investment service. Lower fund expenses have meant that customers are able to realize higher returns on their investment portfolios. Thus, Vanguard represents a good example of how a firm can achieve what some people commonly characterize as disparate and competing objectives, and shows how the simultaneous pursuit of such objectives can actually be complimentary.

Discovering the secret of excellent organizations

At this point, one might ask what is the secret of IKEA, Vanguard, and similar firms? What enables them to excel across a variety of performance fronts? The answer appears to be that these firms have a special knack for designing structures, processes, and policies that interlock and reinforce to produce spin-offs or synergies that enable a further sharpening of the organization's identity and an augmentation of the value customers receive. Vanguard offers a good example of how organizational structure, processes, and policies can enhance customer value. In particular, Vanguard's business structure (maintaining only three retail locations), trading practices and operating processes (emphasizing bond and equity index funds and encouraging clients to invest for the long term), and various operating proce-

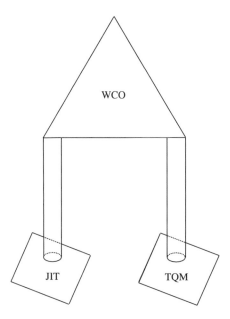

Figure 2.1 Traditional conception of a WCO

dures and policies (tying employee bonuses to cost savings and prohibiting first-class travel for executives) have helped it to develop a solid reputation as a low-cost yet highly reputable stock and bond investment service.

As already mentioned, there are but a small number of organizations throughout the world that have successfully mastered today's imperative of achieving across a wide array of customer-valued dimensions. For this elite group of organizations a special name has been coined: world class organization. Richard Schonberger appears to have been the first to use this term in his book *World Class Manufacturing*. But ever since Schonberger, business writers and consultants, realizing the very appealing nature of the term, have overused it to the extent that the pause and reflection that were once accorded the term has vanished. It now appears alongside such other similarly emaciated terms as retention management and partnering, and has been transposed into another of the three letter acronyms that litter the business landscape. Unfortunately some of the initial meaning and distinction that once applied to the term has been lost.

Today's organizations must begin reaching beyond the marketable jingo WCO has degenerated into and start to rediscover its roots. The original concept of WCO remains an appropriate and energizing battle cry to all organizations who seek to understand the competitive threshold that will separate tomorrow's survivors from the non-survivors.

According to Schonberger, a WCO develops from the successful implementation and integration of JIT and TQM. As illustrated in Figure 2.1, JIT and TQM form the supporting substrata from which a WCO is built.

Before exploring in greater depth the nature and functioning of a WCO, it is appropriate to explore briefly the supporting substrata that make its achievement possible. For those readers interested in obtaining a more thorough understanding of JIT and TQM, there are a number of management texts that are specifically devoted to these two subjects. References to some of these texts can be found at the end of this chapter.

Working definitions of JIT and TQM

The goal of JIT is quite simple and straightforward: the minimization of inventories. Ideally there should be no raw materials or finished goods inventories. Raw materials should be purchased to arrive just in the nick of time to be unloaded straight from the supplier's truck and directly onto the production floor. Likewise, finished production units should flow directly from the production floor straight to the customer's showroom or household. Beginning and ending inventory buffers are wasteful and hide business inefficiencies. As for work-in-progress, JIT advocates would minimize this as well, suggesting that batch sizes of one should become the goal. Some of the business activities that are implemented as part of a JIT initiative include redesigning products to feature a greater number of common parts, reducing the number of suppliers, increasing the frequency of parts delivery, and providing more accurate predictions of customer demand.

TQM comprises a set of business activities that seeks to create an organizational culture encouraging pride in one's work and an urgency to continuously improve upon the set of product or service attributes a customer receives. Interestingly, and importantly, customers are defined as anyone who receives a good or service from an employee within the organization. Consequently, customers can reside both externally (the common definition of a customer) as well as internally (e.g. when an auditor in an accounting firm receives the working papers pertaining to the client's tax liability from a member of the accounting firm's tax department). Some of the business activities that are implemented as part of a TQM initiative include continuous improvement programmes, employee empowerment, and benchmarking.

Hopefully the above definitions make clear the fact that JIT and TQM are much more than simple business practices or techniques. To view them in this manner is to underestimate their potential. Instead it is more appropriate to view JIT and TQM as complementary and reinforcing organizational philosophies. As a consequence, an understanding of the individual definitions of JIT and TQM provides only a partial picture of how a WCO is formed. The sum of the parts is much less than the whole. Instead there is something unique about the combined use of JIT and TQM that must be explained before a clear understanding of a WCO can be formed. In particular, an examination of the connective tissue between JIT and TQM must be undertaken, as well as an exploration of how this tissue promotes and reinforces the use of the two management philosophies.

JIT and TQM are related to each other by virtue of their unceasing commitment to continuous improvement. Both philosophies strive to eliminate organizational

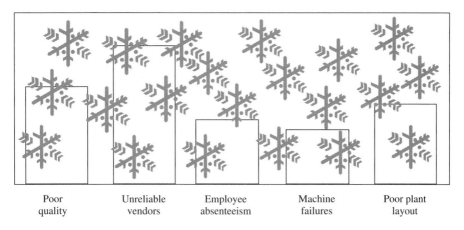

| Poor | Unreliable | Employee | Machine | Poor plant |
| quality | vendors | absenteeism | failures | layout |

Figure 2.2 Illustration of how inventory serves to conceal organizational problems

waste and inefficiency and seek to promote business effectiveness. They strive to achieve this common end, however, in subtly different ways.

JIT as a business philosophy

JIT promotes continuous improvement through its constant attempts to reduce inventories. Its ideal goal of no inventories is meant to energize people and reorient the way they think about how products are made and services rendered. Accordingly, the successful implementation of JIT is as much a cultural issue as it is a matter of production logistics.

JIT advocates argue that inventories are wasteful in two ways: they tie up valuable working capital and they hide inefficient operating practices. The loss of working capital is straightforward and easy to understand. Just how the presence of inventories hides inefficient working practices, however, merits further discussion.

Inventories can be likened to a blanket of newly fallen snow. Just as snow can conceal a city's dirt and grime, so too can inventories conceal an organization's ills and inefficiencies. Of course, the sense of security and well being that inventories foster is as false and ephemeral as the snow that covers an urban landscape.

Imagine, for example, an organization that is plagued by such problems as unreliable vendor deliveries, poor quality, frequently missed production quotas, high employee absenteeism, repeated occurrences of unscheduled machine downtime, and poor plant layouts. As shown in Figure 2.2, the existence of such problems can be minimized, if not entirely hidden, by an abundant supply of inventories, which are represented by the snowflakes.

As Figure 2.2 illustrates, the first problem that will surface as a result of a systematic reduction of inventories is the problem of unreliable vendor deliveries. Such a problem can have serious consequences for a business, with the internal consequences ranging from plant slow downs to plant shut downs, and the external consequences ranging from customer dissatisfaction about late shipments to lost sales orders.

As inventories are further reduced, the next problem to crop up would be the issue of poor quality (see Figure 2.2). Poor quality will, at a minimum, disrupt production and, if undetected prior to the product's shipment, result in high warranty costs, customer dissatisfaction, and possibly even the loss of future sales.

Of course, for some service organizations, the negative consequences of unreliable vendor deliveries or poor quality seldom stay within the confines of the organization. Instead the customer invariably and almost immediately suffers the consequences as well. For example, should a vendor fail to deliver hamburger buns on schedule and McDonald's runs out, such a shortage would immediately affect the customer, i.e. the Big Mac would arrive without its renowned sesame seed bun. Likewise, if a bank teller at a Credit Suisse branch is surly or provides erroneous information, the consequence (i.e. poor quality) is immediately experienced by the customer.

While it is true that the problems of unreliable vendor deliveries can be minimized by the maintenance of ample levels of raw material inventories and the problems associated with poor quality can be mitigated by ample levels of work-in-process and finished goods inventories, such a strategy merely treats the symptom and not the cause. JIT advocates detest and recoil from such an approach. Instead, and logically so, they look to develop solutions that will treat the root cause(s). An interesting aspect of JIT's search for acceptable problem solutions is its involvement of parties both within and outside the organization. Unlike some organizations that perceive very hard and rigid lines between themselves and the outside, JIT proponents view the boundaries as more permeable. As a result, JIT organizations will typically involve a larger set of parties from a greater length of the value chain throughout the various brainstorming and problem-solving stages than their non-JIT counterparts.

In sum, JIT serves to activate and direct employee behaviour toward an ideal goal of zero inventories.[1] While the idea of going 'cold turkey' and introducing a zero inventory edict is a sure recipe for failure, many businesses have been successful at gradually reducing inventories over the course of several successive business quarters. For example, back in the late 1980s and early 1990s, when the successes of JIT were being paraded through the management literature, companies such as Hewlett-Packard, Xerox, and Harley Davidson radically slashed their inventory levels. In fact, one US multinational, Dover Corporation, reported how as the result of implementing JIT its Fueling Components Group (a manufacturer of products

---

[1] It should be noted that not all employees find the idea of zero inventories a motivating goal. There are many employees who, if given the choice, would prefer to have large stocks of inventory. For example, a machinist who is paid on a piecemeal rate would prefer large amounts of WIP queuing in front of his or her work station as a means of reducing the probability that he or she will be left stranded because of insufficient incoming inventory. Likewise, a hotel concierge would prefer an abundant number of empty rooms to accommodate the possibility of a guest rejecting a particular room because it does not meet his or her standards for size, layout, or cleanliness.

for the petrochemical industry) reduced its inventory stocks from approximately 15 weeks supply on hand to less than 1.5 weeks. Although none of these mentioned companies achieved a level of zero inventories, and is unlikely to ever do this, it nonetheless provides the impetus for an organization to continually strive to eliminate waste and promote business effectiveness. As a consequence, improvements are made to its products and services, and customers reap the benefits through the greater value they receive.

TQM as a business philosophy

TQM shares JIT's goal of continual improvement. However, its starting point is quite different. Unlike JIT and its focus on inventory reductions, TQM adopts a customer value focus. The basic tenet of TQM is to ensure that customers, at each and every opportunity, receive the greatest value possible.

Interestingly, and very importantly, TQM defines the word 'customer' in a radically different way from the word's traditional definition. Instead of defining a customer as an external purchaser of the organization's goods or services, TQM expands the concept to include all parties, both within and outside the organization, who receive a good or service from some other member of the organization. Accordingly, a company that fabricates and assembles furniture would define its assembly department as a customer, for it relies on products supplied to it by the fabrication department, in exactly the same manner as it would define the various wholesalers and retailers to which it supplies. In a like manner, an insurance company's Claims Department would be a customer of its Adjustment Department.

The more encompassing definition that TQM ascribes to the definition of a customer has two important outcomes. First, everyone in the organization now has a customer. The idea of pleasing customers, which has been translated into such slogans as 'meeting customer expectations' and more recently as 'exceeding customer expectations', becomes a shared vision and valued activity of all members of the organization. Second, the cumulative effect of the enhanced supplier–customer transactions that occur along the entire length of the organization's internal value chain can be quite dramatic. As a result, the external customers will enjoy superior products or services, and typically for less cost, than they would otherwise.

The successful implementation of TQM requires a systemic or organization-wide approach. According to such notable TQM luminaries as Deming, Juran, and Crosby, managers must evolve their thinking from a focus on the individual employee to a focus on the *organizational* systems that either aid in the delivery of high quality or detract from it. Invariably the design of these systems requires the breaking down of individual and functional responsibilities. For many organizations, especially those that have developed in a western culture, the ability to see beyond the individual can be difficult. These organizations have been schooled for so long on the need for bureaucratic structures, the separation of activities into a multitude of specialized jobs, and the granting of rewards based on individual efforts that it is difficult for them to change to a group or organization-wide way of thinking.

Some of the more popular TQM practices include quality circles, Pareto analysis, and statistical process control (SPC). A common theme among these practices is the central role that employee empowerment plays. It is commonly acknowledged that without an empowered work force TQM is hollow and will fail. As a consequence, middle level managers must be willing to relinquish some of their power and control. They must start allowing employees the freedom to decide how, when, and by whom the work will be accomplished. Instead of their traditional field marshal role, the new directive for managers is to act as 'work facilitators'. Accordingly their new duty is to run interference, break down divisive work barriers, and cut through the various kinds of red tape that prevent employees from getting on with and performing to the best of their abilities the task at hand.

In addition to the need to empower employees, TQM success also depends on having a sufficiently educated work force. The use of employee empowerment in situations where employees fail to possess adequate skills and training is a sure recipe for failure. Before empowerment can work, employees must be fully conversant not only in the operation of their specific job, but also in the job of all other members of their work group. Additionally, because empowerment requires employees to organize and schedule their work, such 'softer' skills as team building, leadership, and time management are also needed.

In sum, TQM seeks to imbue the organization with a customer focus. This customer focus, as embodied in TQM's omnipresent slogan that 'everyone has a customer', highlights the need and urgency to continuously improve. Employees quickly learn that customer expectations are seldom static, but rather are constantly increasing. Once employees understand this lesson, they realize that an unimproved product or service is the equivalent of going backwards. They must, and this is generally accomplished through employee empowerment, make continuous improvements to the products they make and services they render.

Attempts to include advanced manufacturing technology as a component of a WCO

Scott Snell and James Dean are embarked on a long-term research programme that investigates the composition of highly competitive organizations. These researchers believe that a firm's simultaneous pursuit of JIT and TQM is not enough. Instead, an organization must expand its efforts and pursue advanced manufacturing technology (AMT) as well.

AMT is defined as the subset of a firm's information technology that assists the firm in offering products and services that are characterized by high quality and flexibility. Some of the specific technologies found under the umbrella of AMT include flexible manufacturing systems, computer-integrated manufacturing, and computer numerical control. Snell and Dean believe that through the combined use of AMT, JIT, and TQM a firm creates 'a streamline flow of automated, value-added activities, uninterrupted by moving, storage, or rework' (Snell and Dean, 1996).

While at first glance it may appear that Snell and Dean's identification and highlighting of AMT helps to distinguish the features of a WCO, a more careful deliberation reveals that they have overlooked the difference between starring roles and supporting roles. In particular, AMT is not at the same conceptual level as JIT or TQM. The latter concepts represent energizing philosophies while the former represents a necessary supporting practice. As such, it is better to view AMT at the same conceptual level as such organizational practices as kanban systems and statistical process control.

Although AMT is at the same conceptual level as kanban and statistical process control, an important difference separates AMT from the latter two organizational practices. Unlike kanban (which supports a JIT initiative) and statistical process control (which supports a TQM initiative), AMT simultaneously supports JIT *and* TQM. AMT's prime objectives of promoting high quality and high flexibility are part and parcel of JIT and TQM. Most probably it is this dual supporting role of AMT that accounts for why Snell and Dean find such an overlap (as indicated by the large and highly significant correlation coefficients) between AMT and JIT and AMT and TQM.

Summary

This chapter has presented and described the various organizational features that are commonly believed to comprise a WCO. It began with a brief study of the structures, systems, and processes used by a number of exemplary organizations to improve their effectiveness and competitiveness. The chapter then proceeded to discuss Schonberger's idea that a WCO develops from the successful implementation and integration of JIT and TQM. The terms JIT and TQM were subsequently defined and further explored. In the final section of the chapter, the term AMT was defined and the contribution it makes to help understand the features of a WCO was examined.

References

Bolwijn, P. and Kumpe, T. (1990) Manufacturing in the 1990s – Productivity, Flexibility, and Innovation. *Long Range Planning*, **23**(4), 44–57.

Dean, J. and Snell, S. (1996). The Strategic Use of Integrated Manufacturing: An Empirical Examination. *Strategic Management Journal*, **17**(6), 459–480.

Flood, R. (1993). *Beyond TQM*. New York: John Wiley and Sons.

Flynn, B., Sakakibara, S. and Schroeder, R. (1995). Relationships Between JIT and TQM: Practices and Performance. *Academy of Management Journal*, **38**(5), 1325–1360.

Schiederjans, M. (1993). *Topics in Just-In-Time Management*. Needham Heights, MA: Allyn & Bacon.

Schonberger, R. (1986). *World Class Manufacturing*. New York: The Free Press.

Snell, S. and Dean, J. (1992). Integrated Manufacturing and Human Resource Management: A Human Capital Perspective. *Academy of Management Journal*, **35**(3), 467–504.

3

World class organizations: the missing link

Chapter objectives

- Question whether the traditional WCO definition is sufficient for explaining what is required to attain today's threshold of business success.

- Explore an alternative WCO conception, one which includes information and reporting systems as a third supporting leg alongside JIT and TQM.

- Describe the characteristics of this information and reporting system leg and in particular demonstrate how it is just as much an energizing philosophy as JIT and TQM.

- Reveal how information and reporting systems combine with JIT and TQM to promote organizational effectiveness.

The preceding chapter presented the argument that a WCO can be identified by its commitment to JIT and TQM. In the current chapter, we question whether this portrayal of a WCO represents a complete picture. In particular, it appears appropriate at this time to ask such questions as, 'Why, if JIT and TQM comprise the necessary ingredients to become a WCO, did General Motors and IBM receive the highly prestigious Baldrige Award for quality when at the very same time their economic and competitive performances were plummeting?' Additionally, it might be asked, 'Why, as pointed out by Keen and Knapp in their book *Every Manager's Guide to Business Process*, is it widely claimed that 50–70 per cent of all reengineering projects end in failure?' Is it possible that some additional ingredient is needed if even some of the best exemplars of TQM and JIT can't seem to attain the plateau of WCO?

The thesis presented in the current chapter is that TQM and JIT are necessary but not sufficient components of a WCO. A third component, comprising information and reporting systems, is also needed. Since information and reporting systems are commonly associated with the function of accounting, this third component of a WCO is captured under the heading 'value added accounting' (VAA).

What is VAA?

Unlike the concepts of JIT and TQM, which have been extensively spoken and written about during the past two decades, VAA is a concept unique to this book. A full exposition of the concept, therefore, must await the completion of this book. In the meantime, however, a working definition of VAA is in order.

VAA, in very crude and simple terms, involves the production of operational and strategic information that aids senior manager decision making *and* provides the information infrastructure to support an organization's implementation of JIT and TQM. As this definition reveals, VAA embodies the traditional management accounting role (i.e. decision-making support), as well as the new role of informational linchpin to TQM and JIT. While it is true that some accounting scholars – such as Michael Bromwich and Thomas Johnson – have attempted to highlight this needed dual role of accounting, much more needs to be done. In essence, the issues exposed to date represent little more than the tip of the iceberg. Missing from these aerial maps of accounting's new destiny is a communication of the immensely larger substructure that lies beneath the surface and is impervious to superficial observations. As such, the new role for management accounting that is commonly championed is little more than a group of unique, but conceptually unconnected, accounting techniques and tools.

To view accounting's new destiny as the equivalent of a handyman's expanded tool belt, which holds an increased number of specialized gadgets, underestimates the potential of and retards the movement to a more fully evolved management accounting system. Instead it is high time that organizations began realizing the increasingly central role that management accounting systems play in promoting organizational effectiveness. One need only listen to the popular business credos being spoken these days, for example, the references being made to such phenomena as 'the information revolution', 'learning organizations', and 'knowledge workers', to see that the development of good information systems will play an ever larger role in an organization's success.

If we take a closer look at such words as 'information', 'learning', and 'knowledge', we can observe a direct and sequential link between them. In particular, information represents the multitude of stimuli, daily episodes, and multidimensional phenomena that comprise the world in which we live. Learning, or understanding, occurs as a result of our interactions and experiences with our world. And finally, knowledge, or repositories of wisdom, begins to emerge as we attempt to reflect upon, make links between, and share living stories with others. In sum, information leads to learning, which in turn leads to knowledge.

Of course, being a learner and knowledge gatherer does not mean that we respond to all forms of information in an equal manner. Some information is given a higher weighting than others are, and some is ignored altogether. Consider, for example, what occurs as you drive a car. While the number of vehicles and their relative position on the road is constantly monitored, such other information as vehicle model and colour are deemed unimportant, at least to the safe operation of the car. In a like manner, an organization makes choices about what information it will monitor and collect.

The more traditional approaches to organizational information collection focus on the events occurring inside the organization's borders and pay much less attention, and some would argue none at all, to what occurs outside these borders. Alternative approaches to data collection, which are commonly deemed as more enlightened, call for an expansion of the traditional information set to include events that occur beyond the organization's borders. Some examples of events that would be monitored under this latter approach include attempts to cost competitors' product and service offerings; attempts to monitor changes in competitors' intellectual capital base that result from their decisions to add workers, shed workers, and/ or commit more resources to worker training and development; and attempts to assess the readiness of competitors to react to such major discontinuities as environmental crises, national consolidations and dissolutions, and regional wars.

The concept of VAA is meant to symbolize the transition in the world's economic orders from those that are based on manual labour to those based on knowledge creation. Accordingly, VAA serves as a pragmatic alternative to traditional labour-, land-, and capital-based management accounting information systems. Additionally, and this is the more easily overlooked aspect, VAA seeks to enshrine the organization's information gathering, learning activities, and knowledge creation as indispensable and defining features of organizational life. In sum, it represents a philosophical departure from traditional conceptions of the role and purpose of management accounting and information systems.

VAA recognizes that just as too little information can retard knowledge creation, so too can too much information. It is important that the information function be selective about what it gathers. Instead of adopting broad but superficial approaches to data collection, it may make more sense to cast the net less widely but more deeply. For example, in today's environment of corporate downsizing, traditional measures of unemployment are becoming less and less reliable. While it is true that these government statistics are comprehensive (generally being the result of a complete census), they typically fail to probe the surface. In particular, because many organizations are now subcontracting the work that was historically performed in-house, a growing group of independent, part-time employees is developing. As a result, the meaning of the government's employment statistics is becoming increasingly dubious. The International Labour Organization practice of counting as fully employed a person who works one or more hours a week appears to be a severe distortion of reality. In New Zealand it is now estimated that about 7.5 per cent of the labour force, which is currently being counted as fully employed, wishes to work more hours.

Due to the premium that is placed on knowledge creation, information that comes in a form as divorced from reality as today's unemployment figures will fail to not only add value, but is likely to actually subtract from it. For if an individual was not spending time analysing information of dubious content and value, he/she could instead be shifting through reliable and relevant information that can lead to

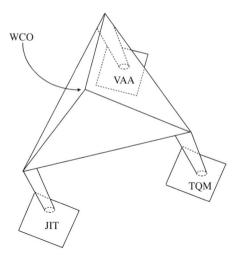

Figure 3.1 Revised conception of a WCO

learning and knowledge creation. Consequently, the idea that not all information is of equal value, and that various techniques for collecting, filtering, and disseminating information can exhibit greater or lesser utility, gives rise to the understanding that VAA, like JIT and TQM, has a mission of continuous improvement. Accordingly, world-class accounting information systems enhance organizational effectiveness and foster initiatives to eliminate waste.

Hopefully the above definition of VAA and the preceding chapter's definitions of JIT and TQM make clear the fact that these three concepts are much more than simple business practices or techniques. Instead they should be viewed as organizational philosophies that support and reinforce one another. By virtue of their mutual commitment to continuous improvement they seek to eliminate organizational waste and promote business effectiveness. It is through this process of combining JIT, TQM, and VAA that an organization is promoted to the ranks of a WCO. Figure 3.1 illustrates this revised conception of a WCO.

Figure 3.1 is drawn to sharply contrast with the WCO representation illustrated by Figure 2.1 in the preceding chapter. Whereas Figure 2.1 is a two-dimensional triangle, Figure 3.1 is drawn as a three-dimensional pyramid and symbolizes an enhanced, more real-world understanding of a WCO. Additionally, the VAA leg is purposely drawn to appear in hidden form at the far end of the pyramid and symbolizes its hitherto overlooked status.

How JIT, TQM, and VAA reinforce one another and support an organization's quest to become a WCO

JIT, TQM, and VAA are connected by virtue of their common commitment to continuous improvement. Although each philosophy offers a different perspective on how to achieve continuous improvement, a listing of the general business approaches, practices, and methods that typically form a part of their implementation reveals the substantial common ground they share. For example, as was previously discussed in Chapter 2, the implementation of JIT and TQM often includes the adoption of advanced manufacturing technology (AMT) as an accompanying business approach. The enhancements in quality and flexibility, which AMT provides, are essential components of an organization's JIT and TQM philosophies.

Similar to the way in which JIT and TQM are supported by an organization's introduction of AMT, VAA and JIT also share a common business approach. In particular, both philosophies are supported by a business approach that emphasizes inventory planning. The tracking of current and anticipated inventory levels is important for evaluating an organization's progress towards achieving JIT's ideal goal of zero inventories. Additionally, because an organization must walk a fine line between the costly effects of excessive inventory on the one side and stockouts on the other – whether the inventory is TVs in a show room or seats on an airline – the inventory planning process provides information that is essential to an organization's continued learning and gaining of knowledge about a business aspect that is at the heart of customer value and satisfaction.

VAA and TQM, the final pairing of organizational philosophies, also share a common business approach. In particular, they share a business approach that involves the need to continuously monitor product and service quality. The recording of product and service quality, especially those that are done on a real-time basis – such as Deming's statistical process control technique – are an essential component of an organization's TQM philosophy. In addition, because product or service quality is often a key determinant of customer satisfaction, quality monitoring provides information that is critical to gaining further learning and knowledge about the organizational operations that can have a profound influence on customer perceptions of value and satisfaction.

Figure 3.2 illustrates the overlapping nature of JIT, TQM, and VAA. It not only shows how these three organizational philosophies combine to create a WCO, but it also reveals the web of interrelated business approaches, practices, and methods that typically underlie the use of JIT, TQM, and VAA. As a means of gaining a better understanding of a WCO, it is worth spending some time identifying and discussing the various elements that are highlighted in the diagram.

Inventory planning

Inventory planning is a business approach that supports organizational philosophies of JIT and VAA. The manner in which this business approach supports these two philosophies was just discussed. Some of its accompanying business practices and methods, however, have yet to be discussed.

Demand forecasting is an essential element of inventory planning. Without reliable forecasts of customer demand, an organization is bound to maintain excessively

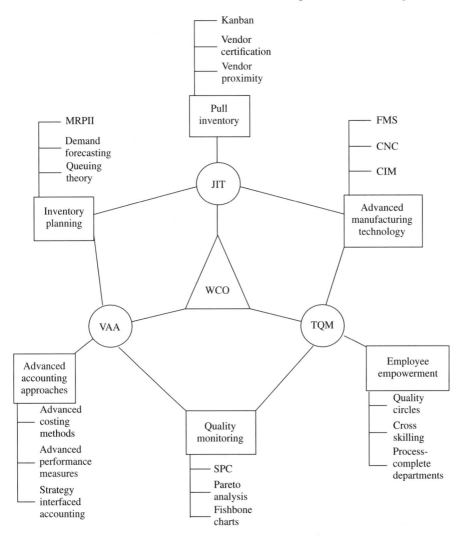

Figure 3.2 The interconnected nature of JIT, TQM, and VAA

large stocks of inventory. Otherwise it will suffer the detrimental consequences of stock outs. Significant improvements in the forecasting of customer demand have occurred through the development of more sophisticated econometric models and the creation of centralized computer databases that are better able to balance customer demand with customer orders.

Manufacturing resources planning (MRPII) represents a system designed to ensure that the necessary materials, labour, and equipment are available in the needed amounts and at the prescribed times so as to properly execute a production task. MRPII typically involves the use of complex computer software to track component lists (commonly termed 'bill of materials') and calculate the necessary quantities and duration lengths of necessary resources.

Queuing theory is the study of waiting times. The Danish mathematician Erlang, who in 1913 studied the effect of fluctuating demand on telephone facilities and the associated service delays, is generally acknowledged as the founder of queuing theory. In very general terms, queuing theory seeks to minimize waiting times by ensuring an equilibrium between arrivals (be they customers, product requiring further processing, or telephone calls) and servers (be they human or mechanical).

Pull inventory systems

JIT is supported by a business approach that emphasizes a pull, as opposed to the traditional push, inventory system. A push inventory system focuses on worker and machine efficiencies. Consequently, it encourages the maximizing of throughput, regardless of the impact that such an obsession with efficiency can have on inventory levels. Meanwhile, pull inventory systems are characterized by production systems that are in balance and harmony, *and* that beat to the metronome of the sales register. It is this attention to customer demand that generally provides the acid test for distinguishing between pull and push systems. For example, while every production line process is predicated on there being equal times between stops or work stations along the assembly line, not every one, and generally very few, of these production line processes are geared to match customer demand. However, with a pull inventory system this is exactly what needs to happen.

Some of the common practices and methods that are associated with pull systems include kanban, vendor proximity, and vendor certification. Kanban is a Japanese formulated inventory card system that determines the rate at which inventory replenishment occurs at any given work station. It is only when a downstream workstation indicates a need for additional inventory, which the colour coded kanban inventory cards visually signify, that inventory is permitted to pass from the neighbouring upstream department.

Vendor proximity is an important feature of JIT. Having suppliers close at hand facilitates the frequent deliverers required under JIT. Close vendor proximity is also helpful when there are unexpected spikes in customer demand.

Vendor certification ensures that only those suppliers that meet stringent requirements for delivery reliability and product quality are certified as acceptable suppliers. In addition to ensuring high levels of delivery reliability and product quality, vendor certification programmes encourage the development of long-term and trusting bonds with a small number of suppliers. This display of loyal ties, and the accompanying implication of mutual destinies, can be sharply contrasted with traditional organizational purchasing habits, which seek to create a large pool of suppliers who compete in a cut-throat fashion among themselves but display little loyalty or allegiance to the organization to which they are supplying.

Advanced manufacturing technology

AMT is frequently employed as a business approach to support an organization's JIT and TQM philosophies. The manner in which this business approach supports both JIT and TQM has previously been discussed. Some of AMT's accompanying business practices and methods, however, have yet to be discussed.

AMT relies heavily upon the integration of computer technology with the organization's production of products and provision of services. As a result of integrating computer technology with the organization's operating processes, whether these processes be machine-based (as is typical with manufacturers) or labour-based (as is typical with service enterprises), delivery is quickened, flexibility is enhanced, and quality is improved. For example, the use of AMT in the automobile industry has drastically reduced the lead time needed to move from initial design to initial production, increased the production flexibility to the point that successive cars moving through an assembly line can be completely different models, and improved quality to the point that defects are measured as occurrences per million versus not too long ago when they were measured per hundred. Likewise, the use of AMT in the airline industry has revolutionized the ticketing process (tickets can now be purchased using e-mail and picked up on the day of departure at the airport), significantly enhanced the in-flight entertainment programme (passengers can choose what programmes they watch and when they watch them), and provided significant improvements to pilot training and flight safety.

AMT is supported by such business practices and methods as computer aided design and computer aided manufacturing (CAD/CAM), computer numerical control, and flexible manufacturing systems. CAD/CAM seeks to slash design and production times and thereby quicken customer delivery. Computer numerical control is designed to improve quality. And finally, flexible manufacturing systems are intended to accommodate the successive production or provision of differing products and services.

Employee empowerment

Employee empowerment represents the primary business approach by which an organization supports a philosophy of TQM. Employee empowerment, as the term implies, provides employees with significant autonomy over how they structure, organize, and execute their work. Such decisions as who should do a particular work activity, how it should be executed, and when it should be accomplished are no longer the exclusive prerogative of middle-level managers. Instead these decisions are directly vested with the workers themselves. Of course, for employee empowerment to work, certain supporting business practices and methods must be in place, including process-complete departments, cross skilling, and quality circles.

Process-complete departments are departments that are capable of performing all the cross-functional steps or tasks required to meet customer needs. Whether an organization has fully evolved its form and structure to accommodate the actual implementation of process-complete departments is not nearly as important as engineering an evolution in employee attitudes and mindsets. In particular, employees must come to understand and embrace the importance of seeing customer needs from the customer's individual and holistic perspective, and not from the perspective of an employee's department. Instead of asking, 'What piece, if any, does my department play in resolving the customer's need?' the employee must say, 'How can I ensure that the customer's problem is fully resolved and his/her needs are completely met?'

Employee empowerment will not work without adequate employee training. Since employee empowerment often results in the formation of autonomous work groups, employees generally need to embody the cricketer's concept of an 'all rounder' versus being a one-task specialist. Cross skilling is therefore assiduously promoted as part of a TQM philosophy and is frequently supported through compensation systems, whereby an employee's base pay is a function of the number of skills that he/she has successfully mastered.

Employee empowerment encourages all employees to come forward with suggestions for improving the organization's systems and processes. Quality circles represent a formalized mechanism for facilitating employee-generated ideas. Similar to the often cross-functional nature of the problem they are meant to address, quality circles are typically composed of a diverse set of individuals, who represent many different organizational functions and sometimes even include supplier and customer representatives.

Quality monitoring

Quality monitoring is commonly used to support an organization's TQM and VAA philosophies. Since a discussion of the supporting role played by this business approach has already been provided, we can turn directly to an examination of the business practices and methods that comprise its use.

Statistical process control (SPC) is a Deming-inspired quality control technique. Its use requires all workers to become familiar with reading and understanding basic statistical properties. SPC's real-time charting of ongoing operations allows employees to detect trends that potentially signify out-of-control operations. The early warning signals provided by SPC allow worker intervention at a very early stage and helps prevent many of the detrimental consequences of poor quality.

Pareto analysis is a technique for helping managers and workers to zero in on business hot spots, especially problem areas. The 80–20 rule of thumb that underlies Pareto analysis suggests that 80 per cent of an organization's outcomes are directly attributable to 20 per cent of its actions. Accordingly, Pareto analysis suggests that 80 per cent of a company's sales are attributable to 20 per cent of its customers. Or, as another example, 80 per cent of a company's quality problems are attributable to 20 per cent of the products/services offered. This 80–20 rule of thumb has proven to be a remarkably reliable forecaster of actual practice. The simplicity and wisdom of Pareto analysis has helped many organizations to focus their attention on the relatively few organizational actions that account for the lion's share of their troubles.

Fishbone charts, which are also commonly called cause and effect diagrams, help a work team to identify, explore, and graphically display the possible causes of a problem. The causes are broken down into increasingly finer detail to uncover the actual root causes to the problem. The purpose of fishbone charts is to find and cure causes, not to attend to symptoms.

Advanced accounting approaches

Advanced accounting approaches (AAAs) comprise the set of business practices and methods used to support an organization's VAA philosophy. AAAs are outward looking and strategically oriented. They contrast with traditional accounting approaches, which are generally inward looking and operationally focused.

Advanced costing methods comprise one element of AAAs. Advanced costing methods include activity-based costing (ABC), cost of quality, target costing, life-cycle costing, and cost modelling. Each of these methods offers a more realistic representation of product/service costs. As a result of the improved costing information these methods provide, organizations are better able to manage activities in a way that will enhance customer value. Part Two of this book, which comprises Chapters 4–6, offers an in-depth look at each of these methods.

Advanced performance measures represent a second element of AAAs. Advance performance measures consist of both financial and non-financial measures. Some of the financial measures include shareholder value analysis (SVA) and economic value added (EVA). Meanwhile, some of the non-financial measures include information about a firm's delivery, flexibility, and innovation performance. One of the more recent and novel attempts to develop a performance measurement system that incorporates financial as well as non-financial measures is Kaplan and Norton's balanced scorecard. Part Three of this book, which comprises Chapters 7–9, provides a fuller discussion of the various methods used by today's WCOs to measure performance.

Strategy interfaced accounting comprises the third element of AAAs. Strategy interfaced accounting promotes the idea that a sound understanding of the organization's strategy should be reflected in the accounting information that is collected, the analyses that are performed on this information set, and the decisions that are finally reached. Shank and Govindarajan have been particularly vocal about the need to link strategy formulation with accounting system design. Part Four of this book, which comprises Chapters 10–12, illustrates how a strategic accounting orientation can be applied to accounting issues that commonly lack a strategic focus and argues that such an approach is an essential feature of a WCO.

Summary

To attain world-class status an organization must not only implement JIT and TQM (the traditional conception of a WCO), but it must also possess an excellent information support system, which this chapter has labelled VAA. JIT, TQM, and VAA exist as three organizational philosophies that reinforce one another and support an organization's quest to become a WCO. In helping the reader to understand the interrelated nature of JIT, TQM, and VAA, Figure 3.2 was presented. This figure can be viewed as a road map. Namely, it lays out the routes an organization must travel to become a WCO, and displays the various connections that exist between these routes.

References

Adler, R. and Everett, A. (1996). *Journal of Socio-Industrial Research*, **10**, 3–11.

Bromwich, M. (1990). The Case for Strategic Management Accounting: The Role of Accounting Information for Strategy in Competitive Markets. *Accounting, Organizations and Society*, **15**(1), 27–46.

Bromwich, M. (1994). Management Accounting: Pathways to Progress. *Management Accounting*, **72**(5), 44.

Bromwich, M. and Bhimani, A. (1989). Management Accounting: Evolution not Revolution. *Management Accounting*, **67**(9), 5–6.

Bromwich, M. and Bhimani, A. (1991). Accounting for Just-in-Time Manufacturing Systems. *CMA Magazine*, **65**(1), 31–34.

Johnson, H.T. (1992). It's Time to Stop Overselling Activity-Based Concepts. *Management Accounting*, **74**(3), 26–35.

Johnson, H.T. (1993). To Achieve Quality You Must Think Quality. *Financial Executive*, **9**(3), 9–12.

Johnson, H.T. and Kaplan, R.S. (1988). Management by Accounting Is Not Management Accounting. *CFO: The Magazine of Chief Financial Officers*, **4**(7), 6–8.

Keen, P. and Knapp, E. (1996). *Every Manager's Guide to Business Process*. Boston, MA: Harvard Business School Press.

Part Two

Advanced Costing Methods

4

Activity-based costing

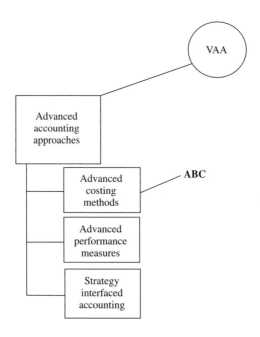

Chapter objectives

- Discuss the distortions that traditional cost accounting systems can create.
- List and describe the warning signals that indicate a cost accounting system has become obsolete and is in need of repair.
- Describe and illustrate how activity-based costing overcomes the problems typically attributed to traditional cost systems.
- Critique ABC and identify recent developments in activity-based thinking.

Over the past 15 years, a number of scholars and practitioners have condemned organizations for using cost accounting systems that are irrelevant and outdated. These critics charge that the product costings generated by traditional costing systems provide insufficient, and sometimes even erroneous, managerial guidance. As a consequence, firms are likely to take incorrect strategic and operational decisions.

The failings of the traditional cost accounting system are poignantly documented in a survey of chief financial officers (CFOs) that was conducted by George Foster. His survey findings point to a sad state of affairs. Fifty-one per cent of the CFOs felt that their cost management systems supplied inadequate information for costing and pricing, 45 per cent said it failed to aid decision making, 35 per cent said it was inadequate for worker performance, 34 per cent said it provided unsatisfactory operating performance measures, 27 per cent said it was not meaningful for competitive analysis, and 11 per cent said it was inconsistent with firm strategy. William Boone, the CEO for Scoville Industries, appears to capture the general sentiment of his managerial colleagues when he says, 'The typical cost accounting system produces product costs that are very precise but totally inaccurate.'

The inability of cost accounting systems to provide managers with what they deem to be critical and necessary information represents a severe handicap for organizations. Today's highly competitive business world is most unforgiving. Should a company fail to understand its costs and consequently misprice its products and services, it is likely that an opportunistic competitor will pounce on such a mistake and turn it to its advantage. Inevitably this will mean a shift in market share from the cost-naïve company to the cost-savvy company.

The problems with traditional cost accounting systems

Companies require accurate product and service costings for pricing, determining optimal product/service mixes, assisting with decisions on whether to and what to outsource, determining preferred channels of distribution, targeting activities for process improvement, managing customer relations, and making investment/ disinvestment decisions. While it is true that the organization's strategy exercises a key influence on each of these decisions, it should be well understood that costs are a vital component of the strategic process, especially in terms of formulating and evaluating a chosen strategy. As several scholars have argued, including most recently Robin Cooper in his book *When Lean Enterprises Collide: Competing Through Confrontation*, even strategies that emphasize non-cost product or service attributes cannot ignore the impact that price exerts on customer behaviour.

Unfortunately, many companies' cost accounting systems lack specificity and precision. Product and service costs are consequently misrepresented. Four of the more prominent causes underlying this problem are the failure to use direct costing where it is economically feasible, the failure to segregate overhead costs into unique cost pools, the failure to apply appropriate cost allocation bases, and the failure to penetrate beyond a gross margin analysis.

In spite of the fact that advances in information technology have greatly reduced the costs associated with tracking and assigning costs to specific products and services, many companies underutilize this technology. Rather than using meters to measure different products' energy consumptions, motion sensors to detect the amount of time employees spend at given tasks, and bar codes to help calculate the costs associated with moving specific materials and finished products, the majority of companies allow these costs to lapse into a general, catch-all category called 'overhead'. These costs are later indirectly assigned to products and services often using a single cost driver that marginally represents the true demands a product or service places on the incurrence of the overhead cost in the first place.

A second cause of many companies' failed cost accounting systems relates to the failure to segregate overhead costs into unique cost pools. The vast majority of companies categorize into one cost pool, or at best a mere handful of cost pools, all costs that cannot be classified as direct materials or direct labour. No attempt is made to separate overhead costs into common overhead cost categories. As a result, the company's ability to associate overhead costs with specific products, services, customers, or some other equally important attribute is blunted.

A third cause behind the failings of traditional costing systems relates to the inappropriate use of cost allocation bases. Just as there is often only one or a very limited number of overhead cost pools, so too there is often only one or a very limited number of cost drivers used to allocate the overhead costs. Frequently direct labour hours or direct labour dollars are used to allocate the overhead costs. Critics have long charged that such a practice is antiquated and outmoded. They argue that labour costs as a percentage of product, and even service, are rapidly decreasing. For many of today's manufacturers direct labour costs represent less than 10 per cent of the product's total cost. Therefore, say these critics, the allocation of overhead based on direct labour is likely to result in distorted product costs.

While some organizational managers have interpreted the criticisms against using direct labour cost drivers as a signal that they should be identifying and using some other cost driver; they often adopt cost drivers that offer only superficial relief. As an example, managers often assume that highly automated production environments should use machine hours as the appropriate cost driver. In reality, however, these managers are only partly correct. It is certainly the case that many overhead costs in a highly automated production environment are closely related to the use of machine hours. For instance, machine depreciation and machine maintenance are undoubtedly associated with machine hours. Nevertheless, there are many other overhead costs that are not related to machine hours such as materials purchasing, materials handling, scheduling, machine set-up, inspection, and product enhancement. If machine hours are used to allocate these costs, then a faulty assumption is being made. In particular, it is incorrectly being assumed that these costs vary with volume. This, however, is not the case. The above costs are a function of the organization's product range, and most particularly the amount of product diversity and complexity that characterizes this range. For many organizations these non-volume related costs range upwards to 25 per cent. As a consequence, it is important not to confuse volume-based cost drivers with non-volume based organizational activities.

A fourth cause behind the failings of traditional costing systems relates to their failure to penetrate beyond a gross margin analysis. In general, companies do not include the costs of marketing, distribution, or administration in the calculation of a product or service cost. The primary reason for this failure is due to the fact that there is no financial accounting requirement to report beyond the gross margin level. And since the mandates of financial accounting often take practical precedence over the extent and shape of the information that will be collected and reported by the management accounting function, a more comprehensive treatment of these 'below the gross margin line' costs is not undertaken.

The potential for erroneously costed products is greatest when marketing, distribution, and administrative costs vary systematically with the type of product or product line. As an example, marketing and distribution costs will vary substantially between products that are sold by travelling salespeople versus products that are sold through a sales catalogue. Over and over again companies have found that the inclusion of these below the gross margin line costs can dramatically affect product profitability. An Australian food manufacturer, for instance, discovered that once it fully allocated its marketing and distribution costs, a product that was originally believed to be 'marginal' was actually losing in excess of $1,000,000 a year.

Symptoms of an obsolete cost system

There are several indicators that a cost system may be providing erroneous cost information. One indication is that difficult-to-produce products exhibit high profit margins even though they do not command a premium price. Difficult-to-produce products invariably consume a greater proportion of the total manufacturing overhead than less difficult-to-produce products. Yet the typical 'peanut butter' approach of averaging overhead costs across products does not reveal the true extent to which organizational resources are being consumed. If it did, then the difficult-to-produce products would either be repriced at a higher figure or be associated with low profit margins.

A second indication of an obsolete cost system is when product margins cannot be easily explained. A product or service's profit margin is influenced by the extent and nature of the attributes that comprise the product or service, as well as by such factors as economies of scale and scope. If management believes it understands the market but cannot explain the patterns in its product profitability, then the cost system is probably at fault.

A third indication that a company's cost system has become obsolete is when the results of competitive bids are hard to explain. If management is unable to predict which of the bids it submits on various pieces of work is likely to be accepted, then the cost system may be reporting inaccurate product costs. The company should be especially sceptical of its product costings when seemingly aggressive bids lose and high priced bids win. Again, its 'peanut butter' approach to applying overheads may be largely responsible for this outcome.

A fourth indication of an obsolete cost system occurs when a company's high volume products are being priced by competitors at what the company believes to be unrealistically low levels. The company should be particularly concerned when it is small, niche-market competitors who offer these lower prices. Often this is a signal that the smaller competitors, who generally produce a more limited range of products, and therefore are less susceptible to cost allocation distortions, have a better understanding of the true costs to manufacture their products.

A fifth symptom of an obsolete cost system is when a decision is made to outsource parts or components, which were previously made in-house, and the vendors' bids are considerably lower than expected. Such a situation casts doubt on the veracity of the computed in-house costs. The process whereby overhead is allocated is the probable culprit.

A sixth indication that a company's cost system is obsolete is when customers ignore price increases, even when there is no corresponding increase in cost. Customers usually react negatively to price increases. If customers show little or no reaction to the price increase or if competitors quickly match the price increase in spite of the fact that the company is not considered to be the market leader, then the cost system is probably underestimating the product's costs.

A final symptom of an obsolete cost system is when product or service profit margins appear to be unrelated to the company's core competencies. If the company finds that its cost system is reporting high profits on products that are not well aligned with the company's core competencies, then it is likely that cost distortions are occurring. For example, in situations where the company is the lone supplier of a product and yet commands no patent protection, brand recognition, or proprietary production processes, it should be especially circumspect. Another telltale sign is when competitors purchase the product, repackage it, and sell it at higher prices. Both circumstances are signs that the cost system is failing to provide accurate product costs.

Developing a better costing system

The presence of an obsolete cost system is equivalent to a catastrophe in waiting. Poor product cost information means that the company is vulnerable to competitors. Competitors will mercilessly prey on the company's naïve product costings.

Generally, the most common reason for product cost inaccuracies results from the overuse of volume-based cost drivers. When companies produce a range of products, featuring varying levels of production volume and production complexity, a sole reliance on volume-based cost drivers means that costs will be under-allocated to low volume and/or difficult-to-produce products and over-allocated to high volume and/or easy-to-produce products. The potential for such errors to occur in today's manufacturing environment is quite high. As Robin Cooper has shown, the fastest growing overhead cost in US manufacturing companies since the 1950s relates to product line diversity and the number of batches put into production; not to the number of units of output.

Companies that operate with distorted product cost information are likely to make incorrect pricing and product mix decisions. In particular, the company, believing it is incapable of matching its competitors' prices on the high volume business, is likely to become increasingly committed to chasing the illusory profits that its cost accounting system suggests are available on the low volume business. Invariably the company ends up with low market share, high per unit overhead costs, and large losses. Ironically, therefore, it is often the company itself, or more precisely the accounting function, that strikes the mortal blow.

Illuminating the 'hidden factory'

Jeffrey Miller and Thomas Vollmann in 1985 wrote an article in *Harvard Business Review* entitled 'The Hidden Factory'. The purpose of their article was to point out how traditional cost accounting systems provide good insight into how to control direct labour and direct materials, but are woefully inadequate in helping companies to manage their overhead costs. Noting that overhead costs are becoming an increasing percentage of a company's total value added, they encouraged companies to undertake a transaction-based analysis of overhead costs as a means of controlling such costs.

Miller and Vollmann's article is truly worthy of the descriptor 'seminal'. Their article served as a wake-up call to businesses and scholars alike. In particular, the authors revealed that in spite of the achievements made in developing models, formula, and sophisticated step-wise techniques for allocating overhead costs, the cost accountant provided little insight into what drives overhead costs or how these costs could best be minimized and/or managed. While it is true that Miller and Vollmann offered a three-pronged strategy for managing overhead costs – analysing the utility of transactions, increasing the stability of transactions, and employing greater automation – an even more important outcome of their article was the implicit challenge it offered. Accountants were challenged to think in creative and unconventional ways about illuminating the 'hidden factory'.

Robin Cooper and Robert Kaplan successfully took up the challenge of Miller and Vollmann. Their development of activity-based costing (ABC) offers substantial insights into what drives overhead costs. While some people continue to see ABC as merely a more accurate costing system, such an understanding of ABC is inchoate and naïve.

ABC represents the culmination of a long crusade of Cooper and Kaplan against the common practice of viewing overhead costs as a *fait accompli*, never to be further pondered or explored. These men have been strident critics of the view that the main job of the accountant is to devise cost drivers and overhead rates for *spreading* overheads from cost pools to products and services. Instead their system of ABC seeks to reverse the chronology of assigning overhead costs to products. ABC advises starting with products and services and trying to establish how these products and services draw upon, and make necessary in the first place, the company's overheads. In other words, they argue that it is the products and services that cause the overhead costs, and not the other way around.

As straightforward and commonsensical as Cooper and Kaplan's ABC approach may sound, they have succeeded in essentially standing the traditional cost allocation system on its head. It is important to understand the inversion they have performed before one can truly appreciate how ABC can be used to manage and control overhead costs, a topic that will be discussed at a later point in this chapter.

What is ABC?

ABC has several objectives. It seeks to inform production and sales efforts, identify hidden profits and losses, suggest ways for improving production efficiency and product design, and reveal the costs of different strategies. Regardless, of the ultimate purpose to which ABC will be applied, the process always begins with trying to establish truer product and service costs.

The process of establishing truer product and service costs begins with an identification of the full set of products or services a company offers. The company's senior managers then ask the question, 'How does our choice of product offerings lead to the incurrence of costs?' Obviously products cause the incurrence of such direct costs as materials and labour. For example, an ice-cream manufacturer incurs costs related to cream, sugar, flavouring, and direct labour.

In addition to these direct costs, however, the ice-cream manufacturer will also incur indirect costs. Some of these indirect costs will be incurred regardless of the manufacturer's choice of product mix. In particular, costs associated with facility sustaining activities, such as heating and lighting, building and grounds, and plant management, will be incurred regardless of whether the plant makes only vanilla ice cream or also makes chocolate, strawberry, walnut, rum raisin, cookies-n-cream, or whatever other combination one might concoct.

Some of the ice-cream manufacturer's indirect costs, however, will vary according to the number of products it produces. Most notable are the indirect costs that are caused by batch-level and product-sustaining activities. For example, the activities of purchasing inventory, storing inventory, moving inventory, scheduling product runs, cleaning equipment, setting-up equipment, expediting orders, and readying product for shipment to customers are all examples of batch-level activities that are complicated by the number of batches of products being produced. Likewise, the activities of process engineering, product specification, product marketing, and product research and development are all examples of product-sustaining activities that are complicated by the number of products being produced. The inevitable consequence of the more complicated production environment is the incurrence of higher

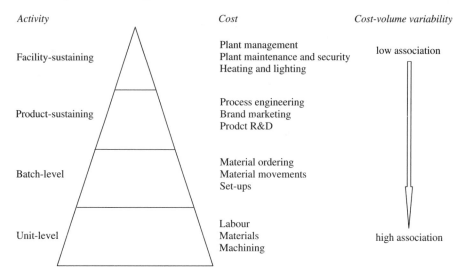

Figure 4.1 Activity and cost hierarchy

indirect production costs. Whether the benefits from producing multiple products are worth the added effort and costs depends upon the manufacturer's ability to benefit from economies of scale and/or scope.

An illustration of the various types of production activities and the type of costs typically associated with each activity is presented in Figure 4.1. These activities are presented as a hierarchy, progressing from activities that are focused at the unit level to activities that are facility sustaining.

The costs associated with unit-level, batch-level, and product-sustaining activities should be assigned to products using the appropriate cost driver. These drivers must relate a product's features to the type and amount of activities it necessitates and consumes. As a consequence, cost drivers are likely to be based on a host of product-related characteristics – such as product quality, product complexity, and product flexibility – and not just production volumes.

Facility-sustaining costs should not be allocated to products. No logical driver exists for allocating facility-sustaining costs, and they are best omitted from any product costing exercise. Facility-sustaining costs will, however, feature in any comparisons the company may make between plants operating in different locations.

There are two further points that should be noted about Figure 4.1. First, as indicated at the right-hand side of this figure, the cost/volume association increases with each step down the hierarchy. Second, the ability to link costs with specific products also increases with each step down the hierarchy. An appreciation for these two points helps reveal the types of situations that are most prone to cost distortions. In particular, we can now see that it is not only product diversity (i.e. volume and complexity) that may lead to cost distortions, but also the hierarchical level at which the majority of the total value-added costs occur. If the majority of the value-added occurs at a low level in the hierarchy, then the potential for cost distortions is low. If, however, the majority of the value-added occurs at a high level in the hierarchy, then the potential for cost distortions is high as well.

The mechanics of ABC

There are five main steps involved in the implementation of ABC. These steps consist of:

1 identifying activities;
2 determining the costs of activities;
3 identifying cost drivers for each activity;
4 determining the annual capacity for the activity; and
5 calculating the activity overhead rate.

In addition to the five main steps, additional factors, such as organizational culture, management leadership, and employee behaviour, will require consideration. While these latter factors are not specifically considered in this chapter, the interested reader is encouraged to read the articles by Norkiewicz and by Bhimani and Pigott, which are listed among the references at the end of the chapter.

The first step in implementing ABC is the identification of activities. Activities are best viewed as groupings of related actions. For example, the activity called 'machine set-up' is the outcome of a variety of individual actions. These actions might include cleaning or flushing the machine of any residue remaining from the previous batch that was run, adjusting the feed and speed of the machine for the new batch's requirements, and inspecting the first item produced to ensure that it conforms to the product's standards for fitness.

Just how general or specific a company wants its identification of activities to be depends on its tolerance for cost distortions. More specific groupings, assuming all other things being equal, result in less distortion. Of course, there is a price to be paid for these more specific groupings. The costs associated with operating the ABC system, due to its more exact and complex nature, will be higher. In the end, it is a matter of management judgement based on how much the company is willing to spend in return for the extra precision that can be achieved.

The second step in implementing ABC involves determining the costs of activities. Continuing with the machine set-up example used above, all the costs involved in executing machine set-ups need to be accumulated. Typically, this process of accumulating costs will require the aggregating of costs across multiple departments. For instance, the activity for setting-up machines often requires the combined contributions of engineering, maintenance, and the line workers themselves.

The process of accumulating these interdepartmental and interfunctional costs is not without its own share of challenges and difficulties. Records reporting the time spent by engineering or maintenance to perform set-ups are rarely maintained. The accountant, or whoever else is responsible for collecting these costs, must therefore consult other possible sources of information, by perhaps interviewing departmental managers, to gain an understanding of the resources that are being devoted to various organizational activities.

Step 3 in the implementation of ABC involves the selection of cost drivers. Actually, this third step consists of two stages. The first stage requires the identification of what are commonly called first-stage drivers. First-stage drivers trace the costs of inputs or resources into the cost pools that comprise each activity. Remember an activity consists of a number of company-defined interrelated actions. It is possible, for instance, that a company may wish to include as a set-up cost the costs of moving material from inventory storage to the shop floor. Consequently, it is for this reason that an activity may consist of a number of cost pools.

The appropriateness of these first-stage drivers has an important influence on the accuracy of the calculated product costs. Poorly chosen first-stage drivers will likely jeopardize the usefulness and accuracy of the ABC system. The cost distortions that may arise will ripple through the ABC system and potentially be exaggerated by the more prone to error second-stage drivers. It is for this reason that companies may wish to trace the consumption of resources directly (as opposed to allocating them) to cost pools.

Second-stage drivers are used to allocate the cost pool overheads to products. The cost driver chosen should relate to the product's consumption of the particular activity's cost pool. This may sound simple on the surface, but in reality it can be a bigger challenge. For example, should the cost pool that comprises the set-up activity be allocated to products based on the number of set-ups or the number of set-up hours? Using the number of set-ups to base the decision assumes that each set-up consumes the same amount of resources regardless of the product being manufactured. This may not be reasonable. Using set-up hours to base the allocation decision assumes that the amount of resources consumed during the set-up activity varies by product, i.e. the difficulty of setting-up the machines for the next batch of production. While this latter approach may sound more reasonable, certain manufacturing realities, or more accurately peculiarities, may compromise this approach as well. Consider, for example, the case of a paint manufacturer and its production of different paint colours. Less time is spent flushing out and cleaning the equipment when it changes from a batch run of white paint to one of red paint than is needed when the change is in the opposite direction. Thus, the order in which batches are performed could substantially influence the costs assigned to a product if set-up hours are used.

The fourth stage in the implementation of ABC requires the determination of the annual capacity for each activity. For example, if set-up hours are used as the cost driver for assigning the costs related to machine set-ups, then the company must determine the number of hours it has made available and therefore committed to this activity. As we shall shortly see, the overhead capacity assigned to each activity is equivalent to a fixed cost. It cannot be exceeded, due to physical capacity issues. Likewise, savings are not possible even on those occasions when consumption rates are less than the assigned capacity. The only way to reduce these activity costs is to

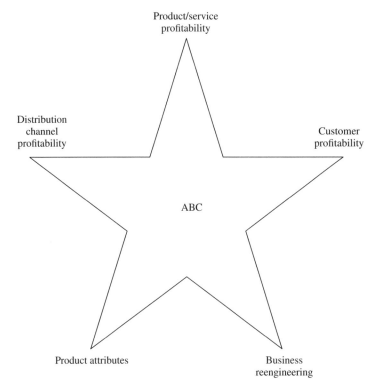

Figure 4.2 Primary applications of ABC information

eliminate or redeploy the resources. Of course, there are important strategic outcomes that are related to such decisions of elimination or redeployment. We will talk more about these strategic implications later in the chapter.

The fifth stage of ABC implementation involves the calculation of activity overhead rates. Let us say for the sake of illustration that 15,000 hours of machine set-up have been made available for the year at a cost of $600,000. Then the overhead rate for the set-up activity is $40.00 per set-up hour. This $40 rate will be used not only to cost products, but can also be used for the purpose of budgeting as well.

Using ABC to cost more than just products

Normally ABC is used to calculate product costs. ABC, however, has the potential to do much more than cost products. As Figure 4.2 tries to indicate, it can be used to assess customer profitability, compare distribution channel profitability, measure product attribute costs, and redesign business processes. The key to ABC's power is based on its segregation of costs into activities. Traditional costing systems merely accumulate costs by function or department. But because many business activities cut across functions, these traditional cost systems offer little insight into managing customers, distribution channels, product features, and the business processes that underlie all organizational action. Meanwhile, ABC, by revealing the costs of activities, illuminates what an organization might do to enhance customer value and organizational profitability.

Product/service profitability

As already mentioned, ABC adds accuracy to the calculation of product and service costs. With this added accuracy comes the ability to discern and differentiate between the profitability of different products and services. The literature is full of stories about companies that have discovered through their use of ABC that products that were thought to be valuable cash cows were actually cash-draining dogs. For instance, Cooper and Kaplan's case study of Schrader Bellows revealed as much as a 645 per cent difference between the costs that were computed using a traditional cost system and an ABC system. By providing more accurate and less distorted cost information, ABC helps companies to enhance product and service profitability.

Customer profitability

ABC reveals the costs of activities that can be related not only to products but also to customers. In particular, there is often a customer-identifiable pattern to the consumption of the organization's resources. High-volume customers often consume fewer resources than low-volume customers do. Remember the cost associated with processing a sales order is typically the same whether the order is for one unit or a thousand units.

Research findings show that it is not uncommon for 30 per cent of the customers to generate 150–200 per cent of a company's profits, 40 per cent of the customers to be profit-neutral, and the remaining 30 per cent of customers to actually be causing losses and destroying company value. Companies need to understand the profile of the customers that they are best matched to serving. Otherwise, competitors who better understand these matches will cherry-pick the profitable customers.

> **Consider this . . .**
>
> A textile manufacturer was asked to quote to retain the business of one of its key retail customers after the customer was approached with significantly discounted prices by one of the manufacturer's competitors. An ABC customer profitability analysis showed the manufacturer made significantly higher profits from this customer than the existing costing system indicated. Profits from this customer had been subsidizing large losses generated by custom work performed for sports, community, and education organizations. The manufacturer quoted prices reduced by 20 per cent to the retailer, retained the business and then went about the difficult job of addressing the profitability of its other customers.
>
> *Source*: Dimonte, R. and Pickering, M. (1997). Activity Based Costing: Strategic Cost Management. Deloitte, Touche & Tohmatsu.   http://www.deloitte.com.au/content/abc.asp, accessed on 7 January 1998.

A good example of a company's awakening to the different profitabilities associated with its different customers is recounted in the side panel on page 40.

Distribution channel profitability

Companies rely upon a variety of mediums to distribute their products and services. For example, companies can wholesale, retail, or sell directly to end customers using a dedicated sales force. Each of these choices implies different levels of organizational effort and expense. While the best distribution channel is not necessarily the cheapest, costs must be borne in mind.

In recent years banks have been particularly aware of, and savvy about, the costs associated with using different distribution channels. Realizing that the transaction costs arising from personal teller service is much higher than automated teller machines, telephone banking, and electronic banking, banks have begun phasing in different fee structures to reflect the different costs associated with each transaction medium. For many banks, ABC information has proved instrumental in costing and pricing its distribution channels.

Product attribute costing

Mike Walker has been particularly influential in extending the ABC frontiers into the realm of measuring and accounting for product and service attribute costs. Essentially he has taken the ABC analysis a level deeper than has traditionally been done. Walker correctly observes that it is not the product *per se* that drives costs, but the various features or attributes that are associated with the product. Accordingly, he encourages companies to cost the attributes of their products and services to ensure that the associated benefit can be justified against the associated cost. Walker calls this extension of ABC, ABCII.

In many ways, Walker's technique, or so it has been argued, is an after-the-fact calculation of what target costing proponents advocate doing during the planning and design of new products. This criticism, however, may not be justified. The product development process is generally ongoing, meaning that what a company makes or provides today serves to inform and guide what it will make tomorrow. It is a bit nonsensical and artificial to separate product evaluation from product planning. By understanding the existing dynamics between product costs and product function, the organization is in a better position to decide the make-up of its next generation of products.

Business process reengineering

ABC information becomes an invaluable source of data for restructuring and redesigning business operations for the purpose of achieving cost savings and boosting operational effectiveness. The cost information that traditional costing systems supply often falls well short of what managers truly need to run their businesses effectively. Too often managers will react to cost accounting numbers by saying, 'We need to achieve an across-the-board X per cent cut in operating expenses.'

Unfortunately, these edicts have no long lasting effect. At best they produce a temporary reduction in costs. Because the across-the-board cuts rarely offer understanding into what causes the costs, and how to eliminate or control their incurrence, the organization's behaviour is effectively unchanged. As a result, these across-the-board cuts frequently produce only the illusion of cost savings. Typically the efforts have only resulted in delaying or pushing into a future period the cost incurrence. Plant maintenance and research and development are two classic examples and perennial victims of cost-cutting exercises.

To achieve a long-term reduction in costs requires managers to control the activities that give rise to the costs in the first place. By focusing manager attention across functional silos, ABC helps them to identify situations where effort is being duplicated or provides minimal value-added. As an example of what might be achieved, one Australian telecommunications company used ABC to both enhance its processes and reduce its costs. This company reduced its customer invoicing lead time by one-third and benefited from cost savings of over $15 million through the removal of duplicated activities.

It is appropriate to sound a note of caution, lest the unwary become sidetracked with their use of ABC. ABC should only be used to help illuminate and control organizational strategy. It should not be used as a substitute. Michael Porter, in his 1996 *Harvard Business Review* article entitled 'What is Strategy?' makes a very impassioned plea for the realization that operational efficiency cannot substitute for strategy. Using ABC merely to chop costs can compromise an organization's strategy and erode its competitive advantage.

Situations most likely to benefit from ABC implementation

Some scholars believe that the usefulness of ABC depends on three factors: the percentage that overhead represents of a product or service's total cost; the number of products or services offered; and the degree of competition. Higher values on these three factors imply that ABC will produce greater benefits. In essence, organizations are urged to plot their particular organizational characteristics against each of the three factors to determine the likely extent to which they will benefit from ABC. Figure 4.3 illustrates this process.

Number of products

Firms that make multiple products (or offer multiple services) are more likely to encounter cost distortions. In the extreme case, when only one product is manufactured, the potential for cost distortions is zero. However, as the number of products manufactured increases, so too does the likelihood for cost distortions.

Some organizations erroneously assume that it is the number of end products that should count. This is false. It is the number of all products, both final products as well as intermediate. Consequently, a New Zealand manufacturer of whitewares, who claimed it only produced a limited line of dishwashers and ranges and therefore did not need ABC, was surprised to learn just how wrong its thinking was. Due

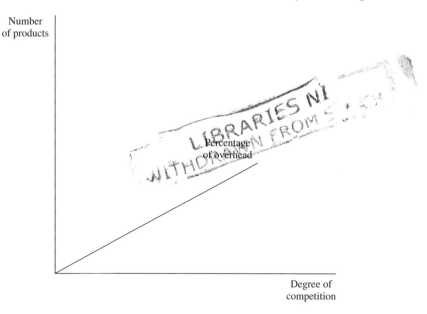

Figure 4.3 Situational determinants of ABC usefulness

to the fact that it produced hundreds of intermediate components, the potential for cost distortions was actually very high and ABC was well suited to this company.

Overhead as a percentage of total product cost

When the amount of overhead to be allocated represents only a very small percentage of a product or service's total cost, then the chance for cost distortions is similarly small. However, as the overhead percentage to total cost increases, so too does the chance for cost distortions. Under these high overhead situations, ABC is deemed to be especially beneficial.

Degree of competition

As previously alluded to in this chapter, an organization's poor understanding of its product or service costs can be like blood to a school of sharks. Competitors will prey upon such a mistake and wrest market share away. Of course, such a scenario assumes that competition exists. In some situations competition is stymied by high initial investments (e.g. the utilities industry) or by government edict (e.g. the defence industry). As a result, some observers believe that ABC only needs to be implemented under conditions of high competitiveness.

The counter argument to the context-specific use of ABC

Not all scholars agree that ABC should be viewed in situational conforming and non-conforming terms. This latter group of scholars sees such an approach as too reactive. They argue that the idea of forgiving and unforgiving environments, a concept made popular by Khandwalla during the 1970s, no longer exists. Any organization that fails to continually learn and improve jeopardizes its ability to survive. ABC, because it promises among other things to assist management with ways to enhance business effectiveness, is seen as a necessity and not a luxury. This idea is particularly well summarized by Mike Walker (1991), who says:

> It is a misconception that ABC applies only to multi-product organizations: in fact it is a key tool in managing any business efficiently.

Before we conclude this discussion of ABC, it is worth noting the cautionary advice that has been raised by Thomas Johnson. In his book *Relevance Regained: From Top-Down Control to Bottom-Up Empowerment*, Johnson puts forward the thesis that ABC has been oversold as a cure-all to whatever ails organizations. According to Johnson, it is not better costing that helps organizations to successfully compete, but the ability to become more customer-focused.

Following the lead of Deming, Johnson argues that today's organizational imperative is to become more responsive to customer needs. In particular, organizations must continually strive to reduce delays, scrap, and variations in the manufacturing or service delivery process. ABC, he believes, does not promote this achievement.

Johnson is right that ABC, at least when it is solely used as a costing tool, will be unable to offer illumination and guidance on what an organization should do to promote effective change. However, as previously noted, ABC is intended to encompass more than simply offering better product or service costings. By illuminating activities, ABC is meant to help managers find creative ways to eliminate non-value-added operations. Product inspection, for instance, only adds value if the organization has poor quality going through its production process.[1] But as TQM advocates have argued all along, if organizations get the job done right the first time, the need to inspect for quality becomes moot. Thus, it would appear that by identifying the amount of resources committed to the organizational effort of inspecting in quality, the organization comes to realize the cost of its poor quality. By developing methods for rooting out the quality problems that plague the organization, the organization will find that it is accomplishing just what Deming and now Johnson are advocating: designing processes that seek to eliminate variation, scrap, and delays. Thus, it seems only when we constrict our view of ABC to being merely a costing tool that Johnson's criticisms appear justified. When we progress beyond seeing ABC as merely a costing tool and begin seeing it as a partner to TQM and JIT, to be used in the organization's quest to eliminate waste and continually improve, then Johnson's criticisms appear to be less appropriate.

---

[1] There are many individuals who feel that product inspections can never add value. Customers expect products to perform to their product specifications 100 per cent of the time. They accept and understand that competing firms' product specifications can vary widely. They merely ask (and demand) that the firm remains faithful to its product specifications. Accordingly, product inspections can never serve to add value.

Summary

ABC offers a very different approach to product and service costing. In particular, ABC highlights the importance of costing activities, rather than merely capturing costs at the work centre or departmental level. The costs of these activities are subsequently assigned to products and services using what are called second-stage cost drivers. This method of product and service costing is meant to improve the accuracy with which product and services are costed.

Of course, ABC offers more than just the ability to cost products and services more accurately. ABC can also help managers to identify profitable customers, determine preferred distribution channels, assess the utility of product/service attributes, and aid with process reengineering. As such, ABC, which is now entering its second decade, is continuing to prove its worth and attract a growing following of organizational users.

References

Bhimani, A. and Pigott, D. (1992). Implementing ABC: A Case Study of Organizational and Behavioural Consequences. *Management Accounting Research*, **3**, 119–132.

Chenhall, R. and Langfield-Smith, K. (1998). Adoption and Benefits of Management Accounting Practices: An Australian Study. *Management Accounting Research*, **9**(1), 1–19.

Cooper, R. and Kaplan, R. (1998). The Promise – and Peril – of Integrated Cost Systems. *Harvard Business Review*, **76**(4), 109–119.

Cooper, R. and Kaplan, R. (1991). Profit Priorities from Activity-Based Costing. *Harvard Business Review*, **69**(3), 130–135.

Drucker, P. (1995). The Information Executives Truly Need. *Harvard Business Review*, **73**(1), 54–62.

Foster, G. Strategic Management Accounting: New Directions and Lessons from Company Experience. (Seminar).

Gooselin, M. (1997). The Effect of Strategy and Organizational Structure on the Adoption and Implementation of Activity-Based Costing. *Accounting, Organizations & Society*, **22**(2), 105–122.

Innes, J. and Mitchell, F. (1995). A Survey of Activity-Based Costing in the UK's Largest Companies. *Management Accounting Research*, **6**(2), 137–153.

Johnson, T. (1992). *Relevance Regained: From Top-Down Control to Bottom-Up Empowerment*, The Free Press.

Lemak, D., Austin, W., Montgomery, J. and Reed, R. (1996). The ABCs of Customer-Centred Performance Measures. *SAM Advanced Management Journal*, **61**(2), 4–10.

Malmi, T. (1997). Towards Explaining Activity-Based Costing Failure: Accounting and Control in a Decentralized Organization. *Management Accounting Research*, **8**(4), 365–480.

Ness, J. and Cucuzza, T. (1995). Tapping the Full Potential of ABC. *Harvard Business Review*, **73**(4), 130–138.

Norkiewicz, A. (1994). Nine Steps to Implementing ABC. *Management Accounting*, **76**(10), 28–33.

Schildbach, T. (1997). Cost Accounting in Germany. *Management Accounting Research*, **8**(3), 261–276.

Walker, M. (1991). ABC Using Product Attributes. *Management Accounting*, October, 34–35.

5

Cost of quality

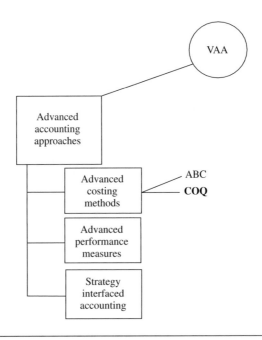

Chapter objectives

- Discuss how quality serves to endow an organization with competitive advantage.
- Trace the roots of the quality movement.
- Identify the leading luminaries of the quality movement and discuss their approaches.
- Discuss how management accountants have tried to construct a cost of quality (COQ) framework.
- Identify the benefits and limitations of this COQ framework.

The importance of good quality has been heard again and again. Case studies from over the past two decades have emphasized the significant cost savings that accompany quality initiatives. For example, Ormon, a leading Japanese supplier of computer control equipment, achieved a seven per cent decrease in market claims, a nine per cent decrease in defective products within the production process, and a 21 per cent decrease in the ratio of total quality costs to sales after introducing its quality cost system. As another example, IBM credits its quality programme with helping its small business units (SBUs) achieve waste reductions that ranged from 15–40 per cent of sales.

The mandate for achieving consistent levels of high quality is highlighted in a recent Gallup survey of US consumers. The survey reveals that consumers would pay 21 per cent more for a better quality car, 42 per cent more for a better quality dishwasher, 67 per cent more for a better quality television, and 72 per cent more for a better quality piece of furniture. The premium value that consumers place on high quality products and services has led some writers to suggest that quality is no longer a competitive weapon, but a prerequisite to survival.[1]

This chapter examines the implications of this quality movement from a management accounting perspective. Before discussing these implications, however, it is important to have a common and well-grounded understanding of the concept of quality. We begin, therefore, by first tracing the evolutionary developments in quality. Following this history, various individuals' attempts to illuminate and provide practical guidance for the enhancement of organizational quality are discussed. Armed with this knowledge, we examine the value-added that management accountants can bring to the subject, as well as the lessons still to be learned.

Tracing the roots of the quality movement

The emergence of quality as a significant organizational issue is often associated with various dates. One group of scholars, for instance, traces its origins to Armand Feigenbaum's article entitled 'Total Quality Control', which appeared in the *Harvard Business Review* in 1956. Meanwhile, there are other scholars who credit Joseph Juran as the founding father, noting that his *Quality Control Handbook* appeared in 1951. In reality, both groups are right, and both groups are wrong.

Juran was certainly the first to write about quality. Feigenbaum, however, was the first to show that quality was an organization-wide issue, including the quality control of supplies, design, production, delivery, and after-sales service. So, in some ways, both groups of scholars are correct.

Predating the work of Juran and Feigenbaum, however, were the quality initiatives of Western Electric in the 1920s and the US Department of Defence (DOD) in the 1940s. Both organizations, and especially the US DOD, provided the groundwork, albeit crude and rudimentary, from which later quality improvements would

---

[1] This idea is evident in Cengiz Haksever's 1996 *Business Horizon's* article and Bolwijn and Kumpe's 1990 *Long Range Planning* article.

emerge. For instance, the DOD's statistical sampling of suppliers' munitions shipments during the Second World War was a first step in the quality movement's evolution from quality control to quality assurance. This change in mindset from quality control to quality assurance is especially evident in the DOD's later approaches to ensuring quality. In December of 1963, it issued a regulation requiring contractors to identify the costs of preventing and correcting non-conforming supplies and to use quality cost data to manage the quality programs. In 1980, the DOD issued a regulation requiring the contractors to record the costs associated with internal and external product failures. Although the contractor was initially required only to collect the quality cost information, not report it to the DOD, this prescription changed. In March of 1985, the DOD issued an amended regulation that required contractors to furnish cost data upon request.

Ever since the early quality initiatives of Western Electric and the US DOD, as well as the seminal work of Juran and Feigenbaum, the field has been ably built upon by such personalities as W. Edwards Deming, Philip Crosby, Kaoru Ishikawa, and Genichi Taguchi and such organizations as Toyota, Xerox, and 3M. Today there is an abundance of literature and practice showcasing the best-in-class quality initiatives.

What is quality?

All too often, discussions of quality occur without a full understanding of what the concept includes. Intuitively the concept may appear simple and straightforward. But in reality, it is anything but simple and straightforward.

Let's begin with a relatively easy example. What does good or poor quality mean when applied to a product such as a laser printer? Some thoughts that are likely to come to mind are the product's ability to produce clear, smudge-free, sharply defined typeface. Such notions seem not only reasonable; they are also common computer parlance, being represented in such terms as draft quality, near-letter quality, letter quality.

Another aspect of a laser printer that is likely to be associated with the concept of quality is product consistency or reliability. In particular, there might be an expectation that the product will be robust enough to withstand prolonged use over an extended period of time, assuming the manufacturer's scheduled maintenance programme is followed.

The identification of these base features of a laser printer's quality is invariably the easy part of the job. But what about such product features as print speed, paper size accommodated, or production of colours? Are they part of the purview of laser printer quality?

Let's now examine a situation that challenges to a greater extent our ability to elucidate quality. What does good or poor quality mean when applied to the service one receives when depositing or withdrawing money from a bank teller? Is it simply accuracy? Or is it more than being properly credited or receiving the correct amount of money? Does timeliness or the speed with which we are served determine quality? What about the friendliness (e.g. greeting a customer by name) or helpfulness (e.g. informing the customer about a new bank service) of the teller? What about the parking facilities, availability of a drive-through service, the convenience of location, and the decor of the bank? Are these also quality matters?

As these two examples are meant to point out, the identification of what constitutes good versus poor quality represents a far more difficult task than might be initially apparent. Quality is commonly an integral and inseparable part of the total product or service experience. A reductionist approach to the identification and measurement of quality may at best only provide an incomplete picture of a product or service's quality. There are times when trying to reduce product or service features into discrete categories of 'quality' and 'not quality' is a bit like the satirical story of the quality assurance manager who was given the CEO's tickets for a symphony by Schubert. When the CEO inquired the next morning about the concert, the quality assurance manager handed him a memo that derided the composer's use of multiple violinists, who were often either silent or playing the exact same notes as the first violinist, and criticized the use of a horn section, which merely repeated (and add no further value to) what had just been played by the string section.

To advance our understanding of quality, we now examine the views of four leading luminaries of the quality movement: Joseph Juran, W. Edwards Deming, Philip Crosby, and Genichi Taguchi. Together the views of these four men will be used to construct a working definition of quality.

Joseph M. Juran

Juran defines quality as 'fitness for use', which has the following five dimensions:

- quality of design;
- quality of conformance;
- availability;
- safety; and
- field use.

A product or service is fit for use when a customer can rely on it for whatever intended purpose he/she had in mind. As an example, a food manufacturer should be able to provide wholesale and retail grocers with food products that are free from damage, correctly labelled, and easy to handle and display. The grocer should, in turn, provide its customers with quick and convenient checkout services and offer food products that are undamaged, easy to find, and correctly labelled and priced.

Juran believes that a comprehensive quality programme is needed to ensure an organization's fitness-for-use mandate. Such a programme is characterized by its establishment of quantifiable goals, a systematic plan for achieving the goals, and a measurement and monitoring system to track organizational progress and performance.

Juran's approach to quality follows the classic 'plan, do, check, act' model. While feeling that this approach was well suited to the needs of shop floor managers and workers, he recognized that it was unlikely to attract senior management attention. These individuals are largely attracted to dollar figures. Accordingly, Juran included a financial analysis as part of his approach to quality, advocating the use of an economic conformance level model.

The economic conformance level approach (ECLA) is an application of microeconomic theory to quality control. Under this approach, the organization seeks to minimize the total costs of preventing, appraising, and reworking defective products. In other words, ECLA encourages the organization to continue to improve its quality until there is no longer a positive return.

An important, and sometimes overlooked, implication of Juran's cost of quality approach is the idea that zero defects is not a practical goal. The organization would have to invest too dearly in prevention and appraisal activities to achieve a zero defect level. Accordingly, a goal of zero defects is uneconomical and wasteful.

W. Edwards Deming

Deming, in stark opposition to Juran, defined quality as reduced variation and maintained that the ultimate goal of any quality programme should be continuous improvement, and ultimately the achievement of zero defects. He loathed the naïve thinking of those people who thought that quality had to be traded-off against productivity. Much to the contrary, he believed that improvements in quality led to a reduction in costs (due to fewer mistakes, fewer delays, fewer snags, and better use of machine time and materials). Meanwhile, a reduction in costs, by definition, leads to an improvement in productivity.

Deming believed that there were two impediments to the achievement of zero defects: common causes and special causes. Common causes are systemic and impact in a general way on departments and workstations. Some typical examples include poor product design, ill-suited machinery, and poor plant layouts.

Special causes are product variations that are attributable to individual employees or activities. They include lack of worker knowledge or skill, worker inattention, and incoming materials characterized by poor quality. It was the responsibility of management to control common causes and shop floor workers to control special causes.

Deming advocated the use of statistical process control (SPC) as a means of ensuring quality control. Although Walter Shewart at Bell Labs originally developed SPC in the 1930s, Deming published his refinement of the technique in a classic article entitled 'On the Statistical Theory of Errors'. SPC requires the worker to take periodic, ongoing samples of work and to compare these samples against some established standard. If a sample data point is within the upper and lower limits associated with the standard, the process is said to be in control. If, on the other hand, the sample point falls outside the upper or lower limit, or if the data displays a trend that implies a limit is likely to be exceeded, the process is deemed out of control. In the event of an out-of-control situation, it is the responsibility of the worker to stop the process and identify and eliminate the cause for the variation.

Management had the ongoing responsibility of enhancing and continually improving upon the underlying production system. In addition to continually improving infrastructural elements (e.g. plant layout), management needed to develop long-term relationships with its vendors and stress the importance of providing consistently high quality incoming materials. Furthermore, managers had to break down department and worker–supervisor barriers, and they had to create a climate that was free of finger pointing and blame.

Philip B. Crosby

Crosby defines quality as 'conformance to requirements'. Quality can be precisely measured by how faithfully the product design has been reproduced. As Crosby wryly notes, 'error is not required to fulfill the laws of nature.' As such, a Lada that meets Lada design specifications is as much a quality product as a Rolls-Royce that meets Rolls-Royce design specifications.

Like Deming, Crosby believed that quality should be measured based on an organization's ability to achieve zero defects. But Juran and Crosby differed in terms of how this defect-free environment can best be achieved. Whereas Deming stressed worker self-control, Crosby stressed the importance of management. In particular, he felt that managers who expected imperfection received imperfection, while managers who were committed to a standard of zero defects received enhanced worker effort and were more likely to achieve their goal of zero defects. Accordingly, Crosby was a champion of any and all techniques that increased worker motivation, e.g. the introduction of a Zero Defects Day.

Crosby, just like Deming, eschewed the belief that an organization could spend too much money on quality. Of course, Crosby was a bit more of a zealot on this issue. According to Crosby, quality is 'free'. The more a firm spends on improving its quality, the more it is recompensed. There is no such thing as too much quality.

Genichi Taguchi

Taguchi criticizes quality programmes that are couched in terms of zero defects. The problem with a zero defect mentality is that it sanctions variations in product quality. Unfortunately these variations, however slight they may be individually, may in combination produce a result that is unacceptable.

To illustrate his point, Taguchi refers to the Ford and Mazda joint auto venture that developed in the late 1980s. Under this joint venture, Mazda was asked to build many of the transmissions that went into Ford's cars. Although the Ford and Mazda manufacturing plants built to identical specifications, it soon became apparent that the Ford-built transmissions were associated with much higher warranty costs.

Ford decided to investigate the matter and was initially quite surprised and perplexed by its findings. Contrary to its expectations, its US plant had met the zero defect standard for every subcomponent comprising the transmission. It wasn't until Ford scrutinized the situation more closely that it realized what was actually happening. The Japanese transmissions exhibited virtually no deviation from the target whatsoever. Meanwhile, the Ford-built transmissions were characterized by a number of seemingly trivial deviations from the target. In actual practice, however, these small deviations tended to stack up and caused greater friction and vibration than either its transmissions or customers were ultimately willing to withstand.

According to Taguchi, zero defects is a recipe for failure. Instead, the organization must strive for zero deviation from the target. This idea of consistently meeting targets, and not the target range, is represented in Taguchi's quality loss function (QLF). The QLF portrays the costs of poor quality as:

$$L = c(x - T)^2 + k$$

Where: L = total cost of poor quality
c = cost of failing to meet the target
T = the target
k = the minimum loss to society

Taguchi's QLF depicts two very important points. First, quality costs increase as the actual result moves away from the target. In other words, there is no such thing as an acceptable or cost-free range of quality. Second, the cost of quality does not increase at a steady rate. It increases geometrically at the squared rate of the difference between actual and targeted. This second observation provides the rationale for Taguchi's often-cited statement, 'You gain virtually nothing from shipping a product that just barely satisfies the corporate standard over a product that just fails.' The difference between Taguchi's conception of cost of quality and conventional thinking on the matter is illustrated in Figure 5.1.

As Figure 5.1 reveals, the conventional loss function only deems a loss to have occurred when either the lower or upper specification has been exceeded. Taguchi, by contrast, believes a loss occurs each and every time the target is missed. The magnitude of this loss is a function of the distance the actual result is from the target.

Taguchi's ultimate approach to quality is to design products that are robust. A robust product is characterized by its ability to withstand the highly variable and demanding conditions to which customers customarily subject products. Customers include both those residing in as well as those residing outside the organization. Just as end customers may mishandle or misuse a product, so too might internal, downstream departments. As an example, an internal process may specify that workers should use extreme care when loading and unloading products, so as to avoid scratching the product's surface. Of course, there are likely to be occasions when employee fatigue or clumsiness overcomes even their best efforts of diligence and the product's surface becomes scratched.

Instead of writing commands and making exhortations, Taguchi believes that the organization's time would be better spent trying to fool-proof the system. Fool-proofing methods need not be elaborate or high-tech. For example, a response to

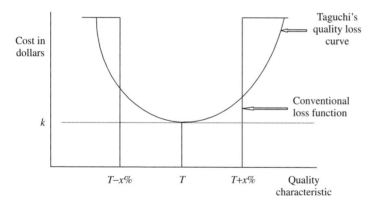

Figure 5.1 Taguchi's loss function

the occasional scratching of a product's surface as it moves through production is to develop a scratchproof surface.

The idea of fool-proofing or *poka-yoke* comes from Shigeo Shingo. He believes that employee mistakes are neither wilful nor the result of incompetence. Rather, lapses in employee attention are the primary causes of errors. As a consequence, it is the organization's responsibility to build into the work process a checklist so that the employee can never 'forget what he has forgotten'.

The end customers of a product are likely to subject the product to an even more hostile set of circumstances than the organization's internal customers do. On most occasions these abuses will be the result of a lapse of attention (e.g. dropping the product), although sometimes ignorance plays a role (e.g. overloading an electrical circuit). Regardless, however, of the origin of the customer's mistake, customers will invariably prefer products that can withstand high variations of use (misuse) to those products that cannot. The former products are characterized by high quality and the latter products by low quality.

The best approach for ensuring high quality, therefore, is to ensure that the product has a robust design. In particular, organizations should strive to design products that can withstand the end customer's wide variations in use, for it is this customer who typically exposes the product to the harshest conditions it is likely to experience. An organization that can reduce product failures in the field will discover a simultaneous ability to reduce defect rates inside its factory. In many ways Taguchi's conception of quality is a lot like 'killing two birds with one stone'.

Summary of the four quality gurus thoughts on quality

Juran, Deming, Crosby, and Taguchi have all significantly contributed to advancing the field of organizational quality. While each is adamant about the necessity for an organizational-wide quality initiative, each offers a different approach to how quality might best be achieved. Table 5.1 provides a summary of their four different approaches.

Table 5.1 A comparison of Deming, Juran, Crosby, and Taguchi's approaches to quality

Characteristic	Deming	Juran	Crosby	Taguchi
Definition of quality	Continuous improvement	Fitness for use	Conformance to requirements	A virtue of design
Why pursue quality	To lower costs, improve productivity, and achieve competitive success			
Cost of quality	Costs of quality initiatives are invariably outweighed by reductions achieved in overall costs	Must be weighed against the benefits using ECLA	Free	Must be matched against the benefits using QLF
Use of quantitative methods	SPC	Reliability programme supported by a broad array of statistical methods	Secondary to motivation	SPC and QLF
Role of top management	Support is critical			
Problem solvers	Workers	Professionals	Managers	Design engineers with workers and managers
Role of workers	Self-control	Incidental	Managerial goals	Self-control
Who causes problems?	85% managers	80+% managers	Unstated	Mostly design, some manufacture
Perpetual improvement	Zero defects	ECLA	Zero defects	Zero deviation
Key tools	SPC	ECLA	Motivation techniques	QLF, orthogonal array experiments
Environment most suitable to approach	High volume	Technical	People-oriented	Some volume plus some complexity
Focus	Process variability	Balancing costs	Management/ labour relations	Customer usage plus process variability
Quality inspection	None, all advocate prevention via on-line checking			
Organizational impact	Repercussions experienced throughout the entire organisation			
Time frame	Long term			
Investment	Expensive, with promise of greater return			
Difficulty	Difficult to implement			
Quality in design	Emphasise as solution			
Major problem	Lacks customer focus	Inappropriate if quality is competitive weapon	Lack of measures and reliance on leadership	Inappropriate if quality is competitive weapon

Adapted from Everett, A., Lecture notes, Operations Management, University of Otago MBA, 3 September 1997.

Based upon the insights provided by Juran, Deming, Crosby, and Taguchi, the following working definition of quality is used in this book:

Quality is the measure of goodness a customer ascribes to an organization's products or services. This measure of goodness is based on how the product/service performs relative to what was expected. Products/services that fail to achieve customer expectations are examples of low quality, products/services that achieve customer expectations are examples of high quality, and products/services that exceed customer expectations are examples of outstanding quality.

Accounting for cost of quality

Prior to the mid-1980s, accountants completely ignored the subject of quality. Even as late as 1989, Shank (1989) observed, with much surprise and puzzlement, that the issue of 'quality analysis is absent from accounting curricula and accounting journals.'

It was not until the early 1990s that accountants showed an appreciable interest in the subject of quality. An article by Shirley Daniel and Wolf Reitsperger, which appeared in the UK journal *Accounting, Organizations and Society* in 1991, followed a year later by Thomas Albright and Harold Roth's article, which appeared in the US journal *Accounting Horizons*, jump-started what had been a largely inactive field of research. While the subject of quality has never been, nor is it now, what one might call a 'hot' topic, it has finally emerged from the backwaters of accounting study.

In fairness to accountants, it is possible that their previous silence on quality is purposeful and not an act of neglect. In particular, if they ascribe to the views of Deming and Crosby, then they would naturally be sceptical of the benefits of trying to account for quality. Rather than promote the idea of analysing the costs associated with quality, especially poor quality, they would argue that the organization is better served when it seeks to ensure its work is accomplished correctly the first time around. In very blunt terms, such accountants would view the exercise of accounting for quality as an utter and complete waste of time.

According to Yoshihiro Ito, an acceptance of Deming and Crosby's views on quality largely explains why Japanese accountants have traditionally not bothered accounting for quality. Japanese accountants, like other members in the organization, see quality as an end in itself and not as a means to an end. As a result, they do not believe it is necessary to collect information that merely confirms what they have accepted as a basic truth: quality can never be too high.

In contrast to Deming and Crosby's views about the irrelevance of accounting for quality, Juran and Taguchi believe that accounting information plays an important role. In particular, they advocate the categorization of quality costs into prevention, appraisal, and failure costs. From this categorization, the organization can track trends in its quality programmes and determine the optimal trade-off between prevention and appraisal costs.

Lately there has been a growing trend in accounting for quality, even among the Japanese. Three recent global developments have substantially contributed to this change in practice. These developments can be listed as the versatility and power of today's computers, the prominence of ISO quality standards, and the growing threat of product liability lawsuits.

Today's computers are not only fast, but they are also becoming increasingly user-friendly. As such, they now offer the necessary platform for running a cost of quality database. The creation of such databases was hampered in the past by size and scope considerations. But with today's computers, cost of quality information – including the interactions between prevention, appraisal, and failure costs, as well as the categorization of costs by responsibility centre – is just a keystroke away.

The emergence of a global business market has been another factor behind the upsurge in the popularity of cost of quality. In their attempt to decrease the uncertainty that a global market – with its many languages and cultures – brings, organizations have been keen to establish a set of standards that commands worldwide recognition and acceptance. Such standardization is especially important for downstream organizations that rely on the incoming product or services of upstream suppliers. The International Organization for Standardization was created with this purpose in mind. It has issued a series of quality standards – ISO9000, 9001, 9002, and 9003 – that establish guidelines for the quality control of everything from product planning to product shipment. A more recently released standard, ISO9004, now requires the measurement of quality costs. Accordingly, cost of quality is no longer a practice of choice, but a practice of necessity.

The third factor that has boosted the use of cost of quality data is the growing threat of product liability lawsuits. While product liability is far from a recent issue in places like the US, it was only introduced into Japan in 1995. Of course, even in the US the spectre of product liability continues to grow. Organizations have responded by establishing quality programmes as evidence of their good faith attempts to reduce and even eliminate the effects of faulty products. As a way of showing the magnitude of their efforts, organizations have begun collecting and disclosing these costs.

As a result of these three recent developments, organizations are increasingly implementing cost of quality reporting systems. In the remaining sections of this chapter, we explore the composition of cost of quality reporting systems and examine how organizations use such systems in practice.

What are cost of quality reporting systems?

A cost of quality reporting system provides the organization with information about its prevention, appraisal, and failure costs. This information helps employees to prioritize quality problems and may offer clues about how such problems can be overcome. Additionally, the cost of quality information is sometimes used to establish the 'correct' amount of costs to spend on the prevention and detection of poor quality.

Table 5.2 Cost of quality categorizations

Category	Definition
Prevention costs	Costs of preventing poor quality, including the costs for training and education, and attempts to enhance quality through product or service design and process improvements
Appraisal costs	Costs of monitoring and selecting out poor quality products, including the costs for inspecting and grading products and services to ensure they conform to established quality standards
Internal failure costs	Costs of fixing a poor quality product or service prior to its delivery to the customer, including the costs of rework and scrap
External failure costs	Costs of fixing a poor quality product or service after it has been delivered to the customer, including costs for return shipment, warranty, and customer 'ill will'

Table 5.2 lists and defines the types of quality costs that organizations commonly collect and analyse. Note that failure costs are often further subdivided into internal and external, depending upon the point at which the quality problem is discovered. In general, there is an inverse relationship between spending on prevention and appraisal costs and spending on internal and external failure costs.

For some organizations, especially service organizations, the potential to detect poor quality before it leaves the organization is severely limited or not possible. Consider, for example, the interaction between a bank teller and a customer. While it is possible to teach tellers effective customer relation techniques (a prevention cost), it is not possible to detect a poor quality interaction before the customer has experienced the detrimental consequence. As a result, quality costs generally fall into either the prevention or external failure categories. There has, however, been a growing trend, whereby an organization's telephone interactions with its customers are sometimes monitored for quality assurance. Such a technique appears to be the service industry's answer to detecting poor quality and correcting the impact such mistakes can have on the customer's future purchasing decisions. Accordingly, one might classify these quality assurance costs as appraisal and internal failure costs.

The Honda approach to quality costing

Honda maintains a large computer network, linking all factories, laboratories, and dealers. Like many organizations, Honda finds that the accumulation of prevention, appraisal, and internal failure costs is the easy task. The accumulation of external failure costs is much more difficult. On the one hand, it is relatively easy to assign a cost for reworking the product or providing a replacement. But how does an organization account for the damage to its image and reputation that also results? Remember too that studies often show that only about 10 per cent of dissatisfied customers will actually make a complaint. The other 90 per cent, however, are unlikely to stew in silence. Instead, these dissatisfied customers are likely to switch their business to a competitor. Additionally, it is possible that they will share their feelings of dissatisfaction with other current or potential customers. It is for this reason that Deming often referred to these 'hidden' costs as the most important figures a manager needs.

Honda shares Deming's belief in the importance of failure costs. Although it routinely collects and calculates costs of quality using the conventional framework of prevention, appraisal, internal failure, and external failure costs, prevention and appraisal costs are mostly considered secondary information. Failure costs, especially external failure costs, receive the lion's share of attention.

Honda's cost of quality programme begins with the decentralized units' entry of external failure costs directly into Honda's worldwide computer network. Honda's Market Quality Management Block then analyses the data according to cause and place of the problem. This information is then forwarded to the factory line managers where the problem originated, as well as to Honda's design laboratory staff. It is the former's responsibility to make improvements in their processes, while it is the latter's responsibility to make improvements in the product's design.

Honda is most adamant about the need to assign quality costs to responsibility centres. The assignment of these costs is intended to stimulate awareness of the importance of and the organization's commitment to quality, as well as to motivate employees to improve quality. Often it is the case that departments will need to work in co-operation to successfully overcome and solve quality problems. It is for this reason that Honda is not overly concerned about the assignment of a quality problem to one particular department. Senior managers simply make larger allocations to the departments they think are most likely to generate quality improvements. As an example, because it is commonly believed that product defects are largely due to faults in product design, a larger percentage of the failure costs are typically allocated to the design department versus the production departments.

In sum, Honda routinely collects cost of quality information across the four categories of prevention, appraisal, internal failure, and external failure costs. However, it predominantly focuses on external failure costs. These external failure costs are analysed and allocated to responsible departments. Although Honda expects all departments to contribute to the elimination of quality problems, it is especially interested in discovering design improvements that can nip quality problems in the bud. As Honda's senior managers are often heard saying, the best way to eliminate poor quality is to improve the design of the product at the product planning and development stages.

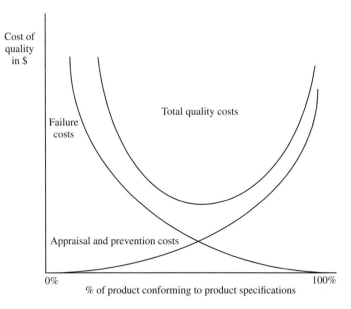

Figure 5.2 Juran's economic conformance level approach

Juran's cost of quality approach

Quality costing under Juran's approach goes beyond tabulating quality costs and assigning them to specific responsibility centres. In addition, Juran uses these quality costs to determine an organization's optimal level of prevention and appraisal costs. The optimal level is determined by reference to a quadratic economic conformance level cost curve. This curve is based on two separate cost curves: (a) the combined costs of prevention and appraisal; and (b) the combined costs of internal and external failure. As shown in Figure 5.2, prevention and appraisal costs increase as defects decrease, while internal and external failure costs decrease.

A total quality cost curve can be derived by combining (summing) the two curves. According to Juran, the optimal point to operate along the total cost of quality curve is determined by taking the derivative of this curve's equation. As it happens, this optimal point is at the same defect rate as where the prevention and appraisal cost curve and the internal and external failure cost curves intersect.

The simplicity of Juran's microeconomic approach to accounting for quality is very alluring and seductive. Just plug in the values for the quality costs associated with different defect rates, and bingo one can solve for the optimal level of quality. But is the answer to organizational quality issues really this easy and straightforward?

In reality, this approach's promise of optimization, though pleasing to the ears, is more a falsehood than a truth. Just as the enchanting music of the sirens enticed Greek sailors to unwittingly sail too close to the island's rocky shores where their ships were broken asunder and the sailors immediately swallowed up by the sea, so too can an overfascination with an economic conformance level approach be equally dangerous.

The main problem with Juran's approach is its wooden and static nature. In particular, the underlying cost curves lack dynamism. Instead they are characterized as hard and rigid. No provision is made for further improvement. Why, for instance, can't we expect the organization to create and then recreate new cost curves, with each cure being below the previous one? Isn't this the very premise of total quality management and the idea of continuous improvement that underlies it? In sum, organizations are cautioned to be wary of the shortcomings of this approach.

Taguchi's quadratic loss function

Taguchi's quadratic loss function (QLF) does not try to specify the correct amount of quality to inject into a given process. Instead, it seeks to identify the costs arising from poor quality. The reporting of these costs helps employees to understand the magnitude of the potential savings that can be achieved. Additionally, these costs provide a benchmark for comparing the costs of countermeasures aimed at eliminating or reducing poor quality.

Taguchi's QLF suffers from the same problem as was noted with Juran's approach for determining the optimal level of quality: it is too static. While the loss that it calculates may be the appropriate quality loss for today, it is unlikely to represent tomorrow's loss. With each passing day, the cost or penalty from failing to meet the target is likely to grow. In particular, customers do not have static expectations regarding quality. They expect better performing, more reliable, and more resilient products that can withstand the vagaries of use that customers commonly subject products.

In fairness to both Juran and Taguchi, however, it should be remembered that their attempts to calculate the dollar impact of varying quality represents only one part of their larger message on organizational quality. Accordingly, we should be careful to target our criticism to those aspects with which we find fault, and not as a general condemnation of their approaches.

Summary

The mere idea of costing quality is anathema to some individuals, e.g. Deming and Crosby. For other individuals – for example, Juran and Taguchi, as well as a growing number of today's organizations – the idea seems far from silly or wasteful. While most scholars and managers who subscribe to the latter view support the practice of categorizing costs into prevention, appraisal, internal failure, and external failure, they are divided in their support of Juran's optimum level of quality or Taguchi's QLF. How adamantly one believes in the concept of continuous improvement largely determines whether he/she will also subscribe to Juran's and Taguchi's attempts to place a dollar figure on quality.

References

Albright, T. and Roth, H. (1992). The Measurement of Quality Costs: An Alternative Paradigm. *Accounting Horizons*, June, 15–27.

Carr, L. (1992). Applying Cost of Quality to a Service Business. *Sloan Management Review*, Summer, 72–77.

Crosby, P. (1979). *Quality is Free*, New York: McGraw-Hill.

Crosby, P. (1986). *Quality Without Tears: The Art of Hassle-Free Management*, New York: McGraw-Hill.

Deming, W. (1982). *Quality, Productivity, and Competitive Position*, Cambridge, MA: MIT Center for Advanced Engineering Study.

Feigenbaum, A. (1983). *Total Quality Control*, New York: McGraw-Hill.

Ishikawa, K. (1985). *What is Total Quality Control? The Japanese Way*, Englewood Cliffs, NJ: Prentice-Hall.

Ito, Y. (1995). Strategic Goals of Quality in Japanese Companies. *Management Accounting Research*, **6**, 383–397.

Juran, J. (1951). *Quality Control Handbook*, New York: McGraw-Hill.

Juran, J. (1988). *Juran on Planning for Quality*, New York: The Free Press.

Juran, J. (1989). *Juran on Leadership for Quality: An Executive Handbook*, New York: The Free Press.

Shank, J. K. (1989). Strategic Cost Management: New Wine, or Just New Bottles? *Journal of Management Accounting Research*, **1**, 59.

Shingo, S. (1986). *Zero Quality Control: Source Inspection and the Poka-Yoke System*, Productivity Press.

Taguchi, G. and Clausing, D. (1990). Robust Quality. *Harvard Business Review*, **68**(1), 65–75.

Taguchi, G., Elsayed, E. and Hsiang, T. (1989). *Quality Engineering in Production Systems*, New York: McGraw-Hill.

6

Target costing activity-based

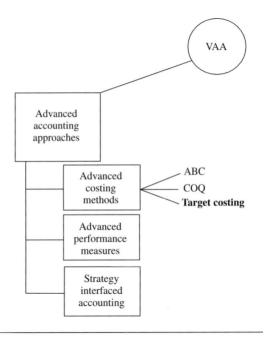

Chapter objectives

- Trace the history of target cost management and reveal the contemporary circumstances that encourage (and what some might say, even mandate) its use.

- Identify and discuss the five stages of target cost management, and show how they relate to the Japanese terms *genka kikaku* and *genka kaizen*.

- Discuss some of the wider accounting and organizational behaviour implications associated with the use of target cost management.

Target cost management involves the systematic process of planning product and service offerings, determining their sales prices, establishing highly challenging target costs, and motivating employees to be ever vigilant for cost reduction opportunities. Under target cost management, the organization seeks to balance quality and functionality with prices that meet both the customer's value-added needs and the organization's profitability needs.

Unlike traditional cost management systems, which have a largely internal focus, target cost management is outward focused and market driven. In particular, target cost management recognizes that the customer comes first. Organizations that forget this truth do so at their own peril. For waiting around the corner is a competitor who understands the importance of meeting (and perhaps even exceeding) customers' expectations about high quality, high functionality, and low cost.

Target cost management is based on the idea that a product or service's quality, functionality, and cost are largely determined during design. Little can be done to improve any of these three elements once the design has been set. For example, the product and production blueprints for a camera specify product features (digital or non-digital), materials (lenses with relatively high precision grinding or relatively low precision grinding), and the production technology (CNC or worker operated). While it is easy to see how these design features influence the camera's versatility (i.e. functionality) and its performance and reliability (i.e. quality), they also substantially influence the camera's final cost. In fact, it is commonly accepted that 80 per cent of a product's final cost is immutable once it leaves the designer's desk. Even the collective forces of employee empowerment, kanban, total preventive maintenance, and the like are only marginally able to influence the product's cost once production has begun.

Target cost management, though often associated with manufacturers, is equally applicable to service companies. They, too, must carefully plan the timing of new service offerings and ensure that each individual characteristic or feature comprising a new service offering is commensurate with the customer value it generates. The idea of balancing a service's cost with its quality and functionality endures for service enterprises as well.

In fact, according to Cooper and Chew (1996), service enterprises may require target cost management even more than their manufacturing counterparts. As they say:

> In people-intensive, customer-responsive service-delivery systems, it is not only possible to add new services, it can be hard not to. Menus are easy to extend. Room services can be easily added. Consulting firms or law firms can always enter a new area of practice. Where is the discipline that ensures that these extensions are profitable?

Target cost management, therefore, is a generic organizational tool, applying equally to all organizations irrespective of their industry classification. All managers are challenged to explicitly consider the product or service's life-cycle costs when planning and designing new products or services. Consequently, although the majority of the academic and practitioner literature discussing target cost management, as well as much of the material presented in this chapter – which is meant to reflect and comment on the literature – focuses on how manufacturers use target cost management, the reader should keep in mind that the concept is equally relevant to service enterprises.

The history of target cost management

Target cost management, like so many of today's supposedly new management techniques, seems so logical and sensible that we are left shaking our heads and asking, 'How could organizations have neglected something as simple and straightforward as the consideration of life-cycle costs when designing new products or services?' In providing an answer, it is best to begin by tracing target cost management's history.

The academic literature's relatively recent discovery of target cost management belies its more mature age. While the literature only began recognizing target cost management in the late 1980s, the concept itself has been around much longer. Toyota, for instance, was using target cost management as early as 1963. An even earlier user, however, dating back to 1947, was General Electric. GE's Lawrence Miles is commonly credited with inventing target cost management – albeit a streamlined and early version of today's highly evolved form.

Age, however, does not always correlate with an ability to command respect; and it appears that target cost management is a prime example of this fact. It is only most recently, during the past 15 years, that target cost management has been implemented in earnest, even in Japan.

Toshiro Hiromoto's often cited *Harvard Business Review* article entitled 'Another Hidden Edge – Japanese Management Accounting' appears to be the first English-speaking journal to feature target cost management. Interestingly, he referred to the concept as 'target costing', the name by which it is mostly referred to today. Unfortunately, this name is a bit of a misnomer. As already alluded to, it is much more than a mere costing system. Rather it is a comprehensive product planning and control process, which also includes a costing element.

The fact that target cost management has recently assumed such a central organizational role appears to be largely due to the intense – and seemingly ever increasing – competitive pressures that organizations now face. Competitive pressures, emanating from the emergence of lean organizations and the increased sophistication of customers, mandate that an organization improves the quality and functionality of its products and services, while simultaneously lowering its cost.

Today's intense competitive pressures no longer make it possible for an organization to survive – let alone prosper – by focusing on technical differentiation alone. The emergence of global markets has shunted aside such an old-fashioned strategy as initially introducing novel products to technophiles at high prices and then subsequently scaling up volume to satisfy the demands of the plainer, more conventional

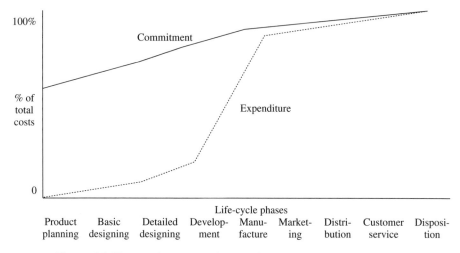

Figure 6.1 New products: commitment of costs versus cost expenditures

customer. The existence of lean competitors means that copycat, me-too product versions can be out on the market in a matter of months. Customers understand this new state of affairs, and now it is only the most ardent of technophiles who is unable to wait the short time necessary for the low-priced, copycat version to appear.

Realizing that the old tactic of using market segmentation to charge differential sales prices is no longer viable, organizations understand that products must display innovation, high quality, and low cost right from their initial launching. Otherwise lean imitators will swoop in and introduce their low-cost copycats.

The implementation of cost reduction programmes may seem to be the name of the game, but this is not really so. There are two reasons why the solution is not as simple as driving costs out of the organization's production, marketing, and distribution activities. First, for the majority of organizations, all the fat has already been squeezed out of the production system, via their ongoing JIT and TQM initiatives. Second, the cost gains from achieving marketing and distribution efficiencies are substantially smaller than the cost gains achieved through better product planning and design. Figure 6.1 illustrates the relationship between the commitment of costs and the actual expenditure of costs throughout a typical product's life cycle.

As revealed in Figure 6.1, although only a relatively small amount of costs have actually been expended by the time a product has been designed, a relatively large amount of costs (about 80 per cent) have been committed. Thus, the greatest potential for cost management occurs during the planning and design of products. It is important to note that the term 'cost management' has been used rather than 'cost reduction'. Cost management is meant to illustrate the idea that successful competition is not simply about having the lowest costs. Instead, success is predicated on having the right quality, functionality, and costs. The mandate for organizations is to ensure that the quality and functionality of every product feature (e.g. the quickness of a car's acceleration, the quietness of its ride, etc.) is commensurate with its cost. Overly engineered, gimmicky product features that provide insufficient customer value must be assiduously avoided. Sophisticated consumers, who can readily choose from a variety of other competing products, will reject such products in the same manner as they will products whose features fail to reach minimum quality and functionality thresholds (e.g. too slow an acceleration, too noisy and bumpy a ride, etc.).

In summary, target cost management, though existing for quite some time, has only most recently attracted organizational and scholarly attention. The intense competition that characterizes today's markets has been the primary force driving its adoption. It is imperative that organizations manage product and service costs in a more active and aggressive manner than they have in the past. Typically this means managing the costs right from the moment a product or service is first proposed.

The five stages of target cost management

There are five stages associated with the implementation of target cost management:

1 corporate-wide product planning;
2 developing new products;
3 determining a new product's basic plan;
4 detailed product design; and
5 transfer of the product plan to production.

The first four stages comprise what the Japanese refer to as *genka kikaku*, while the last stage is part of what the Japanese call *genka kaizen*. *Genka kikaku* describes the various processes that are used to manage the costs associated with the design of new products. Meanwhile, *genka kaizen* describes the processes that are used to produce continuous cost improvement once the product has entered production. Both *genka kikaku* and *genka kaizen* are distinctive Japanese management techniques, which are intended to help the organization achieve production of high quality, high functionality, low cost products.

Before discussing the five stages of target cost management, it is important to point out the following caveat: not all products undergo the process to the same extent. In particular, target cost management is often only applied to base models within a product line and the major components of the higher level products. A study of Japanese manufacturers' practices, for example, shows that only about 22 per cent of companies apply target cost management to all models, whereas 78 per cent apply it to the base model and/or to major components of other models (see Tani *et al.*, 1994).

Corporate-wide product planning

Target cost management is linked from the start with the organization's strategy. The introduction of new products is done in the context of the organization's existing range of products, and the model changes and model modifications that have previously been scheduled. By virtue of such scheduling, the organization seeks to ensure that it has products in various stages of their life cycle, from infancy to divestment. This product planning strategy should sound familiar. It is an application of the Boston Consulting Group's (BCG) four-phase product life cycle: question mark, star, cash cow, and dog.

The BCG model suggests that successful products progress in an orderly fashion through the four life-cycle phases. Meanwhile, unsuccessful products move more swiftly and erratically through the various life-cycle phases, perhaps even skipping an intermediate phase or two, before reaching the dog phase. The dog phase ultimately heralds the end to the product's life.

In addition to suggesting the sequence of life-cycle phases a product moves through, the BCG model is also important in revealing the different levels of cash that are produced or used during different phases of the product's life. The question mark phase consumes cash during the development and readying of the product for production. The star stage is also generally characterized by its heavy use of cash. Although the product has proven successful, there is a critical need to build market share and consolidate the product's reputation. It is typically only in the cash cow phase that the product is finally returning cash (or at least cash in a substantial amount) to the organization. Finally, in the dog phase cash is again being consumed; but this time there is no hope for a change in future cash flows. As such, products in the dog phase require their immediate divestment.

The competitive environment has changed dramatically since the BCG model was first introduced. Accordingly, the belief that products progress in a linear manner through the life-cycle phases has been challenged. It has been proposed that more complex progressions, such as recursive, may occur. Additionally, some scholars have questioned the impact that today's significantly shorter, and seemingly ever shortening, product life cycles have on the relevance of the BCG model. In spite of these criticisms, however, the general thrust of the BCG model appears as applicable today as when it was introduced. Products, at a minimum, require cash during their conception (i.e. design and development) and only later in their life do they generate positive cash flows.

Unlike most managers' general practice of maintaining in the back of their minds the understanding that different phases of a product's life cycle result in either the generation or use of cash, target cost management goes further and incorporates this general understanding into the organization's long- and medium-term profit plans. In particular, an organization that uses target cost management is constantly working from a profit plan that extends several years (generally 3–5) into the future. This profit plan shows contribution margin (sales price minus variable costs), marginal income (contribution margin minus traceable fixed costs), and operating profit (marginal income minus allocated fixed costs). It is up to all members of the organization to ensure that the profit goals are achieved. In accomplishing this objective, the organization must carefully plan its portfolio of products to ensure that there is a balance among products that consume cash, but offer substantial future cash flow promise, and products that generate cash but are unlikely to gain further market share growth.

Developing new products

The second stage of target cost management involves the embryonic development of the new product. Although the genesis of the new product was initially called for in the preceding corporate-wide product planning stage, it was little more than a 'glimmer in someone's eye'. It is only in the second stage of target cost management that some of the new product's substance begins to take form.

The new product development typically starts when the product planning department presents the engineering planning department with a request for a model modification, a model change, or an entire new product. Remember that these modifications, changes, and new product requests have already been called for and approved by top management in Stage 1.

Value engineering, which is a prominent feature of target cost management, helps guide the engineering planning department's development of the new product. Value engineering is a systematic, interfunctional process involving the examination of factors that affect the cost of a product. The goal of value engineering is to achieve the established product standards for quality, functionality, and target cost.

The extent to which value engineering is performed during this early stage of the target cost management process is admittedly much less than what is done during later stages. Daihatsu Motors and users of target cost management frequently refer to this stage's preliminary use of value engineering as 'zero look value engineering'. Nevertheless, function tables, which contain information about the performance characteristics of components, and cost tables, which contain information about components' costs, are often used in combination to help determine the best components for a given project. Meanwhile, cost reduction databases also guide the value engineering process. For instance, Olympus (the Japanese camera manufacturer) discovered that production costs for a given product could be reduced by approximately 35 per cent across the product's production lifetime. Such estimates, when available, can be usefully factored into the estimate of the initial product's cost.

Once completed, the new product plans are forwarded to the cost management department. Preliminary financial analyses are performed. Quite frequently, the payback method is used. (The Japanese have a particularly affinity for the payback method, especially when making capital investment and new product introduction decisions.) As a point of illustration, Japanese automobile companies often use an eight-year payback period. This eight-year period, however, is commonly reduced to four years when the product proposal calls for the construction of a model-specific facility. A two-year payback period is quite common when the proposal calls for only minor model changes.

Should the preliminary financial analyses indicate that the project is unlikely to be profitable, the project is sent back to the engineering planning department. This department is asked to make cost-saving modifications to the product. It is also encouraged to consider the elimination of certain product features that provide dubious value for customers. Such modifications and/or eliminations are performed in consultation with the product planning department. This collaboration helps ensure that the product will still meet customer expectations for quality and functionality.

Determining a new product's basic design

Proposals for new products that have successfully emerged from Stage 2 undergo greater design specification, as well as closer performance and cost scrutiny, during Stage 3. Spearheading this Stage 3 process is the product development manager, who in Japanese is termed 'shusa'. The shusa is responsible for shepherding the new product proposal through to its eventual acceptance or rejection. Due to the substantial amount of interfunctional input that is received during the product's creation, it is highly important that one individual should serve as a 'go-between' or person capable of integrating and facilitating communication between the various organizational functions.

The shusa begins by requesting each department to review the material requirements, manufacturing processes, and estimated costs that presently characterize the new product proposal. As an example, it frequently happens that employee groups, who are working on a previous generation of the product or perhaps a related product, have ideas for improving the production process. Although these ideas may not be applicable to the current production process – perhaps because of commitments that have been made to the scale, scope, complexity, and technology of the product's design, manufacturing, and distribution – these ideas may apply to the new product proposal. The shusa will consider the relevance of any suggested refinements and, as appropriate, incorporate them into the project's design and cost.

Calculating the allowable cost

Based on the preliminary product design and the market research conducted to date, an allowable product cost is calculated. This allowable cost is the difference between the target sales price and the target profit. It is important to note that the target profit is product-specific rather than a single figure that applies universally across all products. The target profit derives from the organization's strategy and financial projections.

The calculation of the target sales price, like any pricing issue, is often a complex matter. One exceedingly reductionist technique suggests that each product feature be separately valued, generally accomplished through the use of a customer survey. The utilities associated with the individual product features are then aggregated to derive a total sales price. There are obvious problems with this pricing technique, including the time, expense, and possibility of overlapping product features.

A second pricing approach takes a more global perspective. The value a customer is expected to receive from the new product is compared with the value another competing product provides and the price at which this product sells. This approach to pricing is essentially a competitor-based approach. When using this latter approach, it is important to view all potential competitors, and not just industry competitors. For example, Olympus discovered that even before a potential customer began deciding between competing brands of cameras, frequently this customer would first decide whether to purchase a camera, a CD player, or a Walkman-type product. Consequently, when determining product prices by reference to one's competitors, it is essential to maintain a sufficiently wide and informed perspective on the composition of one's competitors.

The role of value engineering

The computed allowable cost is often well below the organization's estimated product cost. At Olympus, only about 20 per cent of its new product proposals met the allowable cost on the first pass. The difference between the currently achievable cost and the target cost is known as the cost gap. It is critical that the organization undertake whatever steps it can to close this gap. Once again, value engineering will play an important role. This time, however, it is referred to as 'first look value engineering'.

First look value engineering is significantly more comprehensive than its cousin zero look value engineering. First look value engineering calls upon a greater number of parties and involves these parties on a more frequent and recurring basis than zero look value engineering. A host of internal functional disciplines – including accounting, marketing, purchasing, product planning, product development, product design, production technology, and manufacturing – as well as the organization's suppliers – typically become involved in the design process. This broad coalition of constantly interacting parties provides three benefits. First, such an approach promotes the old adage that 'two heads are better than one'. Second, the process of involving the parties who will ultimately be responsible for producing and selling the product will likely boost their motivation and commitment to achieving the allowable cost. And third, it decreases the lead-time necessary to bring the product to market.

The Japanese have a special name for the process whereby reductions in lead-time are achieved. They refer to it as simultaneous engineering. (An equivalent term sometimes used in the target cost management literature is concurrent engineering.) This process is characterized by an array of techniques, including the Taguchi design method, design for manufacturability, design for assembly, and quality function deployment (QFD).

Simultaneous engineering represents a radical departure from the traditional approach to product development, which is commonly referred to as the 'baton relay' approach. Under the traditional approach, the design of a product follows a clear sequence of product planning, product development, detailed design, production preparation, and finally manufacturing. Simultaneous engineering, by contrast, is characterized by a significant amount of concurrent co-operation between departments. As a result, the product is designed more quickly. Additionally, the simultaneous involvement of a wide cross-section of departments helps to ensure that the product design–product cost relationships are seen in a holistic as opposed to atomistic fashion. In particular, simultaneous engineering exposes and makes evident the impacts that one department's decisions on product design have on the design decisions that are made by other departments. Accordingly, the allowable cost is more likely to be achieved than would be the case with a 'baton relay' approach.

Throughout the value engineering process, the broad coalition of contributing parties compares estimated costs with the allowable cost. Variances between the two are fed back to all the participating parties and the process of balancing quality and functionality with the allowable cost continues. Several iterations may be required before senior management accepts a final design.

To aid the various departments with their value engineering activities, function tables, cost tables, and cost reduction databases will once again be referenced, just as they were during zero look value engineering. In addition, however, the departments will analyse cost drivers, undertake comprehensive product cost and function decompositions, and apply cost modelling techniques.

The role of cost driver analysis

Cost driver analysis, at least the part that focuses on executional cost drivers, is an integral part of Japanese management accounting and features prominently during the target cost management process. In Japan the management of cost drivers is referred to as *kousuu* management. The Japanese commonly undertake a detailed analysis of various conversion costs, tracking the origin of these costs back to the very activities that cause or give rise to the type and amount of conversions cost in the first place.

Robin Cooper (1996) and Takeo Yoshikawa (1994) provide a practical example of *kousuu* management. They report and show how the Japanese divide labour costs into basic working hours and production support. Each of these two categories is in turn further subdivided. Basic working hours are classified as net working hours and incidental working hours. Meanwhile, production support hours are classified as set-up hours, artificial delay hours, waiting hours, or incidental work hours. As a final step, each of these subclassifications is divided into and associated with specific tasks. Net working hours, for example, can be associated with such activities as the loading and unloading of machines, the operation of machines, the washing of products, the measurement of products, etc. Alternatively, waiting hours can be associated with waiting for materials and parts, machine breakdowns, machine maintenance, etc.

While basic working hours are commonly termed value-adding and production support are commonly termed non-value adding, the aim of *kousuu* management (just as with cost driver analysis) is to consider ways of reducing or, where possible, eliminating activities. Typically the organization will look to simplify products (e.g. using fewer and more common parts) and the production process (e.g. efficient production layouts and optimal levels of machine and human production).

At all times, however, the organization must ensure that its streamlining efforts are promoting and not interfering with its strategy. It wants to cut fat and enhance its nimbleness, not amputate a limb and impair its responsiveness.

The role of product cost and function decompositions

Another technique that is commonly used during first look value engineering is the undertaking of comprehensive product cost and function decompositions. Under this approach, every basic and secondary function associated with a given product is identified and its value analysed. A basic function is defined as the principal reason for the existence of the product, while a secondary function is defined as a side effect (either beneficial or non-beneficial) that occurs as the result of the way the basic functions have been designed. As an example, the primary functions of a refrigerator are to keep food in the refrigerated compartment chilled; to keep food in the frozen compartment frozen; and, assuming such a feature is present, to make ice. Secondary functions include the energy it uses and the environmental hazard its cooling system may pose.

Through the process of decomposing product costs and functions, a product's multiple functions are clearly identified. Often the organization will ask customers to assign a value to each of these functions. The identification of customer-determined function values can serve to provide the motivation whereby each department, both singly and in unison, seeks to meet these cost-function targets. As Cooper (1996) notes, the target costing approach of 'designing to a *specified* low cost appears to create more intense pressure to reduce costs than designing to an *unspecified* minimum cost' (emphasis in its original).

It should be recognized that it is the overall product cost and not each individual product feature that matters most. It is possible therefore to trade-off the cost of one product feature against another. Accordingly, product features with easily achievable target costs may require cost reductions below their customer-determined value as a means of helping to achieve the overall target cost.

The role of cost modelling

Cost modelling is yet another technique that forms a part of first look value engineering. In most basic terms, cost modelling is a technique for anticipating product costs. Usually it is undertaken by using computer simulation.

Cost modelling consists of four main steps: identification of cost drivers; comparative cost estimation; sensitivity analysis; and risk analysis. Together these four steps help product designers to simulate the cost effect of different combinations of product quality and functionality. In essence, cost modelling is meant to ensure that product designers do not unknowingly include more product features than necessary, ultimately making the product needlessly complex and too costly to satisfy customer needs.

Breaching the allowable cost

The objective of the *genka kikaku* stage of target cost management is very explicit: to design a product that achieves the prescribed quality and functionality at the calculated allowable cost. The discipline that such an approach imparts on employee thinking and behaviour is substantial. Fudging results and/or boosting prices are not acceptable. Either the company achieves the product design at the allowable cost or one of its competitors will.

Of course, every rule seems to have its exceptions; and target cost management does not prove unique in this regard. There are two key exceptions to the 'never exceed the allowable cost' rule: price point considerations and strategic factors.

A situation whereby the allowable cost is exceeded due to a price point consideration may technically be a violation, but in reality it is an admission that the product should have been designed with a different (more demanding) customer group in mind. An example provides the best means of illustrating this exception to the general rule.

A large number of in-line skate manufacturers, as is the case with many manufacturers of sporting goods, produce a range of different product models. Each skate type is designed with a particular customer in mind. For example, some skates are produced for recreational users, some for people who skate to work, and still others for people who are stunt skaters (commonly known as aggressive skaters). These broad skate categories are further broken down into subgroups. In very crude terms, there is a low-priced skate (intended for the occasional or infrequent skater), a medium-priced skate (for the regular hobbyist), and a high-priced skate (for the highly discerning skate enthusiast).

It is possible that during the design of a new skate intended for, say, the infrequent recreational skater that the features of the proposed skate are of a sufficiently enhanced nature to suggest its promotion to a higher price point (i.e. suited to the needs of the regular hobbyist). Again, this exception to the general rule is less a true violation than an admission that the skate was initially designed with the wrong customer market in mind.

The other time that the allowable cost rule is sometimes exceeded is when strategic factors suggest that it would be detrimental to do otherwise. In particular, many firms believe that it makes poor business sense to leave a 'hole' in the product line. Such issues as building customer loyalty and the marketing strategy of persuading people to buy now and trade-up with their next purchase may require an organization to fill an empty slot in its product range by accepting a product proposal even when it fails to achieve the allowable cost.

Before leaving this topic of the circumstances under which the allowable cost rule can be breached, it is interesting to note the apparent divergence between what is said and what actually occurs. In particular, writers such as Yutaka Kato and Robin Cooper consistently stress the idea of the discipline, commitment, and motivation to achieve what the allowable cost engenders. According to Cooper (1996), although 'the 'never exceeded' rule is [sometimes] broken, . . . the conditions must justify it and specified procedures must be followed to authorise it.' It is interesting to note, however, that while Cooper and others speak about the stringent controls that limit the occasions when the allowable cost can be exceeded, Takeyuki Tani's (1994) survey of Japanese practice shows that a majority of companies (57 per cent) make some adjustment to the allowable cost. Typically the target cost, which is the goal toward which everyone works, represents a middle ground between the currently achievable cost and the allowable cost.

When choosing a target cost, the company seeks to ensure that the cost goal is challenging without being perceived as unattainable. Goals that are perceived as unattainable serve only to defeat and discourage employee effort. Accordingly, the Japanese have developed what they call tiptoe objectives, or objectives that require employees to extend themselves to their fullest.

Whether or not senior management will establish a target cost that is different from the allowable cost is only made after the *shusa* has submitted his/her report on the new product's feasibility. Based on this report, senior management will decide whether to proceed with or put a stop to the product's further development. Should senior management decide to proceed further, they will issue a development order and establish a target cost. This development order sets up Stage 4 of the target cost management process.

Detailed product design

Stage 4 of the target cost management process begins with senior management's issuance of a development order. The design department is responsible for executing the development order. It will draft a trial blueprint for every part. When drafting these trial blueprints, as well as the overall product blueprint, it invariably must seek further information from various organizational departments and suppliers.

Once the overall product blueprint is completed, the design department executes the blueprint and builds a trial product. The cost management department then calculates the product's cost and compares it to the target cost. Should a gap exist, the departments and outside suppliers will undertake further value engineering. The product blueprint will be adjusted accordingly. After several iterations, the final blueprint is established and presented to senior management for its approval.

Transfer of the product plan to production

Following the detailed product design stage, the product is readied for production. The purchasing department finalizes purchased materials' prices; makes preparatory checks of the production equipment; and derives standard values for the material consumption, labour hours, machine times, etc. These standards are used for financial accounting reporting and to provide the data needed by the organization's MRP/MRPII systems.

After a three-month break-in period, whereby teething problems will surface and solutions will be found, performance is evaluated. In particular, the actual cost is compared with the target cost over a certain period of budgeted months (e.g. six months at Toyota). If the target cost is not achieved, investigations are undertaken to determine where the gap arises and with whom the responsibility lies. This comparison of actual and target costs also serves to evaluate the effectiveness of the target costing process.

It is important to recall that this fifth stage of target cost management includes the process of *genka kaizen*. Accordingly, the achievement of the target cost is only a starting point. Over the course of the year, the target cost is further reduced. In each succeeding period of evaluation, the actual cost of the previous period becomes the starting point for further cost reduction. This continual tightening of standards creates a cost reduction dynamic that operates for as long as the product remains in production. A critical source for these cost improvements is the frontline workers and their supervising managers. They are expected to propose new cost and technological improvements on a daily basis. The norm in Japan is 50 suggestions per employee per year (Japan Economic Research Centre, 1986).

Further target cost management issues

When describing the five stages of target cost management, two features that stand out are:

1 its highly disciplined approach to planning and designing products and services; and
2 the increased worker motivation it promotes.

In addition to these two main features, however, there are a few further management accounting issues that deserve at least a passing mention. These issues include an accelerated consideration of several key product and service decisions, a modification of the conventional standard costing system, and an understanding of the barriers that may inhibit the successful implementation of target cost management.

The emphasis that target cost management places on the planning and design of new products and services means that decisions, which were once made at a later point in time, must now be considered right from the outset. For instance, decisions about the price to charge, whether to make a subpart internally or to outsource it, the distribution network to use, and the establishment of cost standards, just to name a few, are all made in conjunction with the product's early planning and design. As a point of illustration, in contrast to the conventional way of waiting until after a product is designed to establish a cost standard, using perhaps a time and motion study, under target cost management cost standards are established in conjunction with the product's design. In other words, target cost management seeks to match a design to the overall cost, and not the other way around.

A company's use of standard costing systems is radically altered when it adopts target cost management. While some writers suggest that standard costs are abolished altogether, this suggestion can portray a misleading picture. Yes, it is true that the application of a conventional standard costing system will prove too rigid.

Remember in particular the *genka kaizen* part of target cost management. The goal is not to meet a static standard, but to constantly improve upon it. Accordingly, management's expectation is that the target cost will be improved upon over the course of the year and that a previous period's actual results will become the current period's target cost. In other words, cost standards still exist, but they do so in a more fluid and downward-ratcheting manner.

Organizations should be aware of the barriers that commonly inhibit the adoption of target cost management. A most notable barrier is the lack of a supplier's commitment to achieving and then continuing to beat the target cost. For instance, cost of living adjustments that need to be made to a worker's salary under a previously negotiated labour contract cannot be allowed to interfere with the attainment of the target cost. Target costs are final. The organization must find ways to offset the higher wage costs with savings that it can achieve in other areas. Additionally, suppliers must be willing to operate in a highly transparent manner. They must be willing, for example, to disclose detailed cost information and permit inspections of their manufacturing sites. For many suppliers, especially in the west where target cost management has a less established history, it is difficult for them to make the required transformation.

Summary

Target cost management involves the systematic process of planning product and service offerings; determining their sales prices; establishing a continuously adjusting set of downward-ratcheting, highly challenging target costs; and motivating employees to be ever vigilant for cost reduction opportunities. The goal of target cost management is to balance quality and functionality with prices that meet both the organization's profitability requirements and the customer's value-added needs.

Target cost management is much more than a cost reduction tool. To view target cost management in this way is equivalent to 'Seeing the trees but missing the forest'. Although the minimization of cost and the maximization of profits are connected, the first is but a subset of the latter.

In this chapter, the history of target cost management was traced. Following this history, a discussion of the five stages of target cost management was presented. The first four stages are characterized by the Japanese term *genka kikaku*, or cost design, while the fifth stage is characterized by the Japanese term *genka kaizen*, or continuous cost improvement. The final section of the chapter discussed several additional issues that are associated with the use of target cost management.

References

Cooper, R. (1995). *When Lean Organizations Collide: Competing Through Confrontation*, Cambridge, MA: Harvard Business School Press.

Cooper, R. (1996). Costing Techniques to Support Corporate Strategy: Evidence from Japan. *Management Accounting Research*, **7**, 219–246.

Cooper, R. and Chew, W. (1996). Control Tomorrow's Costs Through Today's Designs. *Harvard Business Review*, **74**(1), 88–97.

Kato, Y. (1993). Target Costing Support Systems: Lessons from Leading Japanese Companies. *Management Accounting Research*, **4**(1), 33–47.

Monden, Y. (1997). *Toyota Management System: Linking the Seven Key Functional Areas*, Portland, OR: Productivity Press.

Nishimura, A. (1995). Transplanting Japanese Management Accounting and Cultural Relevance. *International Journal of Accounting*, **30**, 318–330.

Tani, T., Okano, H., Shimizu, N., Iwabuchi, Y., Fukuda, J. and Cooray, S. (1994). Target Cost Management in Japanese Companies: Current State of the Art. *Management Accounting Research*, **5**, 67–81.

Tani, T. (1995). Interactive Control in Target Cost Management. *Management Accounting Research*, **6**, 399–414.

Yoshikawa, T. (1994). Some Aspects of the Japanese Approach to Management Accounting. *Management Accounting Research*, **5**, 279–287.

Part Three

Advanced Performance Measures

7

Financial performance measures

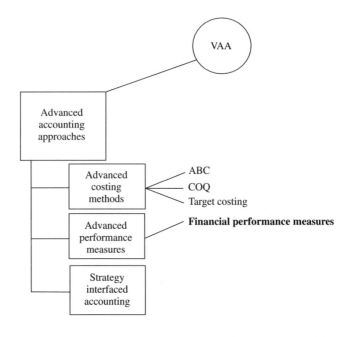

Chapter objectives

- Show how to calculate return-on-investment, residual income, shareholder value analysis, and economic value added.
- Identify and discuss the various shortcomings of the four performance measures.
- Discuss the common threads that bind together these four performance measures.

Descartes once said, 'I am as I am measured'. Although the wisdom of this state-ment has not dimmed with age, many organizations adopt performance measures that run foul of the advice. Too often, misunderstood or poorly constructed mea-sures of performance are used.

This chapter is devoted to a discussion of financial corporate performance mea-sures. It begins by briefly examining some of the older and more traditional perfor-mance measures. Following this brief review, a detailed examination of shareholder value analysis (SVA) and economic value added (EVA) is undertaken. The chapter ends with a look at the common threads that bind these various corporate perform-ance measures together.

Return-on-investment (ROI)

ROI is a relatively old corporate performance measure that was developed during the early part of this century. Despite its age, it continues as one of today's most popular performance measures. Part of the reason for its popularity is its simplicity. Not only is it simple to compute, but unlike many of the other performance mea-sures that have been constructed by accountants, it is easily understood by the average manager.

ROI is computed as the ratio of net income to capital investment. Essentially it is a measure of the return that a company (or subunit of the company) is generating on the investors' funds. A greater (lower) ROI from one period to the next implies a greater (lower) return on investors' funds.

Other than the fact that high net incomes generated from low capital investment bases are preferred, the basic ROI formula offers little additional advice or insight for managers. Fortunately there is another formula, called the DuPont formula, which provides a more detailed mapping of the connection between operating activities and higher or lower ROIs. The DuPont formula decomposes ROI into a sales margin ratio (an important barometer of profitability) and a turnover ratio (an important barometer of operating efficiency).

The sales margin ratio is computed by dividing net income by the total sales. This ratio indicates the amount of profit that each sales dollar is earning. As an example, a net income of $100 that was generated from sales of $500 results in a sales margin ratio of 20 per cent. Assuming all other things are equal, a high sales margin ratio is preferred.

The turnover ratio is computed by dividing the total sales by the amount of capital invested. This ratio indicates the number of times that the investors' capital was invested in the business' money-making enterprise (e.g. making TVs, flying passengers, etc.) and a successful sale was made. As an example, total sales of $500 generated from a capital investment base of $200 produces a turnover ratio of 2.5. Assuming all other things are equal, a high turnover ratio is preferred.

Using the sales margin and turnover ratio numbers presented above, the company's ROI is computed to be 50 per cent (20 per cent sales margin multiplied by a turnover ratio of 2.5). The 50 per cent ROI is, of course, the same number that would have been calculated had the ROI been computed directly as net income divided by total capital invested (i.e. net income of $100 divided by capital invested of $200 equals 50 per cent).

The simplicity of ROI has been both the key to its success and its more recent undoing. In particular, ROI has been criticized for promoting poor decision making. First, it often encourages subunit managers to snub investment opportunities that, although attractive from a company perspective, do not match the average rate of return that the subunit is currently generating on its portfolio of invested capital. Such a resistance against 'diluting' one's rate of return has been a commonly cited reason for the lack of long-term thinking and subsequent decreased competitiveness that Anglo-American managers and their organizations exhibited during the 1970s and 1980s (see Hayes and Abernathy, 1980 and Hayes and Jaikumar, 1990).

A second way that ROI impedes sound decision making is that it encourages managers to pursue increasingly higher ROIs. Such a predisposition, however, can be dangerous. A strong and positive association exists between investment projects' expected returns and their risk. In other words, projects that promise high rates of returns are commonly (and almost invariably) associated with increased risk. As a consequence, managers, who in their scramble to attain ever higher ROIs, are exposing their organizations to high levels of risk.

Residual income has been proffered as a remedy to ROI's twin ills of inconsistent investing objectives and increased risk taking. We now turn to a discussion of residual income.

Residual income (RI)

RI, like ROI, represents an older and more traditional corporate performance measure. Although its use has been steadfastly advocated by academics, for it overcomes ROI's problems of inconsistent investing objectives and increased risk taking, it has never caught on as a popular technique. Instead it has always been the poor cousin to ROI.

RI is computed by subtracting a 'cost of capital' charge from a company's reported net income. The cost of capital represents the return that a company must earn on its total capital in order to pay interest on its debt obligations and provide an acceptable return to its shareholders. A positive residual income means the company's sales are of a sufficient amount to cover not only the costs incurred in making the sales but also the implied costs, or what others might call the opportunity costs, that are associated with the capital invested in the company. As an example, assume a company reports net income of $100, has invested capital of $200, and has a weighted average cost of capital of 20 per cent. The RI for this company would be $100 − ($200 × 20 per cent) or $60.

RI calculations will lead to either positive or negative values. Positive values indicate acceptable performance, while negative values indicate problems and the need for remedial action.

The good news–bad news signals provided by RI apply equally to all subunits throughout the organization. As a result, the existence of inconsistent subunit versus organizational objectives is not present. Also, because RI rewards any project that can generate more income than the associated cost of capital, managers will be content to pursue projects that meet the cost of capital requirement and not feel compelled to reach for projects with ever higher, and generally more risky, ROIs.

Calculating the cost of capital

While the decision rules associated with RI may be a straightforward matter, the calculation of the cost of capital is generally anything but a straightforward matter. The cost of capital is a weighted measure of the firm's borrowing costs and its shareholder equity costs. While the former can be directly observed (i.e. by examining the bank loan or bond agreement) the latter requires a significant amount of teasing out.

There are two ways to calculate shareholder cost of capital. The first method, known as the financing approach, involves calculating a firm's beta, or its business risk relative to other firms within its industry. This beta is then multiplied by the market risk premium, or the incremental risk that is associated with investments in common stock versus such 'risk-free' investments as high rated government bonds. The combination of the firm-specific business risk and the general market risk are then added to the risk-free rate to compute the firm's shareholder cost of capital.

The second method for calculating shareholder cost of capital, known as the operating approach, involves an analysis of the risk inherent in a firm's operations, chosen strategy, asset management, and size and diversity. The number of standard deviations that a firm's assessed risk on each of the four categories is from the industry average determines its overall firm-specific business risk. In a similar manner to what was done under the beta approach, the calculated firm-specific business risk is multiplied by the market risk, and the product is added to the risk-free rate to compute the shareholders' cost of capital.

Once the shareholder and debt costs of capital are computed, the next step in calculating the weighted cost of capital is to compute the proportion of a firm's total capital that shareholder and debt capital represent. The proportion of the firm's total capital represented by shareholder capital is multiplied by the shareholder cost of capital to determine the weighted cost of shareholder capital. Likewise, the proportion of the firm's total capital represented by debt capital is multiplied by the cost of debt capital to determine the weighted cost of debt capital. Since the interest costs related to debt financing are a recognized expense for tax purposes, the 'tax shelter' provided by the presence of debt must be included in a computation of the weighted cost of debt capital. Accordingly the weighted cost of debt capital is multiplied by the inverse of the prevailing tax rate (i.e. 1 minus the tax rate) to determine the tax adjusted weighted cost of the debt capital. Now, adding the two weighted cost of capitals (shareholder and debt, that is) together yields the firm's weighted average cost of capital.

The following formula represents the multi-step process that must be followed when solving for a firm's weighted average cost of capital:

$$c* = (s \times Sc \: / \: K) + [(d \times Dc \: / \: K) \times (1 - t)] \qquad (10.1)$$

where: $c*$ = weighted average cost of capital
s = shareholder cost of capital
Sc = dollar amount of shareholder capital
K = dollar amount of total capital (both shareholder and debt)
d = debt cost of capital
Dc = dollar amount of debt capital
t = firm's tax rate

As an illustration of how the formula works, assume the following facts:

s = 15.5%
d = 10%
t = 38%
Sc/K = 60%
Dc/K = 40%

Plugging the above values into Equation 10.1 and proceeding to solve the equation results in:

$$\begin{aligned} c* &= (15.5\% \times 60\%) + [(10\% \times 40\%) \times (1 - 38\%)] \\ &= 9.3\% + (4\% \times 62\%) \\ &= 9.3\% + 2.48\% \\ &= 11.78\% \end{aligned}$$

Consequently, based upon the above computed weighted average cost of capital, a capital charge, consisting of 11.78% of the firm's total capital, would be subtracted from the reported net income when determining RI.

Weaknesses of RI

RI, although a conceptually superior performance measure to ROI, has never reached the same level of acceptance as ROI. Apparently there are two main problems that plague its use. First, many managers have difficulty understanding the rationale for a cost of capital charge being levied against net income. While managers generally understand the need to allow for and deduct from net income the interest that banks and bondholders charge, they are often confused by the need to include a capital charge associated with shareholder capital. The bank and bondholder capital charge mirrors actual practice in the sense that cash payments of interest are periodically made to the firm's debtors. The shareholder capital charge, however, does not have any equivalent real-world counterpart. In fact, a common question posed by many managers is, 'Doesn't the firm's payment of dividends constitute its fulfilment of the shareholder charge?' In other words, managers are unused to the economist's and accountant's definitions of wealth and opportunity costs, respectively.

A second problem that plagues the use of RI is the manner in which the cost of capital is calculated. Even if managers are able to understand the need for subtracting a cost of capital charge from net income, they are often less than satisfied by its computation, viewing it as just another arbitrary accounting artefact. In particular, managers hold a great dislike for the inferential analysis that is used to compute the firm's shareholder cost of capital. These managers, especially when their compensation is linked to RI performance, as is often the case, view such RI lingo as 'firm-specific business risk' and 'betas' with grave suspicion and disdain.

As a result of these two problems, RI has largely remained in the backwaters of corporate life, until recently that is. Most recently, although presented and marketed under another name, there has been a rediscovery of the value in using RI. But more will be said about this at a later point in the chapter.

Shareholder value analysis (SVA)

SVA is a measure of corporate performance developed by Alfred Rapport. According to Rapport, shareholder value is gained or lost as a result of the following five value drivers:

1 sales
2 operating profit margin
3 cash tax rate
4 investment in fixed capital assets
5 investment in working capital assets

While each of these value drivers affects firm performance, it is important to maintain a holistic view of the firm before any terms such as 'favourable' or 'unfavourable' can be applied to the observed movements, either up or down, in any of the value drivers. As an example, an increase in the firm's operating profit margin can be good, bad, or a mixture of good and bad news depending upon the underlying cause(s). If, for instance, the increase in operating profit margin was the result of the firm's ability to reduce costs without any customer perceived reduction in the value of the product or service purchased, then the increase is good news. If, however, the increase in operating profit margins occurred as the result of a sales price increase, which alienated customers and is likely to produce a loss in the firm's market share, or occurred as the result of skimping on product/service attributes, which negatively impacted on customers, then the increase might be more appropriately viewed as bad news.

As one further twist on how to interpret a change in a firm's operating profit margin, imagine a situation in which a set of customers is serviced by five competing firms. Imagine further that one of the competitors is forced out of business and the surviving competitors increase their sales prices, thereby increasing their profit margins, and still gain market share. Finally, imagine that two of the surviving firms experience a relatively greater increase in market share than the other two. Under such circumstances, the increase in profit margins for the latter two firms might be viewed as a mixture of good and bad news. Suffice it to say that an interpretation of the movement in any one value driver must be viewed as part of a wider and more encompassing picture of the entire organization.

Using the five value drivers and plotting the anticipated growth in each driver over a chosen period of time allows one to calculate what are termed the 'free cash flows'. Free cash flows are the cash that is expected to result from a continuance of current operations or the introduction of a new product, process, investment, or whatever other potential business opportunity one might be considering.

As the final step in arriving at SVA, the cost of capital must be computed and used as the basis for discounting or time valuing the projected free cash flows. The cost of capital is calculated in exactly the same way as was described in the above discussion of RI.

SVA provides for trade-offs to be made among the five value drivers. For example, a firm that is considering introducing a new product will likely incur significant fixed and working capital investment costs. The investment may represent a significant drain on the firm's immediate cash flows. While the firm's immediate cash flow may dip, there is undoubtedly an expectation that the investment will produce greater future cash flows than if the new product were not introduced. The calculation of SVA explicitly allows for this trade-off of cash flows between short term and long term by looking at the entire set of expected cash flows and not some abbreviated set as many other business models might do.

An example of how to compute SVA is provided in the following illustration.

Palo Alto Software
Income statement
For the year ended 31 December 1998

	1997 ($ in 000s)
Revenue	1,500
Cost of goods sold	1,000
Gross margin	500
Operating expenses:	
Selling and administration	108
Depreciation	75
R&D	60
Miscellaneous expense	27
Total operating expenses	270
Net income before interest and taxes	230
Interest expense	20
Net income before taxes	210
Tax expense (at 30% tax rate)	63
Net income	147

Palo Alto Software
Balance sheet
As of 31 December 1997 and 1998

	1997 (in 000s)	1998 (in 000s)
ASSETS		
Cash	50	50
Inventories	20	20
Prepaids	10	10
Land	170	170
Office and equipment	470	500
TOTAL ASSETS	720	750
LIABILITIES		
Accounts payable	105	125
Bonds payable	200	200
TOTAL LIABILITIES	305	325
SHAREHOLDERS' EQUITY		
Common stock	350	350
Retained earnings	65	75
TOTAL SHAREHOLDERS' EQUITY	415	425
TOTAL LIABILITIES AND SHAREHOLDERS' EQUITY	720	750

In conjunction with the above income statement and balance sheet, assume the following facts:

Sales growth rate	15%
Operating profit margin	10%
Cash tax rate	30%
Incremental working capital investment (IWCI)	10% of the increment in sales
Incremental fixed capital investment (IFCI)	15% of the increment in sales
Cost of capital	10%
Planning period	5 years
Capital asset replacements equal annual depreciation	
No further growth past 2003 or Year 5	

Table 7.1 provides a five-year projection of the cash flows associated with Palo Alto Software.

Using the free cash flows computed in Table 7.1, we can now calculate the expected SVA. This is done in Table 7.2.

Table 7.1 Palo Alto Software's five-year cash flow projections

	1998	1999	2000	2001	2002	2003	Beyond
Sales	1,500,000	1,725,000	1,983,750	2,281,313	2,623,509	3,017,036	3,017,036
Operating profit		172,500	198,375	228,131	262,351	301,704	301,704
Tax		−51,750	−59,513	−68,439	−78,705	−90,511	−90,511
Depreciation		75,000	80,000	85,000	90,000	95,000	100,000
Operating cash flow		195,750	218,863	244,692	273,646	306,193	311,193
Capital asset replacement		75,000	80,000	85,000	90,000	95,000	100,000
IWCI		22,500	25,875	29,756	34,220	39,353	0
IFCI		33,750	38,813	44,634	51,330	59,029	0
Free cash flows		64,500	74,175	85,301	98,096	112,811	211,193

Table 7.2 SVA calculation for Palo Alto Software

Year	Free cash flow	PV of free cash flow	Cumulative PV
1999	64,500	58,636	58,636
2000	74,175	61,302	119,938
2001	85,301	64,088	184,026
2002	98,096	67,001	251,027
2003	112,811	70,047	321,074
PV of continuing value			
(the continuing value shown in Year 5 and beyond)			1,092,783
Additional shareholder value expected			1,413,857

Similar to RI, positive SVAs are favourable, while negative SVAs suggest caution and/or the need for remedial action. Additionally, in a like manner to RI, SVA reduces a firm's operating profit by a cost of capital charge. More, however, will be said about the similarities between these two techniques at a later point in the chapter.

Economic value added (EVA)

EVA is a measure of corporate performance that was developed by Joel Stern. It was created to reinforce management's supposed prime imperative: to enhance shareholder value. In particular, EVA alerts managers to the necessity of earning rates of return on total investor capital that are, at a minimum, equal to the required prevailing market rate of return that applies to the particular business. When a firm exceeds the required rate of return, shareholder value is added. When it fails to meet the required rate of return, shareholder value is lost.

Although EVA was only introduced in the late 1980s, it has already developed a long list of corporate converts. Included in this list are such US behemoths as AT&T, Briggs & Stratton, Coca-Cola, GE, NCR, Quaker Oats, Scott Paper, Trans-America, and Whirlpool. Of course, there are a score of large and small companies from throughout the world that have also adopted EVA. For instance, in New Zealand, Airways Corporation, Fay, Richwhite & Co., Fletcher Challenge, New Zealand Dairy Industry, Sanford, Skellerup Group, Wrightson, Telecom, and Trans Power use EVA. In fact, for Fletcher Challenge EVA has become the cornerstone of the bonus plan covering its top 300 executives. The following excerpt is taken from its executive compensation brochure, dated August 1994:

> Creating value for shareholders is fundamental to Fletcher Challenge. Our share-holders expect us to produce superior returns by performing better than our competitors. Executives at every level of the group are able to add value by developing and executing successful strategies and managing resources effectively. . . . We have adopted [economic] value added measures to assess financial performance across the different businesses within the group. . . . The same measures are used in the Value Added Incentive Remuneration plan to determine rewards for executives who have created value in the businesses.

EVA is calculated as the difference between the net operating profit after tax and the cost of all capital employed to generate such profit. Does this definition have a familiar ring to it? It should. But more will be said about this momentarily.

The following formula is used to calculate EVA:

$$EVA = (r - c^*) \times K$$

Where: r = return on capital employed
c^* = cost of capital
K = economic value of capital invested in the business

The return on capital employed is essentially ROI, with some adjustments made to both the profit figure and investment base as a means of better approximating the economist's definition of wealth creation. Some of the more common adjustments include deferred income taxes; operating leases; LIFO inventory reserves; unre-corded goodwill and its amortization; asset revaluations; successful efforts expens-ing; unusual gains and losses; provisions for bad debt, inventory obsolescence, warranties, and deferred income; and such intangibles as R&D, patents, trademarks, new product development, and upfront marketing costs. Table 7.3 sets forth the effect each of these items has on the computation of a firm's net operating profit after tax (NOPAT) and capital employed.

An adjustment should also be made to the depreciation charge whenever the book amount (i.e. the amount appearing on the financial statements) does not closely approximate the economic depreciation. Should this occur, the asset should be revalued at its current economic cost, minus any estimated residual value, and depreciated on a straight-line basis over the estimated life of the asset. Estimated

Table 7.3 EVA adjustments needed to capital and NOPAT

Items to add to capital:	Items to include in NOPAT:
Deferred tax reserve	Increase in deferred tax reserve
Present value of the next five years' worth of minimum lease payments	Operating lease expenses
	Increase in LIFO reserve
LIFO reserve	Goodwill amortization (Note: no adjustment
Cumulative goodwill amortization	is needed for unrecorded goodwill)
Unrecorded goodwill	Asset revaluations
Asset revaluations	Increase in full cost reserve
Full cost reserve	Unusual loss (gain) after tax
Cumulative unusual loss (gain)	Increase in reserve for bad debt
Bad debt reserve	Increase in reserve for inventory
Inventory obsolescence reserve	obsolescence
Warranty reserve	Increase in reserve for warranty costs
Deferred income reserve	Increase in reserve for deferred income
Capitalized R&D	R&D expense
Capitalized patents	Patents expense
Capitalized trademarks	Trademarks expense
Capitalized new product development costs	New product development expense
Capitalized upfront marketing costs	Upfront marketing expense

asset lives should be based on such considerations as likely obsolescence through technological change, deterioration through use, and the effects of the competitive environment.

In addition to the various adjustments noted above, NOPAT must always be adjusted for interest expense. In particular, interest expense must be added back to net income when calculating NOPAT. This adjustment is made for the purpose of maintaining the division between a company's operating performance and how it chooses to finance its activities (i.e. the proportion of debt versus shareholder funds used).

The following example provides a comprehensive illustration of the various equity and NOPAT adjustments that are necessary for calculating EVA. When reviewing the example, keep the following two points in mind: the company's first year of operations was 1997, and its cost of capital is assumed to be 12 per cent.

Solar Panel, Inc.
Income statement
For the years ended 31 December 1997 and 1998

	1997 (in 000s)	1998 (in 000s)
Revenue	1,000	1,200
Cost of goods sold	500	600
Gross margin	500	600
Operating expenses:		
Selling and administration	63	75
Depreciation	75	100
R&D	50	60
Amortization of goodwill	10	10
Miscellaneous expense	10	11
Total operating expenses	208	256
Net income before interest and taxes	292	344
Interest expense	64	56
Net income before taxes	228	288
Tax expense (at 25% tax rate)	57	72
Net income	171	216

Solar Panel, Inc.
Balance sheet
As of 31 December 1997 and 1998

	1997 (in 000s)	1998 (in 000s)
ASSETS		
Cash	10	30
Inventories	30	52
Prepaids	6	10
Land	450	450
Factory and equipment	1,000	1,000
Intangibles – Goodwill	40	30
TOTAL ASSETS	1,536	1,572
LIABILITIES		
Accounts payable	35	35
Provision for deferred taxes	10	20
Provision for warranties	20	30
Short-term bank loan	200	0
Bonds payable	700	700
TOTAL LIABILITIES	965	785

	1997 (in 000s)	1998 (in 000s)
SHAREHOLDERS' EQUITY		
Common stock	400	400
Retained earnings	171	387
TOTAL SHAREHOLDERS' EQUITY	571	787
TOTAL LIABILITIES AND SHAREHOLDERS' EQUITY	1,536	1,572

Before calculating Solar Panel, Inc.'s EVA, let's first perform some traditional financial accounting analyses. First, an examination of the income statement reveals that net income has increased from $171,000 to $216,000. This is an increase of 26.3 per cent. Next looking at the balance sheet we see that total assets have increased from $1,531,000 to $1,572,000, an increase of 2.3 per cent. Combining these measures of net income and total assets we can calculate Solar Panel's return on assets (ROA). In 1997 its ROA was 11.1 per cent. In 1998 the ratio rose to 13.7 per cent. In sum, traditional accounting performance measures are providing signals that the company is performing well. Now let's look at the answers that an EVA analysis provides. This EVA analysis is presented in Tables 7.4–7.7.

There are two important lessons to be learned from the above EVA example. First, accounts payable is generally not included in the calculation of a firm's capital employed. Instead, due to what is a generally constant or expanding dollar amount of vendor financed working capital it is commonly viewed as a free source of capital.

The second lesson to be learned from the EVA example is the sometimes contrary signals that EVA and other accounting performance measures may provide. In contrast with the improvement in performance that ROA indicates, EVA suggests a very different view. In particular, although Solar Panel, Inc. has managed to add shareholder value in both 1997 and 1998, its performance slightly *worsened*

Table 7.4 Calculating NOPAT for 1997 and 1998

	1997 (in 000s)	1998 (in 000s)
Net income	171	216
Add:		
Interest	64	56
Amortization of goodwill	10	10
Increase in deferred tax	10	10
Increase in provision for warranties	20	10
Total NOPAT adjustments	104	86
NOPAT	275	302

Table 7.5 Calculation of economic capital for 1997 and 1998

	1997 (in 000s)	1998 (in 000s)
Capital employed per balance sheet:		
Common stock	400	400
Retained earnings	171	387
Bank loan	200	0
Bonds payable	700	700
Add:		
Cumulative goodwill amortization	10	20
Capitalized deferred taxes	10	20
Capitalized provision for warranties	20	30
Adjusted capital employed	1,511	1,557

Table 7.6 EVA for 1997 (assuming a 12% cost of capital)

EVA = NOPAT − (Capital employed x 12%)
  = 275,000 − (1,511,000 x 12%)
  = 275,000 − 181,320
  = 93,680

Table 7.7 EVA for 1998 (assuming a 12% cost of capital)

EVA = NOPAT − (Capital employed × 12%)
  = 302,000 − (1,557,000 × 12%)
  = 275,000 − 186,840
  = 88,160

between the two years. EVA fell from $93,680 in 1997 to $88,160 in 1998. Due to EVA's focus on company performance in relation to what its investors expect, it is a preferred technique for measuring corporate performance and should therefore be relied upon.

A comparison of the four corporate performance measures

At this point it is time to compare and contrast the four corporate performance measures. Essentially the four measures divide into two camps: those that include a cost of capital charge and those that do not. RI, SVA, and EVA occupy the former camp, while ROI alone occupies the latter camp. Unlike its counterparts, ROI simply provides a measure of the accounting return on the company's invested capital. Whether this return is sufficient to provide for investors', and in particular shareholders', expectations of company returns is unknown under an ROI analysis. RI, SVA, and EVA, however, all highlight the need to earn a return that equals or exceeds the investors' required rate of return expectations.

The practical and conceptual similarities between RI, SVA, and EVA have been uncovered by a variety of authors. Mills and Print, for example, have shown the similarities between SVA and EVA. In one of their articles, which appears in *Management Accounting*, they discuss the equivalence of the two measures and include a numerical example that yields an identical SVA and EVA. Meanwhile, Adler and McClelland, in an article that appears in the *Chartered Accountants' Journal*, reveal the equivalence of RI and EVA.

It is interesting to note that while some individuals rebel against the idea that RI, SVA, and EVA are equivalent in nature, the originators of the various performance measures are the first to admit this equivalence. For example, Stern, in a very straightforward and unabashed manner says in one of his pioneering articles on EVA, published in *Financial Executive*, 'In essence, this [EVA] is best described as "residual income" – the only internal measure of corporate performance to tie directly to value. We [members of his consulting firm] like to refer to it as economic value added (EVA).'

Those individuals who try to divide RI, SVA, and EVA into measures that are economic-based versus accounting-based are merely fooling themselves. In particular, to say that SVA and EVA are economic-based, as the argument is typically presented, ignores two very important facts. First, both SVA and EVA are based on accounting numbers. Second, while it is true that certain adjustments are made to these accounting numbers, the adjustments are generally no different from what managers who use RI might do. As any good accounting or finance text that discusses RI will note, there are a variety of ways to account for and determine what should be included in a company's investment base. Also, such issues as the necessity to revalue depreciable assets and recompute depreciation charges have long been a topic of earnest discussions. These discussions have in turn led to the formulation of several suggested alternative approaches depending on the nature of the situation encountered.

Such seemingly new concepts as SVA and EVA have their compelling allure largely because Rappaport and Stern have been so successful at codifying a set of comprehensive rules for calculating their respective measures. It is obvious that these men have spent substantial time thinking about the subtleties and nuances of their performance measures. Truly, and this is especially the case for EVA, no stone has been left unturned.

RI, meanwhile, appears in stark contrast to SVA and EVA's highly formalized systems of calculation. RI highlights all the questions that need to be asked and poses the various alternative approaches that can be taken, but steers clear of mandating any one particular approach. Instead, RI maintains the idea that the company must choose an approach based upon its unique set of organizational factors.

Of course, some people do not like the additional work involved in making choices. Furthermore, RI's encouragement of companies to tailor measures of the investment base and operating profit to unique organizational factors, though offering emancipation from potentially ill-suited measurement approaches, poses the danger that the company may make the wrong choice. As a result, there are many people who prefer the easier and safer passage provided by SVA and EVA.

When all is said and done, SVA, to a partial degree, and EVA, to a large degree, represent a shrewd rediscovery of RI – albeit a multi-period, time discounted RI. As Anthony Atkinson, a prominent accounting scholar, has very aptly noted about EVA, 'The conceptual basis of EVA is residual income, which has been around for a long time. What Stern and Stewart have done is to promote EVA and MVA heavily' (see Adler and McClelland, 1996). A major source of this consulting firm's marketing success comes from the fawning platitudes that accompany its EVA seminars, such as 'Making Managers into Owners', and the near cookbook approach to calculating EVA that its newly created Finansee™ computer software programs allow.

Of course, the important point to bear in mind is that members of the business community are finally benefiting from the use of residual income. This news should be welcomed and not made an issue for recrimination. Stern and Rappaport should be praised for their genius in persuading managers of the need to earn operating profits that provide sufficient returns for debt holders and equity holders alike. Nevertheless, as sensible people, who are in control of (and hopefully not controlled by) the various accounting concepts we use, it seems sensible that we understand that SVA and EVA are in reality a rediscovery of RI.

Summary

This chapter discussed the use and calculation of ROI, RI, SVA, and EVA. Several numerical examples were used to illustrate the required computations.

The four measures of corporate performance can be divided into techniques that include, versus those that do not include, a cost of capital charge. RI, SVA, and EVA are representative of the former, while ROI characterizes the latter. Further comments about the similarities between RI, SVA, and EVA were noted in the final section of the chapter.

References

Adler, R. and McClelland, L. (1996). EVA: Reinventing the Wheel. *Chartered Accountants' Journal*, **74**(4), 35–36.

Hayes, R. and Abernathy, W. (1980). Managing Our Way to Economic Decline. *Harvard Business Review*, **58**(4), 67–77.

Hayes, R. and Jaikumar, R. (1990). Manufacturing Crisis: New Technologies, Obsolete Organizations. *Harvard Business Review*, **68**, 77–85.

Mills, R. (1993). Strategic Value Management: Towards a Financial Framework for Developing the General Manager. *Journal of General Management*, **18**(4), 34–56.

Mills, R. and Print, C. (1995). Strategic Value Analysis. *Management Accounting*, 35–37.

Mills. R. and Weinstein, W. (1996). Calculating Shareholder Value in a Turbulent Environment. *Long Range Planning*, **29**(1), 76–83.

Pare, T. (1994). GE Monkeys with its Money Machine. *Fortune*, February, 49–53.

Rappaport, A. (1986). *Creating Shareholder Wealth: The New Standard for Business Performance*, The Free Press.

Rutledge, J. (1993) De-jargoning EVA. *Forbes*, October, 148.

Solomons, D. (1965). *Divisional Performance: Management and Control*, Financial Executive Research Foundation.

Stern, J. (1990). One Way to Build Value in Your Firm, à la Executive Compensation. *Financial Executive*, Nov/Dec, 51–54.

Stewart, G. (1991). *The Quest for Value: A Guide for Senior Managers*, Harper Business.

Tully, S. (1993). The Key to Creating Wealth. *Fortune*, September, 34–42.

8

Non-financial performance measures

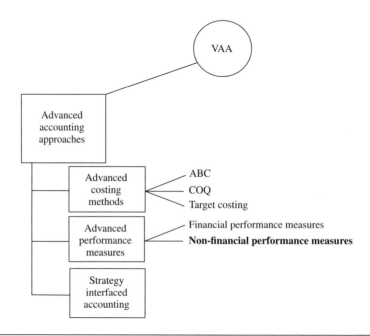

Chapter objectives

- Explore why the development of non-financial performance measures has become such a critical corporate imperative.

- Show how the development of non-financial performance measures can only proceed when clearly defined statements of organizational mission and strategy are present.

- Offer and discuss a variety of the non-financial performance measurement systems that have been recently developed.

- Provide advice on what to do when the non-financial performance measures provide contradictory evidence.

Today's organizations are increasingly adopting non-financial performance measures. Seldom does a day pass without someone preaching the importance of customer satisfaction or the need to develop measures that probe an organization's ability to be street savvy and light on its feet.

Of course, noting this upsurge in non-financial performance measures is not the same as saying that financial performance measures are unimportant. Nothing could be further from the truth. Instead, today's organizations need a combination of both financial and non-financial measures. Organizations have too often, and for far too long, relied almost exclusively on the former performance measures and either ignored or paid mere lip service to the latter.

Before diving headlong into a discussion of the latest and newest non-financial performance measures, it is appropriate to examine why there is this relatively sudden urgency to develop and implement non-financial performance measures. For the cynic might argue that non-financial performance measures are merely a here-today and gone-tomorrow craze that will burn out as quickly as it appeared.

Impediments to the adoption of non-financial performance measures

Organizations are often slow to change their behaviours. According to organizational theorists, an organization's inbred survival instinct is to resist change. Thus, for organizational change to occur, the change catalyst must be sufficiently hardy and persistent.

The introduction of non-financial performance measures, however, is not only handicapped by an organization's predisposition to inertia, but also by two further factors: the general suspicion it invokes in managers and the continued obsession organizations have with financial performance measures. For instance, there are many managers who are suspicious of and unimpressed with the 'soft' nature of non-financial performance measures. There are also many other managers who appear to have been hoodwinked by EVA's representation as the organizational cure-all. This state of affairs has led Thomas Peters (1989) to lament, 'our fixation with financial measures leads us to downplay or ignore less tangible non-financial measures. Yet these are increasingly the real drivers of corporate success over the middle to long term.' Meanwhile, C.J. McNair and William Mosconi (1987) have set the blame squarely at the feet of accountants, blaming them for being 'myopic, focusing solely on cost and ignoring the non-financial critical success factors.'

Catalysts of non-financial performance measures

In spite of these obstacles to the adoption of non-financial performance measures, there are two reasons for believing that the introduction of non-financial performance measures is not a passing fad. First, the size and scale of today's organizational operations and the type of CEO who directs the organization's activities are markedly different from what they once were. Organizations are becoming increasingly diversified and multinational, while CEOs are becoming more akin to the roving sheriffs during the days of the American Wild West. They enter as outsiders (CEOs are headhunted from what has developed into a class of professional CEOs), are expected to bring law and order (commonly translated as new drive and strategic direction), and are summarily dismissed the minute they show the slightest signs of weakness (the average CEO's tenure is barely half of what it was 10 years ago).

As a consequence of businesses' and CEOs' evolved nature, today's CEOs rarely possess the same level of knowledge about company operations and people as their predecessors did. Unlike such CEOs as Carnegie, du Pont, and Sloan, who had a visceral feel for the companies they ran and were able to see beyond the reported financial performance measures, today's CEOs are often less knowledgeable about the business operations they oversee and less able to make the same *ad hoc* adjustments.

To successfully manage, senior executives must either include other sources of information in their decision making – such as measures about shipment dates missed, machine utilization, and lead times required to introduce new products – or risk the consequences of taking action on a set of incomplete data. Unfortunately, at least until recently, the majority of senior level managers appeared to be taking the latter approach. In the process, they committed some unfortunate blunders, including the encouragement of excess inventories, the overlooking of cost reduction opportunities, and the failure to harness the organization's intellectual capital.

The second catalyst behind the emergence of non-financial performance measures is the changed nature of firm competitiveness. In the past, cost efficiency largely determined an organization's success. As a result, the need for financial information, particularly cost information, was essential and, by itself, largely sufficient. Over the last 20 years, however, there has been a shift in the basis of competition. In the 1980s it was cost and quality, and in the early 1990s it became cost, quality, and flexibility. Now as we approach the new millennium it has changed to cost, quality, flexibility, and innovation.

Once firms started down this new path of competitiveness, shifting from a unidimensional cost focus to a multidimensional customer focus, it was only a matter of time before the holes in traditional performance measurement systems became too egregious to tolerate. Today's organizations appear to have reached this point and are now seeking to redesign their performance measurement systems to include non-financial performance measures. No longer are they satisfied with what Thomas Stewart (1990) terms the 'golf scorecard' approach to performance measurement. Instead of being told such things as 'what club you used, how far you hit each drive, whether you made par on the ninth hole, and whether you shot a 72 or an 84', what firms really want to know about is why they shot the score they did. Was it because of a poor stance, poor backswing, or a poor grip? These latter pieces of information are what are needed to play a better round of golf the next time out.

The need for non-financial performance measures, therefore, appears to be the result of a dual occurrence. On the one hand it is partly in response to the changed characteristics of businesses and CEOs, while on the other hand it is partly due to the changed basis of firm competition.

How strategy precedes the development of non-financial performance measures

The importance of basing a firm's performance measures on its strategy may appear so eminently sensible that no further mention is required. Yet time and again organizations fail to fully consider the effect that their performance measures will have on employee motivation and commitment, especially in terms of how the measures will contribute to or detract from the organization's implementation of its strategy and attainment of its goals and objectives. As Robert Kaplan and David Norton (1992) have noted in an article entitled 'Putting the Balanced Scorecard to Work', 'Today's managers recognize the impact that measures will have on performance. But they rarely think of measurement as an essential part of their strategy.' This frequent failure to connect performance measures with strategy is often the reason behind a poorly performing performance measurement system.

The need to start with a clear understanding of the firm's strategic mission and vision is well underscored by an article of Robert Eccles entitled 'The Performance Measurement Manifesto'. In this article, Eccles stresses the importance of linking performance measures with firm strategy. In particular, he demonstrates how the development of performance measures must first begin with managers asking themselves such basic questions as, 'Given our strategy, what are the most important measures of performance?' Typically, says Eccles, future corporate performance measurement systems will require a greater representation of non-financial performance measures as a means of reflecting the organizational trend of using service and innovation to promote customer satisfaction.

As we shall see at a later point in this chapter, several of the more highly evolved systems of non-financial performance measures explicitly note the need for strategy to illuminate the development of non-financial performance measures. For example, Kelvin Cross and Richard Lynch's (1990) performance pyramid places organizational strategy at the top of the pyramid, indicating that the development of performance measures can only proceed when an exact and explicit understanding of the organization's strategy exists. Meanwhile, Robert Kaplan and David Norton prominently include as the first step in the development of a balanced scorecard the need to have a clearly defined organizational vision and strategy.

Examples of non-financial performance measures

Various systems of non-financial performance measures have been proposed throughout the past 10 years. These systems range from the *ad hoc* to the highly engineered. This chapter identifies and discusses four of the most popular systems.

Drucker's views on non-financial performance measures

Peter Drucker has written extensively about the need for organizations to collect information about their core competencies. While he believes that the set of core competencies of one organization may, and typically does, differ from the set of core competencies of another organization, he is quick to add that 'Every organization – not just businesses – needs one core competence: innovation' (1995). As a consequence, Drucker devotes most of his attention to fleshing out the various performance measures that help an organization record and appraise its innovation.

According to Drucker (1995), the starting point for assessing a company's innovation begins not with a review of one's own performance, but with a careful assessment of the innovations in one's industry over a given period of time. Accordingly, the organization asks such questions as: 'Which of them [the innovations] were truly successful? How many of them were ours? Is our performance commensurate with our objectives? With the direction of the market? With our market standing? With our research standing? Are our successful innovations in the areas of greatest growth and opportunity? How many of the truly important innovation opportunities did we miss? Why? Because we did not see them? Or because we botched them? And how well did we convert an innovation into a commercial product?'

Unlike some of the other non-financial performance measurement systems we will soon discuss, Drucker's system, if one can label it as such, stays well clear of providing formulas or setting forth categories on which to judge performance. Instead he seeks to highlight the management mindset that must prevail during the development of measures of performance. The qualitative measures he proposes, which are actually more akin to open-ended questions, are more concerned with assessment than they are with measurement. But, as Drucker properly points out, the ability to answer questions is not nearly as important as the ability to raise the right questions. Senior management's value-added is less about answering questions, for this is typically the job of the various operating and support groups. Instead, their value-added comes from posing the right questions, and in particular the type of questions that alert employee attention to truly important matters, and providing a framework within which the employees may address these matters.

Hall's four dimensions of performance measurement

Robert Hall proposes a performance measurement system consisting of four broad measures:

- quality;
- lead-time;
- resource use; and
- people development.

These measures are primarily geared for manufacturers. Nevertheless, with a little bit of imagination they can be adapted to service enterprises.

Quality

Quality measures are divided into three main groups: external quality; internal quality; and quality improvement processes. External quality is defined as the product or service goodness that customers or other people outside the organization ascribe to its products or services. Examples of external quality measures include customer surveys, service-call effectiveness, and warranty and reliability rates.

Internal quality represents the calibre of the organization's operations and processes. Examples of measures include overall yields, process capabilities, inspection ratios, and defect and rework rates.

The quality improvement process is defined as the programme or set of formalized steps an organization adopts to ensure high levels of external and internal quality. As such, today's quality improvement process determines tomorrow's internal and external quality. Although generally difficult to measure, Hall points to the measurement and scoring criteria used to determine the winner of the Malcolm Baldrige National Quality Award as an excellent point of reference when trying to assess an organization's quality improvement process.

Lead-time

Lead-time is defined as the length of time required to transform raw materials into finished product. Examples include tooling turnaround time, equipment repair time, time to change plant or process layout, engineering change time, tooling design time, and tooling build time.

The measurement of lead-times is important for two reasons. First, such measures help the firm to focus on potentially rich areas of value-added or, more to the point, non-value-added activities. Any lead-time measure greater than zero implies waiting time. While it may be said that wines improve with age, this relationship seldom holds with other business activities. How, for instance, does waiting on line at the supermarket or waiting for product to be shipped improve value? Surely it does not.

A second important reason for measuring lead-times is the valuable information such measures provide about an organization's flexibility. In today's business markets, where the 'customer is king', the ability to tailor products and services to customers' unique needs is critical. To accomplish this, organizations must evolve their businesses in the direction of make to order. Lead-time measures show just how far an organization has progressed.

Resource use

Measurements of resource use quantify the amount of particular resources consumed and the cost associated with their consumption. Examples of some typical measures of resource use are direct labour dollars, materials consumption, space utilization, and machine utilization. While the first two measures quantify the direct costs associated with using labour and materials to make products or provide services, the latter two measures contain both a direct costing element and an indirect, opportunity cost element.

One of the factors that limits the precision, if not usefulness, of resource use measures is the reliance that is placed on the accountant's conception and formulation of costs. As Hall points out, the various assumptions and aggregations that generally go into the computation of a cost figure make its use suspect. In particular, how can one distinguish between small, but still unfavourable, changes? Might they be indications of something wrong or mere 'measurement chatter?'

People development

People measures comprise Hall's fourth category. Other than noting the need for organizations to maintain human resource inventories and implement systems that fairly and appropriately recognize and reward employees, Hall offers little additional advice on this category. This is an unfortunate occurrence, especially in light of the fact that scholars and managers alike are underscoring the increasingly important role played by an organization's human resources.

It appears that Hall's underdeveloped set of people measures could be substantially improved by incorporating into it Thomas Stewart's work on intellectual capital. In particular, Stewart has studied various companies' attempts to record and report their intellectual capital. One company, Skandia Assurance and Financial Services (AFS), a Swedish company selling annuities, variable life insurance policies, and other savings and insurance instruments, appears to be leading in this area. Rather than relying on such conventional practices as the skill levels attained by its employees or the amount of money spent upgrading employees' skills, AFS is more interested in developing ratios that reveal how effectively it leverages its intellectual assets. As Stewart (1994) notes in his summary of AFS's approach to intellectual capital, 'It is less important to find the grand total value of intellectual capital than to develop gauges that show whether AFS is moving in the right direction – creating more of the stuff this year than last, and using it better.' Some of the trends that AFS charts are the growth in its broker network and the size of the accounts they manage.

Hall stresses the need for the average organization to make substantial improvements across all four performance fronts or risk elimination by its competitors. While Hall realizes the difficulty (if not impossibility) of making a simultaneous across-the-board improvement, he is confident that organizations can make incremental improvements over time to each of the four performance criteria without jeopardizing the organization's past achievements. For instance, improvements in lead-times should be sought without regression on some other measure, such as quality. Similarly, improvements in quality should occur without sacrificing resource use.

Kaplan and Norton's balanced scorecard

Robert Kaplan and David Norton's balanced scorecard is a hybrid performance measurement system consisting of financial and non-financial measures. The balanced scorecard assesses enterprise performance from four broad perspectives:

- financial;
- internal business;
- customer; and
- learning and growth.

The financial perspective offers insight into how well the organization is meeting its shareholder needs. Some of the typical measures used to assess financial performance are return on capital, cash flow, project profitability, and profit forecast reliability.

The internal business perspective sheds light on how well the organization is executing its core activities. Some of the measures that commonly appear under this category are cycle times, unit costs, yield rates, scrap rates, machine utilization, set-up times, and manufacturing lead-times.

The customer perspective provides insight into how well the organization is meeting its customer needs. Some of the measures that characterize the customer perspective are customer surveys, customer satisfaction indices, market share trends, and on-time delivery statistics.

The learning and growth perspective, which was originally named innovation and learning, sheds light on an organization's ability to improve and create value. Some of the measures that are commonly associated with this perspective are employee satisfaction, employee retention, employee productivity, percentage of processes with real-time feedback, and number of employee suggestions, as well as indices of team building and team performance.

Information from each of these perspectives is vital to the organization's continued success. As Kaplan and Norton like to point out, the successful management of an organization requires the ability to view performance in several areas simultaneously. Similar to an aeroplane pilot – who needs constantly updated information on fuel, air speed, altitude, bearing, and destination – so too do an organization and its managers need information comprising a broad set of performance criteria.

While all organizations need information from each of the four performance perspectives, the specific set of items comprising each perspective will most likely be different for each organization. The differences will arise from differences in organizational strategies, as well as factors that are unique to an organization's internal or external environment. As Kaplan and Norton (1992) note:

> The balanced scorecard is not a template that can be applied to businesses in general or even industry-wide. Different market situations, product strategies, and competitive environments require different scorecards.

Accordingly, effective balanced scorecards are ones that have been tailored to fit the organization's mission, strategy, and internal and external environments. The acid test of a well-designed balanced scorecard is an observer's ability to see through the specific scorecard measures and correctly divine the organization's strategy.

A number of organizations have adopted the balanced scorecard. A partial list of such adopting organizations include Apple Computers, Rockwater, CIGNA Corporation, Bank of Montreal, Airways Corporation, Telecom New Zealand, ICI Australia, New Zealand Post, and Ericsson Australia Limited. According to Kaplan and Norton, the typical company testimonial centres on the balanced scorecard's ability to help drive organizational change and enhance management planning and control.

If there is one major shortcoming with the balanced scorecard it is the often inconsistent set of performance measures that appears under the innovation and learning perspective. For example, in their *Harvard Business Review* article showcasing Rockwater's experience with using the balanced scorecard, Kaplan and Norton place under the innovation and learning perspective such measures as percent revenue from new services, rate of improvement index, staff attitude survey, number of employee suggestions, and revenue per employee. It seems, however, that many of these performance measures can be, and perhaps are better, categorized under different performance perspectives from the ones under which they currently appear. Percentage revenue from new services, which is essentially a specific type of market share statistic, appears better categorized with customer performance measures. Likewise, the rate of improvement index, which is defined for Rockwater as the improvement made in relation to product rework and safety issues, appears better categorized with internal business performance measures. Furthermore, staff attitude surveys might be better placed with measures of internal business performance, and revenue per employee might be better placed with financial performance measures. In sum, it appears that Kaplan and Norton have yet to iron out the inconsistencies associated with their innovation and learning perspective.

In fairness to Kaplan and Norton, they appear to be aware of the deficiencies inherent in their learning and growth perspective. In their book, *Translating Strategy into Action: The Balanced Scorecard* (1996), they admit that the measures of the learning and growth perspective are 'less developed than those of the other three perspectives.'

As a first step in resolving the problems associated with the balanced scorecard's learning and innovation perspective, it is suggested that the name of this perspective be changed to the 'learning perspective'. In actual truth, such a name change is more a rediscovery than a reorientation. In the balanced scorecard's original version, the perspective was labelled 'learning and innovation'. Additionally, the name change would mirror the importance that today's writers are ascribing to an organization's ability to learn.

By steering clear of the word 'growth', Kaplan and Norton's model will not only be conceptually clearer, but it will also be in greater harmony with the management literature on continuous improvement. In particular, the idea of growth or improvement should not be seen as unique to any one perspective. Improvement is required across all four perspectives. To operate otherwise jeopardizes an organization's survival. Remember from Chapter 2 that when organizations become complacent and seek to merely maintain performance, they are in danger of slipping backwards and losing competitiveness.

The measures to assess this renamed fourth perspective can be researched in the management literature focusing on learning organizations. Generally speaking, measures of an organization's learning capacity will draw attention to the organization's ability to generate new ideas and subsequently generalize and disseminate them on an organization-wide basis. In more specific terms, items likely to feature under this learning perspective are measures of an organization's ability to harness its human asset resource and include employee empowerment, the creation of flatter organizations, and the marrying of people and structural capital.

Before leaving this topic of the balanced scorecard, it is worth noting some similarities between Kaplan and Norton's work and the work of Brignall and his colleagues. Based on a multi-year field project seeking to uncover key performance measures in for-profit service businesses, Brignall *et al.* (1991) propose a set of six generic performance dimensions:

- competitiveness;
- financial;
- quality;
- flexibility;
- resource utilization; and
- innovation.

While in some respects the framework is very much like Hall's, sharing many of the same performance category names, it shares even more in common with the balanced scorecard. The similarity becomes increasingly evident when the performance measures underlying Brignall *et al.*'s six dimensions are compared with the performance measures underlying the balanced scorecard's four perspectives. In particular, the competitiveness and financial performance measures tap the same theme as the balanced scorecard's financial perspective. Additionally, the quality performance measures map onto the balanced scorecard's customer perspective, while the flexibility and resource utilization performance measures equate to the balanced scorecard's internal perspective. And finally, the innovation performance measures are similar to the balanced scorecard's learning and growth perspective. It is interesting to note how the Brignall *et al.* and Kaplan and Norton performance measurement systems were developed at about the same time, although on different sides of the Atlantic, and largely ended up with the same results.

Cross and Lynch's performance measurement hierarchy

Kelvin Cross and Richard Lynch propose a performance measurement system that links operational and strategic goals and integrates financial and non-financial information. To help underscore their message about the importance of linking strategy

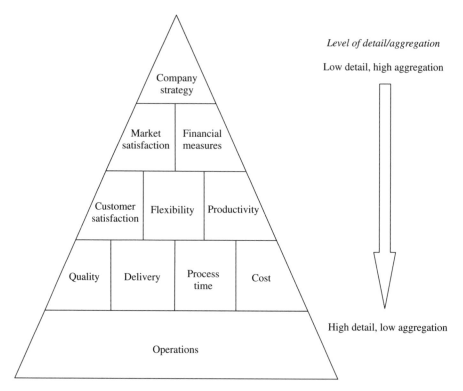

Figure 8.1 The performance pyramid. Adapted from Cross, K. and Lynch, R. (1990). Tailoring Performance Measures to Suit Your Business. *Journal of Accounting and EDP*, **6**(1), 17–25.

with measures of performance, they illustrate, using what they have termed a performance pyramid, the intertwining nature of strategic objectives and operational performance measures. An adapted version of the pyramid is presented in Figure 8.1.

At the top of the pyramid is the organization's strategy. Strategic objectives are developed from this strategy and translated down the organization, ultimately to the very work centres themselves. With a sound knowledge of the organization's strategic objectives, the work centres can now begin developing appropriate operational performance measures to indicate how well they are meeting the strategic objectives. Data in the form of these operational performance measures will then be filtered back up the organization. Based on the feedback contained in these measures, senior managers can, as needed, fine-tune either the presentation or substance of future strategic objectives.

The process of communicating strategic objectives is cascading in nature. Strategic objectives are first communicated down to the business unit levels. Here, market satisfaction and financial performance targets are developed. In terms of Kaplan and Norton's balanced scorecard, these terms resemble the customer and financial perspectives, respectively.

The strategic objectives are next translated down to the business operating systems as customer satisfaction, flexibility, and productivity. Customer satisfaction and flexibility combine to comprise market targets, while productivity comprises financial targets.

Finally, the strategic objectives are translated down to the work centre level. Here they are represented by quality, delivery, cycle time, and waste. Quality and delivery combine to comprise customer satisfaction, delivery and cycle time combine to comprise flexibility, and cycle time and waste combine to comprise productivity.

Performance measurement information is meant to percolate up through the organization. As this information moves up the organization, it is subject to increasing aggregation and summarizing. Senior managers, the ultimate target of the performance information, will use the information to fine-tune the presentation or substance of future strategic objectives.

In addition to highlighting the critical role played by organizational strategy in determining performance measures, Cross and Lynch's performance pyramid makes two further important contributions. First, they show the intertwined nature of performance targets and performance measures. Second, they reveal the cascading and iterative process by which strategic targets move down and operational measures move up various levels of an organization's hierarchy.

The main weakness of the Cross and Lynch performance pyramid is its failure to recognize or mention the importance of organizational learning. As noted above, scholars and practitioners are increasingly emphasizing this critical organizational factor. Perhaps, therefore, it is this lack of comprehensiveness that explains the model's low rate of adoption by organizations.

Striking the right balance

It is important to operate a sufficiently broad-based performance measurement system. Otherwise, employees' strategies for maximizing their own goals, typically at the expense of the organization's goals, may develop.

As examples of the dysfunctional behaviour that can occur when the performance measurement focus is too narrow, consider the following two real-life stories. The first story is about an airline company that tried to speed delivery of passengers' luggage to the baggage collection area by measuring how long it took for the initial bag to arrive at the baggage carousel. Although the airline's measurement approach appears quite logical, it didn't take long for the baggage handlers to figure out a successful, at least when viewed from their perspective, strategy. Upon a plane's arrival, one of the baggage handlers would quickly unlock the cargo door, disappear for a few moments inside the cargo hold, reappear with as small a bag as he/she could find without spending too much time searching, throw this bag to another waiting baggage handler, who would then sprint directly to the baggage claim carousel. Based upon the company's performance measurement system, the baggage handlers' performance was judged excellent. In reality, however, their performance was anything but exemplary. They stepped on other passengers' bags in the process of selecting the small and easily portable bag, they sometimes dropped this bag when making the throwing exchange, and generally undertook a lot of wasteful activities trying to beat the system.

A second story about a performance measurement system that had too narrow a focus involves Penfold Wineries. Penfold implemented a performance measurement system that measured productivity as the number of litres of wine per man-hour worked. The employees quickly recognized that they could improve this productivity measure by decreasing their performance on a range of other non-recorded activities, including product waste and overtime. As a consequence, although the measured productivity was quite high, the performance measurement system was actually undermining the firm's competitiveness.

As the above two case examples highlight, performance measurement systems must tap a broad range of organizational activity or risk unleashing dysfunctional employee behaviour. Of course, it must also be said that just as there is a danger in having too few and too narrow a focus, there is also a danger in having too many and too broad a focus. The existence of too many performance measures may produce information overload or may trivialize the importance of any single performance measure. Either way, the performance measurement system breaks down and loses its motivational purpose.

But even when the 'right' number of performance measures are used, which according to Kaplan and Norton is about 15–20, there is still the problem of knowing what to do when the performance measures provide mixed messages. In other words, when one measure signals good news and some other measure, either within or across performance categories, signals unfavourable news.

There appear to be two approaches a manager can take when confronted with conflicting performance signals. The first approach is based on Hall's idea that performance on a given measure should be maintained or improved without any sacrifice of performance on any other criterion. Performance is unacceptable when slippage or backtracking occurs.

The second approach involves the weighting of the various performance criteria for the purpose of constructing a composite score. The weighting scheme is based upon senior management's preferences for successfully achieving on the various performance measures. There are multiple methods that can be used to develop a weighting system, ranging from Delphi techniques to paired comparison rankings. A discussion of these techniques, however, is beyond the scope of this book. Readers who are interested in gaining more information about these weighting techniques can examine the ample, primarily management-based literature that exists on this topic. Also, a *Journal of Management Research* article by Chan and Lynn, which is referenced at the end of this chapter, can be consulted.

Summary

This chapter identified and discussed four of the more popular approaches to the development of non-financial performance measures. These approaches were compared, and the various shortcomings and weaknesses of each were noted. In addition, the possibility of and potential remedies for the existence of conflicting performance signals were explored.

A theme that repeatedly occurred in this chapter is the idea that strategy must illuminate the development of non-financial performance measures. It is only after an organization has clearly defined its strategy that it can then begin the process of translating its strategy into strategic objectives and subsequently its strategic objectives into tangible non-financial goals and actions.

References

Brignall, T., Fitzgerald, L, Johnston, R. and Silvestro, R. (1991). Performance Measurement in Service Businesses. *Management Accounting*, 34–36.

Bruns, W. (1992). *Performance Measurement, Evaluation, and Incentives*, Boston: Harvard Business School Press.

Chan, Y.C. and Lynn, B.E. (1991). Performance Evaluation and the Analytic Hierarchy Process. *Journal of Management Research*, **3**, 57–87.

Cross, K. and Lynch R. (1990). Tailoring Performance Measures to Suit Your Business. *Journal of Accounting and EDP*, **6**(1), 17–25.

Dixon, J., Nanni, J. and Vollman, T. (1990). *The New Performance Challenge: Measuring Operations for World-Class Competition*, Homewood, IL: Dow Jones-Irwin.

Drucker, P. (1995). The Information Executives Truly Need. *Harvard Business Review*, **73**(1), 54–62.

Kaplan, R. and Norton, D. (1992a). The Balanced Scorecard as a Strategic Management System. *Harvard Business Review*, January–February, 71–79.

Kaplan, R. and Norton, D. (1992b). Putting the Balanced Scorecard to Work. *Harvard Business Review*, September–October, 134–142.

Kaplan, R. and Norton, D. (1996). Using the Balanced Score as a Strategic Management System. *Harvard Business Review*, January–Febuary, 75–85.

Kaplan, R. and Norton, D. (1996). *Translating Strategy into Action: The Balanced Scorecard*, Boston: Harvard Business School Press.

Lynch, R. and Cross, K. (1992). *Measure Up – Yardsticks for Continuous Improvement*, Cambridge, MA: Basil Blackwell.

McNair, C. and Mosconi, W. (1987). Measuring Performance in an Advanced Manufacturing Environment. *Management Accounting*, **69**(1), 28–31.

Peters, T. (1989). *Thriving on Chaos: Handbook for a Management Revolution*, London: Macmillan.

Simons, R. and Davila, A. (1998) How High is Your Return on Management? *Harvard Business Review*, **76**(1), 71–80.

Stewart, T. (1990). Why Budgets Are Bad for Business. *Fortune*, June, 103–107.

Stewart, T. (1994). Your Company's Most Valuable Assets: Intellectual Capital. *Fortune*, 10 October, 2–10.

Thorne, H., Gurd, B. and Southwick, A. (1995). Performance Measures in Manufacturing: Lessons from the Balanced Scorecard and Dynamic Modelling Approach. *Accounting Forum*, **18**(4), 27–44.

9
Benchmarking

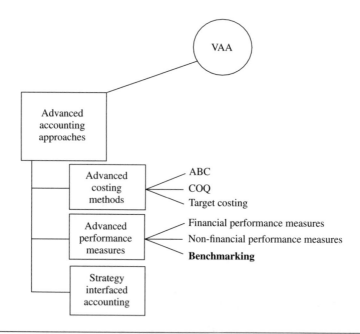

Chapter objectives

■ Examine the definition, history, and purpose of benchmarking.

■ Identify and discuss the different kinds of benchmarking that exist.

■ Explore the steps involved in benchmarking.

■ Discuss the limitations of benchmarking.

Benchmarking is a powerful management technique. The success stories associated with its use have practically achieved legendary status. Xerox, the supposed pioneer of benchmarking, is claimed to have reduced its manufacturing costs by 50 per cent, reduced its product development cycles by 25 per cent, increased its revenue per employee by 20 per cent, and increased its incoming working materials defect-free rate from 92 per cent to 99.95 per cent! Added to this already impressive list of accomplishments was an industry source's rating of Xerox as being first on four out of six categories for copier and duplicator reliability and quality.

In addition to the shining example of Xerox, further tributes to benchmarking's prowess can be readily found. Milliken, for instance, credits benchmarking with increasing its on-time delivery rate from 75 per cent to 99 per cent. Meanwhile, a senior executive with Bluebird Foods Ltd, the giant New Zealand food company, reports that in 13 months his company 'went from being very average to being first on 7 of the 11 measures that it benchmarked' (Simmons, 1995).

In light of the seemingly endless praise that has been heaped on benchmarking, it is not surprising to learn that such US corporations as Xerox, Ford, Eastman Kodak, GTE, General Motors, Motorola, AT&T, Du Pont, Alcoa, Milliken, Corning, and NYNEX have been enthusiastic adopters of benchmarking. Of course, it is not just the US corporate behemoths that have turned to benchmarking. Benchmarking has attracted a large following of organizations both big and small, service and manufacturing, for-profit and not-for-profit. In fact, the benefits from benchmarking have been so widely acknowledged that a researcher with Kreigsmann Research in New Zealand has recently claimed, 'If all manufacturers could achieve to perform in line with the best in the industry, manufacturing sales could be 54 per cent above their current level, value added could be 85 per cent higher and EBIT [earnings before interest and taxes] could exceed the current level by 214 per cent.'

In many respects the emergence of benchmarking has been similar to the sports world's intermittent discovery of its latest new-wonder athlete. Just like the athlete who streaks across the field leaving the opposition behind and the spectators gasping in disbelief, benchmarking has been trumpeted as the competitive weapon that all organizations must have.

Benchmarking is undoubtedly one of today's fastest growing and most touted advanced management techniques. Accordingly, it seems appropriate to examine how this technique may relate to an organization's attainment of world-class status and, in particular, how it may serve to guide an organization's selection and development of key performance measures. We start this examination by investigating benchmarking's distinguishing characteristics and issues related to its use.

Benchmarking: what it is and where it came from

Various writers have defined benchmarking in various ways. Robert Camp (1989), who is often acknowledged as the founding father of benchmarking, defines it as:

The continuous process of measuring our products, services, and business practices against the toughest competitors or those companies recognized as industry leaders.

Meanwhile, Roy Simmons (1995), the logistics executive at Bluebird Foods Ltd, defines benchmarking as:

The ongoing activity of comparing one's own process, product, or service against the best known similar activity, so that challenging but attainable goals can be set and a realistic course of action implemented to efficiently become and remain best-of-the-best in a reasonable time.

While the definitions offered by Camp and Simmons provide a good starting point for understanding benchmarking, neither definition sufficiently illuminates the full extent of organizational action that is likely to occur. Benchmarking is more than merely comparing oneself with the best. It also involves, and this is the considerably harder part, understanding what it is that makes the 'best' so good. In other words, it entails a close scrutiny of the 'best' organization's, as well as one's own organization's, numerous practices and methods that ultimately underlie the provision of its product or the rendering of its service. For the purposes of this book, the following definition of benchmarking will be used:

Benchmarking involves making systematic and rigorous comparisons of the products, services, and work processes of one's own organization against a suitably chosen partner. The comparisons highlight performance achievement and serve to motivate the focal organization to make improvements. Often these improvements require changes in organizational processes, technology, and work practices as a way to either maintain superiority or bridge performance deficiencies.

The actual practice of benchmarking often leads to the development of tables, graphs, and charts that are intended to plot the focal organization's performance against its chosen partner(s). As an example, the following two bar charts (Figures 9.1 and 9.2) contrast four different organizations' customer and employee retention rates. Assume that 'Firm W' is the focal organization.

As Figure 9.1 reveals, Firm W scores relatively poorly on its customer retention rates. Compared to all four organizations it is the worst at retaining customers. The performance gap, which is measured as the difference between Firm W and the best-in-class organization, which in this case is Firm X, is meant to highlight the improvement that Firm W must achieve. As part of the process of closing the performance gap, and hopefully even one day surpassing the best-in-class, Firm W will need to undertake a thorough examination of the factors associated with customer retention and compare its practices on these factors against those of Firm X.

Meanwhile, as revealed in Figure 9.2, Firm W enjoys the best employee retention rate. It is currently the best-in-class, albeit by a slim margin. The performance gap, which in this case is the difference between Firm W and Firm Y, indicates just how much of a lead it has on the firm currently running in second place. Of course, what Firm W now must do is devise a strategy for maintaining, or even increasing, its superiority. Again, this may entail identifying all the factors related to employee

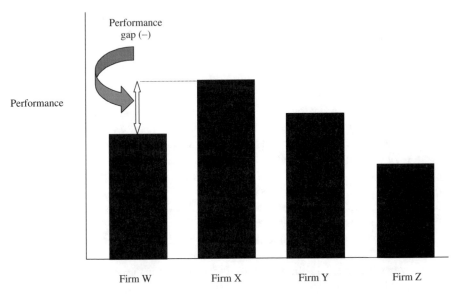

Figure 9.1 Benchmarking customer retention rates

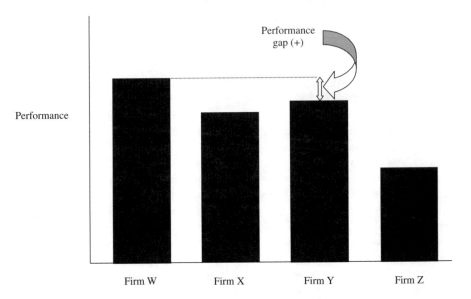

Figure 9.2 Benchmarking employee retention rates

retention and examining how it can improve its performance on these factors. To help spur improvement, Firm W might adopt GE's Jack Welsh's 10–4 programme. Under the 10–4 programme, a goal is set to improve performance by a factor of 10 over the next four years.

Before progressing too far into the subtleties of benchmarking, it is appropriate to raise the often-asked question, 'Is benchmarking anything new?' The short answer to this question is 'no'. As John Gibb (1995), benchmarking co-ordinator at Telecom New Zealand, tells it, the concept of benchmarking has been around since the dawn of mankind. Starting with the world's first man (woman), 'mankind has continuously observed and adopted new ideas and practices.'

While the caveman analogy may be too far removed from the boardroom for some or too fanciful for others, the following organizational examples should help uncover the falseness of benchmarking's newness. Chrysler Motors, under the direction of its then CEO Walter Chrysler, used to tear apart each Oldsmobile model to determine what went into the car, how much it cost, and how it was made. This practice of buying one's competitors' products, or sampling their services, is a standard organizational practice, and probably was even before Walter Chrysler did it. Today we call it 'reverse engineering'.

A second example of benchmarking's relatively mature status involves Toyota. In the 1930s, Toyota executives visited Ford's motor vehicle plant in the USA to witness what the 'best' in the world were doing so that they might learn how to emulate and improve upon this success. The Japanese even had a word for this practice: *dantotsu*. It means striving to be the best of the best. Of course, Toyota's practice of learning from other companies' operational practices was itself hardly new. BHP, the steel maker, had been comparing steel-making processes with steel makers in Europe since 1907.

The practice of benchmarking, like so many of today's other management practices, gains its uniqueness not from the set of ideas that comprises it, but from the thorough and thoughtful approach that has been applied to formulating its features. As a result of the efforts of Robert Camp and Michael Spendolini, the various sets of organizational tools that have been applied in the past to the process of comparing one organization's achievements against another have now been drawn together under one umbrella.

In addition to the efforts of Robert Camp and Michael Spendolini, benchmarking has been given a further boost from today's powerful, yet relatively inexpensive, computers. The advancements in computer technology have enabled the development and upkeep of large-sized databases of myriad organizational activity and performance measures. There are now a number of organizations that specialize in maintaining benchmarking databases. Some of the better-known benchmarking organizations are the International Benchmarking Clearinghouse, headquartered in Houston; the Benchmarking Competency Centre, headquartered in Milwaukee; the Benchmarking Centre, headquartered in Europe; and the Australian Centre for Best Practices.

Why is benchmarking important?

According to Michael Sweeney, benchmarking is the 'in vogue solution' to the question 'How can senior management find the right catalyst for the development

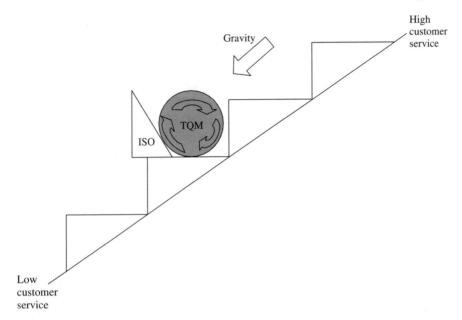

Figure 9.3 A customer service staircase showing the interrelationships between benchmarking and TQM

of a corporate culture that is motivated to transform its operations to better those that are recognized as world class?' It is unclear whether Sweeney's choice of the words 'in vogue' is meant to convey his scepticism about the worth of benchmarking or merely to note benchmarking's popularity. There appear, however, to be three good reasons for believing in the value of benchmarking.

One of the benefits of benchmarking is the boost it gives to an organization's TQM initiatives. TQM – with its focus on quality enhancement, waste elimination and continuous improvement – is often aided by the revelations that benchmarking provides. Benchmarking, by measuring an organization's performance on various key success factors and comparing this performance to a best-in-class organization, helps illuminate where the organization must devote its improvement efforts. As one senior manager, who was responsible for the benchmarking activities of a large international food-processing firm, said, 'Without benchmarking it is like walking through the dark.'

Another way of seeing the synergy that exists between benchmarking and TQM is through the use of the diagram illustrated in Figure 9.3. This figure shows customer service as a staircase, ranging from low to high customer service. The organization's present achievement on customer service is represented by the step that the ball occupies. While it is the organization's intention to seek improvements in its customer service, as represented by the fact that the ball is labelled 'TQM', the vertical plane of the next staircase is preventing this occurrence. A breakthrough is needed to lift the organization's customer service to the next level. Benchmarking is intended to play this breakthrough role.

There are three further elements to note in this diagram. First, there are times when the infectious nature of continuous improvement can give way to organizational lethargy and inertia, which are symbolized in the diagram as the forces of gravity. Second, it is the organization's policies and procedures on quality, typically captured in its ISO efforts or their equivalent, that serve to prevent the back slipping. Third, once a higher level of customer service has been achieved, the cycle repeats. In particular, the organization's quality standards will be revised to represent the organization's new set of operating procedures, and the benchmarking exercise will serve to cast a new beacon of light on organizational areas that are ripe for further improvement.

In addition to being a catalyst to the organization's ongoing TQM efforts, benchmarking can also aid the organization's activity-based costing (ABC) initiative. Benchmarking is a logical extension of ABC. As noted earlier in this book, the use of ABC does not stop with the development of better product and service costs. Instead, attempts should be made to eliminate all non-value-adding activities. These efforts are made easier by the connection ABC draws between the performance of a given activity and the costs such an activity generates. Armed with this information, the organization is in a position to understand the cost implications of its various activities and begin the process of redesigning these activities so that they will become best in class.

A third benefit of benchmarking is the boost it gives to employee motivation. Benchmarking shows employees the extent of the performance gap that exists between their firm and the best in class. As employees learn to appreciate the nature of this gap, i.e. how to measure it and why it is important to overcome it, they develop a deeper understanding of their organization's business and what must be done to remain competitive. Additionally, as Edwin Locke has revealed through his goal-setting research, the actions associated with setting goals and measuring and communicating performance relative to the attainment of those goals increases a person's motivation. Benchmarking, therefore, with its goal-setting emphasis, has the ability to enhance employee motivation.

Types of benchmarking

There are two types of benchmarking: product (service) benchmarking and process benchmarking. Product benchmarking involves the process of reverse engineering. Accordingly, the superior products or services of another organization are stripped down and compared to what one's own organization produces or provides. Through the process of reverse engineering, an organization learns about its competitor's product design/service characteristics, the costs involved in making the product or providing the service, and sometimes even the procedures that went into either making the product or providing the service.

Process benchmarking involves comparing one's own organization's operational processes against those of another organization that is deemed to have superior operational processes. The goal is to improve one's processes so that they are at a minimum equal to, but hopefully better than, the pace-setting organization's processes.

Process benchmarking can in turn be broken down into three separate kinds of benchmarking: strategic, operational, and management. Strategic benchmarking involves the process of comparing different business strategies with the objective of identifying key elements in a successful strategy.

Operational benchmarking makes comparisons between the core operating, as opposed to support, activities of one's own organization and those of the benchmarked partner(s). In general, operational benchmarking involves the collection and comparison of information about competitive cost and competitive differentiation.

Management benchmarking involves comparing the support activities of one's own organization against those of the benchmarked partner(s). Essentially any support function can be benchmarked. Some typical examples include financial management, billing and collection, human resource management, information technology management, and logistics and inventory management.

Table 9.1 displays a variety of support functions that are potential candidates for benchmarking. Included in this table is a listing of the work activities that can serve as the basis for collecting benchmarking information.

Table 9.1 An illustrative example of organizational support processes and associated activities to benchmark

Organizational process	Activities to benchmark
Order fulfilment	Order processing
	Scheduling
	Customer preparation
	Staging and preinstallation
	Delivery/removal
	Installation/deinstallation
	Product production
Logistics and inventory management	Physical asset acquisition
	Inventory management
	Physical asset planning
	Logistics planning
	Logistics operations
	Logistics engineering
	Vendor management
Billing and collection	Invoicing
	Bank operations
	Cash application
	Collection
	Third-party leasing administration

Table 9.1 (*cont.*)

Organizational process	Activities to benchmark
Product maintenance	Service call management
	Service dispatching
	Product servicing
	Service call closure
	Product maintenance planning
	Equipment performance monitoring
	Technical information provision
	Service territory planning
Information technology management	Information strategy planning
Systems analysis and design	Systems development
	Production systems support
	Research and development
	Business systems management and co-ordination
Market management	Market planning
	Product planning and development
	Pricing
	Market tracking
	Product life-cycle management
	Marketing communications
Human resource management	Workforce requirements planning
	Hiring and assignment
	Benefits and compensation management
	Personnel management
	Workforce preparedness
	Employee communications
Business management	Business strategy development
	Business planning
	Business process and operations management
Financial management	Financial planning
	Financial analysis and reporting
	Financial forecasting
	Tax planning and management
	Accounting operations
	Financial auditing
	Disbursements
	Financial asset/cash planning
	Financial asset control

Adapted from Simmons, R., Benchmarking Conference, Auckland, New Zealand, December 1995.

The stages of benchmarking

Different organizations have different ways of specifying the various stages involved in benchmarking. For instance, Xerox has a 10-step approach, AT&T a 12-step approach and Alcoa a 6-step approach. Tables 9.2–9.4 present the specific benchmarking approaches of the three firms.

The common thread among Xerox, AT&T, and Alcoa's benchmarking approaches, as well as those of other companies, are the following five stages: determine what to benchmark, identify benchmarking partner(s), locate and collect information, analyse the collected performance data relative to the benchmark goals the

Table 9.2 Xerox's approach to benchmarking

Planning	1. Identify what to benchmark
	2. Identify benchmark candidates
	3. Determine data collection method and collect data
Analysis	4. Determine current performance gap
	5. Project future performance levels
Integration	6. Communicate benchmark findings and gain acceptance
	7. Establish functional goals
Action	8. Develop action plans
	9. Implement specific actions and monitor progress
	10. Recalculate benchmarks
Maturity	◆ Leadership position attained
	◆ Practices fully integrated into processes

Table 9.3 AT&T's approach to benchmarking

1. Identify clients (process owners and planners)
2. Advance the clients from the literacy stage to the champion stage (encourage to visualize how to achieve best practices)
3. Test the environment (spend time with clients to determine commitment and identify barriers)
4. Determine urgency
5. Determine the scope and type of benchmarking needed
6. Select and prepare the team (a six to eight member team that will work with clients)
7. Overlay the benchmarking process onto the business planning process (this reinforces benchmarking's status as part of the business planning process)
8. Develop the benchmarking plan (identify benchmarking candidates, determine data collection methodology, etc.)
9. Collect and analyse data
10. Integrate the recommended actions
11. Take action
12. Continue improvement

Table 9.4 Alcoa's approach to benchmarking

1. Decide what to benchmark (what is the importance to the customer, mission statement, business needs?)
2. Planning the benchmarking project (choosing a team leader, team members and submitting project proposal)
3. Understanding own performance (self-study in order to examine factors which influence performance positively or negatively)
4. Studying others (identifying candidates for benchmarking, short-list, prepare questions of interest, conduct the study)
5. Learn from the data (identify performance gaps and which practices should be adopted)
6. Use the findings (for the benefit of the organization and its employees)

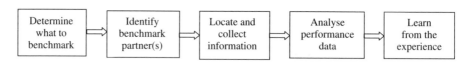

Figure 9.4 Flow diagram of steps to benchmarking

organization has set, and learn from the experience. These five stages are illustrated in Figure 9.4.

Determining what to benchmark

The first part of any benchmarking programme involves deciding on what to benchmark. In general, those activities that undergird an organization's competitive advantage should be selected. Many organizations that have only just started along the road of benchmarking find that their employees focus on product and service costs. Senior managers should be wary of this tendency and must stand ready to reorient employee effort toward its critical success factors.

Of course, even when there is a shared understanding of the need to concentrate on critical success factors, the selection of exactly what to benchmark is seldom an easy matter. As a way of providing instructive guidance on this matter, a number of qualitative and quantitative selection frameworks have been proposed.

Examples of some of the qualitative selection frameworks are Camp's, Altany's, Spendolini's, and Pryor's. Camp's (1980) highly intuitive approach suggests that the process should start at a high strategic conceptual level and cascade down to individual deliverables. Altany suggests that the organization should look for an area of weakness in the value chain that, if corrected, would generate a substantial improvement in the organization's competitive advantage. Spendolini (1992), meanwhile, simply reiterates the need to focus on the organization's critical success factors, without elaborating any further. And finally, Pryor offers three rules: identify key success factor business areas; next identify the areas that represent the greatest portion of the organization's total cost or value added; and finally use customer feedback to highlight a competitive gap, with the most serious gap determining the area to begin benchmarking.

A quantitative approach to the selection of what to benchmark has been proposed by Partovi (1994). Partovi suggests using an analytical hierarchy process (AHP) approach. This approach involves the creation of preference matrices, the derivation of relative weightings, and finally the prioritization of the list of activities being considered for benchmarking. According to proponents of the AHP approach, AHP formalizes and makes specific what is otherwise a largely subjective decision process. This claim is a bit exaggerated since the process of creating preference matrices is a subjective process in itself. However, a discussion of the merits of AHP is beyond the scope of this book. Readers who are interested in learning more about the technique should consult Saaty's book, which is included among the references at the end of the chapter.

Identifying benchmarking partners

The determination of one's benchmarking partner(s) represents the second stage of benchmarking. Benchmarking partners can come from one of five possible areas. They can be examples of best practice found:

1 in-house;
2 among domestic competitors;
3 among foreign competitors;
4 throughout one's home country (sometimes termed 'national class'); or
5 throughout the world (sometimes termed 'world class').

In-house or internal benchmarking is generally the easiest to accomplish. At times, due to the reticence of other organizations to disclose information about themselves, internal benchmarking is the only avenue available. While the costs of implementing internal benchmarking rather than external benchmarking are invariably lower, so too are the benefits. Instead of aiming to initially match and later exceed the performance of a best-in-class organization, internal benchmarking's goal is generally less ambitious.

The other four methods of benchmarking represent forms of external benchmarking. Industry type and geography are the two factors that distinguish between and characterize these different methods. Domestic and foreign competitor benchmarking entails the selection of partners from among one's group of either domestic or foreign competitors and ensures that the benchmarking comparisons are unaffected by industry type. Meanwhile, national class and world class benchmarking involves the selection of partners on a generic, that is unconstrained by industry type, basis. Accordingly, the list of potential benchmarking partners is expanded.

While world class benchmarking may seem like the pinnacle of benchmarking, it is often easier to implement than competitor benchmarking. As noted above, organizations, especially competitors, are reluctant to disclose what is often viewed as commercially sensitive information. Consequently, organizations are often more successful recruiting a willing partner from outside one's industry than from within it.

National benchmarking, although not as comprehensive in its selection process as world-wide benchmarking, avoids the cultural problems that can affect world-wide benchmarking. In particular, language and legislative differences can make world-wide benchmarking unwieldy to administer and difficult to interpret.

Locating/collecting benchmark information

When the chosen benchmarking partners are all willing candidates, the collection of performance information is a simple matter. But what happens in situations where the selected partners are not willing to share information? What, if any, alternatives are available to the organization?

Surprisingly there are quite a number of alternative information sources to which an organization can turn. There are five main groups of sources: customers, suppliers and distributors, government, news media, and competitor intelligence.

Customer perceptions about competitors' products, service, and pricing can be gathered using surveys. This technique appears to be gaining in popularity. Banks, airlines, manufacturers, and telephone companies, just to name a few, commonly ask their customers to rate product and service attributes of their company against their competitors.

Suppliers and distributors are also a valuable source of information. Just like customers, suppliers and distributors are often exposed to a variety of organizational practices. The benchmarking organization can query the suppliers and distributors about these contacts.

The government represents a third source of information. There are many aspects of corporate life that come under the jurisdiction of governments, including financial reporting, safety, patents and copyrights, court actions, and several more. As a consequence, financial information may be gathered from the government-mandated annual report filings. Meanwhile, safety information can be obtained from occupational safety authorities for worker-related safety and from specific governmental agencies for product- and service-related safety, e.g. aviation departments for airline safety records and highway departments for car safety. Patents and copyright information can be acquired from patent and copyright offices. And finally, information on court actions can be collected from court proceedings.

The fourth source of information is the news media. Television, newspapers, and magazines sometimes showcase individual companies' practices. While it is often the case that the company itself has released – and sometimes in a slightly embellished form – the information to the media, there are also occasions when the news story is the result of investigative journalism and offers a very open and blunt look at the company's practices.

The fifth source of information is competitor intelligence and surveillance. Some of the common information-gathering techniques that are included under this category are visits to trade shows, attendance at professional meetings and conferences, perusal of trade publications, perusal of academic research (especially case-based work), and the obtaining of (through legal means) competitors' price lists. One additional and extremely powerful technique is to query company employees, who worked for competitors, about the competitors' practices.

It should be noted that this fifth source of benchmarking information is inherently fraught with ethical issues and should be carefully approached. At times, the line is quite fine between what are acceptable and unacceptable practices of competitor surveillance. In an attempt to provide guidance to its members, the Council on Benchmarking, the Clearinghouse, and other benchmarking organizations have recently developed protocols and codes of conduct.

Analysing the benchmark data

The fourth stage of benchmarking involves the analysis of the collected data. The data serves to allow the organization to monitor movements in the performance gap and compare these movements to the benchmark goals that were set. The results of this analysis should be communicated widely throughout the company.

The data analysis stage should, of course, go beyond the mere tabulation of performance results. Additionally, the organization should investigate the reasons for the observed performance differences. For instance, charting the difference between one's unit costs, set-up times, or customer satisfaction rates is only the beginning. It is important that the organization move ahead with the task of restructuring organizational processes, technology, and work practices.

Learning from the experience

The final stage of benchmarking is learning from the experience. Benchmark learning takes a variety of forms, and is not just limited to reshaping organizational processes and practices. In addition, the organization's benchmarking experience may suggest a need to recalibrate how performance is measured, or it may even expose deficiencies in the process used to select bench-marking partners. In essence, this learning stage of benchmarking is intended to embody the idea of continuous improvement. The organization must continuously learn from its benchmarking experience so that it is in a better position to capitalize on the benefits that benchmarking provides.

The limitations of benchmarking

There are three main limitations of benchmarking. The first limitation concerns the difficulty of obtaining benchmarking information. This problem is especially evident when the chosen benchmark partners are competitors. These partners may be unwilling to share information, and the costs involved in tapping other information sources may prove too costly or time consuming. As a consequence, it may be more feasible to study non-competitors. The side panel at right shows how one organization, Xerox, chose to benchmark non-competitors.

The second limitation of benchmarking concerns its applicability to different organizational environments. In particular, benchmarking is best suited to environments that are characterized by high certainty, high stability, and high repetition. Benchmarking requires not only an ability to measure outcomes, but also a sound understanding of the processes that underlie the outcomes. Remember that the measurement of outcomes – whether it be unit costs, customer satisfaction, etc. – and the calculation of a performance gap is not the end point. The identification of a performance gap is meant to energize and direct employee behaviour toward finding ways to close the performance gap and eventually become the best in class. The accomplishment of this task presupposes that the processes, technology, and work practices are sufficiently understood and the effects of planned modifications can be anticipated. If

Consider this . . .

Xerox, when implementing its highly acclaimed benchmarking programme chose to select non-competitors as its benchmark partners. It benchmarked its automated inventory control against American Hospital Supply; its billing and collection against American Express; its distribution against L.L. Bean Inc., Hershey Foods, and Mary Kay Cosmetics; its employee suggestions against Milliken Carpet; its computer operations against Deere and Company; its marketing, participative management, and employee involvement against Procter & Gamble; its research and product development against AT&T and Hewlett-Packard; its manufacturing operations and quality management against Fuji-Xerox, Toyota, and Komatsu; its strategy implementation against Texas Instruments; its factory layout against Ford Motor Company and Cummins Engine; and its quality improvement against Florida Power and Light.

these conditions do not apply, then the activity is less likely to benefit from benchmarking.

There are some benchmarking experts who believe that service organizations are less likely to benefit from benchmarking. However, such a black-and-white approach is false and misleading. Many service activities fit the definition of high certainty, high stability, and high repetition (e.g. a bank's processing of a mortgage application). Likewise there are many examples of manufacturing activities that do not fit the definition of high certainty, high stability, and high repetition (e.g. research and development).

The third limitation of benchmarking concerns its frequent misuse. Although this is more a problem of management and not the concept of benchmarking *per se*, it still remains that benchmarking is frequently misunderstood and misused. Instead of functioning as a proactive organizational practice, which is meant to complement an organization's programme of continuous improvement, it is often hijacked along the way and becomes a reactive, me-too approach. Organizations that merely use benchmarking to emulate or 'copycat' others' practices will find only short-lived benefits from benchmarking. In essence, such organizations will always be playing 'catch-up'. Ultimately these organizations' perceptions of benchmarking will sour and their commitment to benchmarking will progressively weaken.

Summary

Benchmarking involves the continuous process of comparing an organization's products, services, and practices against a best-in-class standard. While some organizations chose a sister department, division, or business unit for benchmarking, most organizations chose external partners. Through the process of measuring and comparing performance, employees are encouraged to suggest and implement ideas for improving organizational activities. The ultimate goal of benchmarking is to transform an organization into or to maintain its status as the best in class.

The topic of benchmarking is closely related to performance measurement systems. But rather than viewing it as a subset of performance measurement, it is better to see it as an extension of this topic. While both benchmarking and performance measurement are concerned with measuring and comparing performance, benchmarking is additionally characterized by its attempt to improve existing organizational processes, technology, and work practices. In this manner, it is quite similar to ABC (activity-based costing) and especially ABM (activity-based management).

In sum, benchmarking is a continuous and unfolding organizational journey toward organizational betterment. Management must eschew characterizations that portray benchmarking as a one-time or intermittent practice. Management must remember, and always be ready to put forward the case, that benchmarking is most powerful when combined with the organization's overall programme of quality enhancement and continuous improvement.

References

Camp, R. (1989). *Benchmarking: The Search for Industry Best Practices that Lead to Superior Performance*, Milwaukee: ASQC Quality Press.

Cox, A. and Thompson, I. (1998). On the Appropriateness of Benchmarking. *Journal of General Management*, **23**(3), 1–20.

Gibb, J., Benchmarking Conference, December 1995, Auckland, New Zealand.

Macneil, J., Rimmer, M. and Testi, J. (1994). *Benchmarking in Australia*, Melbourne: Longman Professional.

Ohinata, Y. (1994). Benchmarking: The Japanese Experience. *Long Range Planning*, **27**(4), 48–53.

Partovi, F. (1994). Determining What to Benchmark: An Analytic Hierarchy Process Approach. *International Journal of Operations and Production Management*, **14**(6), 25–39.

Saaty, T. (1980). *The Analytic Hierarchy Process*, New York: McGraw-Hill.

Simmons, R., Benchmarking Conference, December 1995, Auckland, New Zealand.

Spendolini, M. (1992). *The Benchmarking Book*, New York: American Management Association.

Xerox Group (1984). *Competitive Benchmarking*, Stamford, CT: Xerox Corp.

Part Four

Strategic Management Issues

10

Strategic cost management

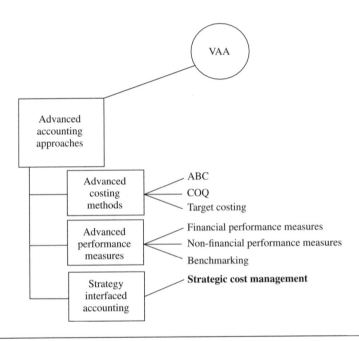

Chapter objectives

- Explore the movement behind the push for a new management accounting cost paradigm.
- Introduce strategic cost management (SCM) as management accounting's revitalized cost paradigm.
- Identify and discuss the three strands of SCM and offer case examples of each.
- Describe the stages for implementing SCM.

The roots of management accounting can be traced to an earlier time when the field was termed cost accounting. Back then, the cost accounting function was primarily, if not entirely, concerned with costing products and services. Through a succession of evolutionary developments, the purpose of today's management accounting, or so contemporary management accounting textbooks would have us believe, is to provide the informational software needed to run the organization's operational hardware.

There are many critics, however, who see such a definition as exaggerated and fanciful. According to these critics, the name change (from cost accounting to management accounting) has not been accompanied by any true change in substance. The field, say these critics, continues to espouse a focus that is predominantly internal and cost-based, focusing on the firm's purchases, products, processes, workers, and customers.

The shortcomings of relying upon internal, cost-based accounting information and the strains it is placing on organizational competitiveness are becoming increasingly evident. Today's organizations compete on a world-wide basis and across a broad range of product and service attributes. Yet management accounting information provides limited illumination and, at times, actually interferes and causes delayed organizational action. As noted by Kaplan and Johnson (1987):

> Typical 1980s cost accounting systems are helpful neither for product costing nor for operational control; they do not provide information useful for cost management . . . When senior management no longer receive accurate information about the efficiency and effectiveness of internal operations, the organization becomes vulnerable to competition from smaller and more focused organizations.

The comments of Johnson and Kaplan, though now a bit dated, appear to still ring true. Dixon and Smith (1993), for example, have reported that strategic planners spend 70 per cent of their time reworking accounting numbers to make them suitable for strategic purposes. Meanwhile, Tony Grundy (1996) laments management accounting's continuing narrow focus on internal costs. He worries that such a misguided preoccupation 'generates weaker financial performance . . . [and] destroys shareholder value.'

While it is certainly the case that the number of proponents for change is growing, a decision as fundamental as the reconstitution of the costing paradigm should be made on the basis of argument rather than the result of a hand count. Any argument for change must reveal why the existing paradigm no longer fits and clearly set out what should be adopted in its place. We begin our exploration into the case for change, therefore, by examining the problems that mar the traditional cost accounting paradigm.

What is wrong with the traditional cost accounting paradigm?

There are three main problems that plague the traditional cost accounting paradigm: its narrow view of the value chain; its short-term focus; and its emphasis on output volume. Each of these problems is discussed in turn.

Traditional costing systems commonly have a narrow focus of value added. Value added is seen as the difference between the cost of materials and the price at which a product or service sells. The key is to maximize this difference.

Unfortunately such a view of the business process is too limited: it starts too late and ends too soon. Starting cost analysis with purchases overlooks all the opportunities for rethinking, recombining, and further exploiting the organization's linkages with its suppliers. In fact, the continuous realignment and improvement of the organization – supplier transacting arrangement, including the business practices and methods adopted by each, is a fundamental characteristic of JIT.

Traditional cost analysis is also guilty of ending too soon. Cost analyses that stop at the point of sale overlook all the opportunities for reconfiguring and reshaping the organization – customer transacting arrangement. As Richard Norman and Rafael Ramirez say in their *Harvard Business Review* article entitled 'From Value Chain to Value Constellation: Designing Interactive Strategy', organizations can pack more value into their product and service offerings by redesigning the roles, relationships, and responsibilities that are traditionally assigned to the organization and the customer. For example, they note how IKEA, the Swedish furniture maker, 'offers customers a brand new division of labour that looks something like this: if customers agree to take on certain key tasks traditionally done by manufacturers and retailers – the assembly of products and their delivery to customers' homes – then IKEA promises to deliver well-designed products at substantially lower prices.'

The organization and customer enhancements that can result from a redistribution of the typical roles assigned to each party are well highlighted by the banking industry's introduction of automatic teller machines (ATMs). In exchange for what has essentially become a self-service transaction, the bank has decreased delivery time (i.e. the amount of time waiting to be served) and increased flexibility (i.e. most ATMs can be accessed 24 hours a day, 7 days a week). According to Norman and Ramirez, the IKEA and ATM examples illustrate how 'work-sharing' and 'co-productive' activities can promote 'denser' or more value-packed offerings. As a result of the process, the customers reap greater product or service value and the organization reports higher profits.

The second problem that plagues traditional costing approaches is the overemphasis given to short-term results. Too much time is spent constructing monthly sales and cost budgets, as well as computing and analysing the myriad price and efficiency variances these budgets spawn. This scorekeeping function has virtually hijacked other important management accounting activities. For example, the design of different management accounting systems to support different strategic orientations has frequently been shunted aside. While it is commonly believed that a cost leader strategy requires a heavy reliance on short-term cost data (see, in particular, Govindarajan and Gupta's work, 1985), a differentiation strategy is believed to be ill suited to a cost-based approach. Instead this later strategic approach requires the use of long-term, non-financial information (again see Govindarajan and Gupta's, 1985). Unfortunately, the traditional cost accounting paradigm is generally unable to provide such information.

The third problem that plagues the traditional cost accounting paradigm is the over-reliance it places on output volume. The organization often inappropriately emphasizes the categorization of costs into one of four categories: variable, fixed, step fixed, and mixed. But the reality of today's business environment, which is characterized by shorter product life cycles and greater amounts of automation, makes such a division of costs increasingly less relevant and often breeds complacency. The growing irrelevance of these cost divisions has occurred as a result of the ever-dwindling pool of variable costs. As Thomas Sheridan says, 'Perhaps the only really significant variable costs left are materials and subcontract labour.' Meanwhile, the continued use of such classical cost categorizations encourages a complacent, scorekeeping mentality. Instead of merely counting costs, today's organizations must begin actively managing them.

A framework that has been proposed to aid in the management of organizational costs is John Shank's generic strategic cost drivers. According to Shank (1989), cost drivers can be grouped into one of two categories: structural and executional. Structural cost drivers are associated with the design phase of an organization's products or services, while executional cost drivers are associated with the implementation or post-design phase. Much more will be said about these two generic types of cost drivers at a later point in this chapter.

The problems inherent in traditional costing systems have led many management accounting scholars to wonder whether it is time to rethink the objectives, definitions, and usage of costing procedures. As a way of sharpening the debate between the current characterization of management accounting and its future evolved state, Shank has offered the following checklist of questions:

- Should conventional management accounting outputs (such as cost variance analysis) continue to be supported in today's radically changed business environment?
- Can conventional management accounting frameworks accommodate the inclusion of new information outputs, such as activity-based costing, that are generally consistent with the conventional framework?
- Can conventional management accounting frameworks accommodate the inclusion of new information outputs, such as cost of quality, that are generally outside the scope of the conventional framework?
- Can conventional management accounting frameworks accommodate the inclusion of new information outputs, such as life-cycle costing, that are largely at odds with the conventional framework?

According to Shank, the faults and inadequacies of the traditional management accounting framework are so serious that a new cost paradigm is required. Shank has enunciated the distinguishing features of this new cost paradigm, which he terms 'strategic cost management'. We now proceed to an examination of this new paradigm, including the steps required for its implementation.

What is strategic cost management?

Strategic cost management (SCM) seeks to manage costs for both financial and competitive advantage and for both long- and short-term control. The accomplishment of this aim is supported by its integration of the fields of management accounting, production, and strategic planning. As such, SCM provides the informational fuel for powering the organization's formulation of strategies, communication of the strategies throughout the organization, development and execution of tactics to implement the strategies, and development and implementation of strategic controls.

To further tease out the distinguishing traits of SCM, it is helpful to identify and discuss SCM's three main activities:

- value chain analysis;
- competitive advantage analysis; and
- cost driver analysis.

Each of these activities is discussed below.

Value chain analysis

Value chain analysis involves the examination of value-creating activities, starting with the suppliers of basic raw materials and stopping with the end-use customer. Instead of limiting the examination to the organization's suppliers and customers, which is what John Shank terms the 'value-added' approach, value chain analysis is more comprehensive and more externally oriented.

Value chain analysis recognizes that senior managers' vistas have been circumscribed by their organization's transaction-based accounting systems. Accordingly, he encourages senior managers to shrug off these blinkers and begin thinking about how supplier and customer roles and relationships along the full length of the value chain can be modified to produce a Pareto efficient outcome. The challenges implied in value chain analysis are simultaneously lucrative and daunting.

The importance of value chain analysis is well argued by Peter Drucker. He notes how time and again a newly formed organization comes out of nowhere and quickly overtakes the established leaders. The common explanation given for the newcomer's success is its superior strategy, superior technology, superior marketing, or lean manufacturing. Yet this is not true, says Drucker. Invariably the newcomer enjoys a tremendous cost advantage. According to Drucker, the cost advantage is usually about 30 per cent. It derives from the newcomer's knowledge of and ability to manage costs along the full length of the value chain, and not just the piece it occupies.

In spite of the substantial benefits associated with value chain analysis, organizations commonly neglect to use it. Too often they succumb to their old habits. They focus on internal, existing business costs and fail to consider the needs of more distant upstream and downstream suppliers and customers. A good case in point is John Shank's description of a US papermill's determination of a sales price for its production of 'narrow' rolls of paper. The industry norm is to include an $11 per ton surcharge for narrow rolls (less than 11 inches). The extra value to the envelope converters, who are the primary consumers of these narrower widths, is substantially greater than the $11 surcharge. In particular, it can cost more than $100 per ton to have an outside subcontractor cut the rolls to a narrower width. The end result, says Shank (1989), 'is an uneconomic price, the impact of which is buried in a mill management accounting system that ignores value chain issues.'

Approaching this situation from the perspective of value chain analysis produces a much different price. The savings to the customer would be examined, and not just the extra costs incurred in cutting the rolls to the customer's narrower specifications.

In contrast to the paper mill example, there are many organizations that have successfully implemented value chain analysis. IKEA is one of these organizations. It has learned to optimally leverage not only its own competencies, but also the competencies of its suppliers and customers as well. We shall examine its shrewd handling of the value chain by first looking at the manner in which it has reinvented the roles and relationships of the furniture manufacturer and customers.

IKEA offers its customers high quality, low cost furniture. But there is one catch: customers must be willing to assume some of the roles and responsibilities that have traditionally been vested with the furniture manufacturer. In particular, customers must be willing to familiarize themselves with IKEA's products (for only a fraction are on display in any one store) and how to place a sales order. Additionally, customers must be willing to take responsibility for transporting the furniture to their home and assembling it.

To facilitate the process whereby customers can reap the benefits of their added inputs (in the form of reduced furniture prices), IKEA provides a variety of self-help support systems. For example, upon entering the store, customers are supplied with sales catalogues, tape measures, pens, and note paper. The IKEA furniture retail stores make an effort to not only have display areas with multiple similar product types (25 different sofas in one area and five dining tables in another), but also include display areas with room-like settings. These latter display areas help the customer to imagine how to co-ordinate the furniture, and therefore potentially helps the customer avoid the need to employ an interior decorator. The furniture items in each of the display areas carry simple readable labels, which include the name of the product, as well as its price, dimensions, features, available colours, instructions for care, and the store location where it can be ordered and claimed.

Since only about 30 per cent of IKEA's roughly 10,000 products are on display in any one store, IKEA's special knack for making clear visual presentations of its furniture offerings is not enough. Instead it is important that the customer quickly becomes adept at using the books displaying various fabric swatches, wood samples, and alternate product styles.

Adjacent to the furnished showrooms is a warehouse. Customers report here to claim their packages. (Remember the customers will need to perform their own assembly.) In the event that customers find their cars are unable to accommodate the size or quantity of their purchases, IKEA will sell at cost a car roof rack. The roof rack can be returned for a refund at the customer's next visit.

As the IKEA example demonstrates, by reshaping the traditional customer–supplier relationship, IKEA helps its customers to reap greater product value. Customers' skills and abilities are harnessed at a much earlier stage in the value chain than is normally the case. No longer do customers merely consume value. They now help to create it as well.

In addition to its enablement and mobilization of customer-created value, IKEA also seeks to enhance the value creation that its suppliers bring to the product. IKEA is very selective about who will be included among its supplying network. Thirty buying offices screen potential candidates from around the world. Those candidates that become part of the IKEA supplier network are offered extensive continuing assistance from IKEA. For example, the suppliers receive technical support, leased equipment, and advice on how to raise their operations to world-class standards. Meanwhile, IKEA's Vienna-based Business Services Department helps its suppliers to locate cost-effective raw materials and is always vigilant for synergistic business opportunities between its suppliers and other outside firms.

In sum, the IKEA example is meant to illustrate how the adoption of work-sharing, co-productive arrangements along the entire length of the value chain can promote the achievement of enhanced product value. By reshaping the roles and responsibilities assumed by itself, its customers, and its suppliers – whereby IKEA's role is expanded to include supplier training and technical assistance; the customer's role is expanded to include the supply of time, labour, information, and transportation; and the supplier's role is expanded to include a working partner commitment to IKEA's low cost, high quality product promise – IKEA has shown the impoverished and inadequate nature of traditional, static views of the value chain. Instead of viewing itself as a company that receives inputs from an upstream supplier, adds value to these inputs, and then passes them downstream to the next actor in the value chain, IKEA has transformed itself into the linchpin of goods, services, management, and support that are shared and traded among itself, its suppliers, and its customers.

Competitive advantage analysis

Strategic positioning involves an explicit recognition of the markets in which an organization chooses to compete. In particular, does an organization choose to emphasize cost leadership or some form of product/service differentiation (e.g. quick delivery, responsive after-sales service, or unique and innovative products and services)? Figure 10.1, which is an illustration of a resource grid, helps to expose and clarify the strategic positioning choices available to an organization. Although Figure 10.1 is a highly simplified representation of the actual strategic positioning process – due to the fact that it pictures the underlying decision process as two dimensional (cost and quality) when in fact the process is multidimensional – it still provides the basic elements for understanding the process of strategic positioning.

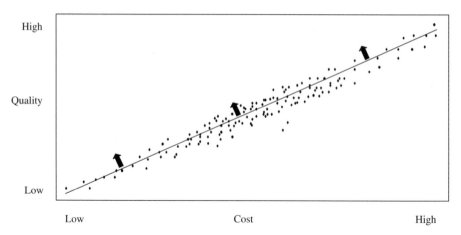

Figure 10.1 An illustration of a resource grid

A resource grid, at least in conceptual terms, underlies every product or service. The points within the grid represent a resource, or more precisely a customer need. Due to different individuals' preferences for trading-off cost and quality, a multitude of different resource points arises. In general, however, these resource points rise from the lower left corner (low cost and low quality) to the upper right corner (high cost and high quality). A line is fitted along the points to illustrate this general trend. Usually, and as is depicted in Figure 10.1, there are a greater number of resource points in the middle of the grid. Such a phenomenon illustrates the fact that although some people are unwilling to trade-off quality for price, the majority of people are willing to do so.

Competitive pressures and ever-rising customer expectations are constantly exerting their influence on the resource grid. Over time, these factors produce an upward migration of the resource points. This trend is denoted in Figure 10.1 by the inclusion of the upward pointing arrows.

The initial and most basic strategic positioning decision an organization must make is whether it will chose to be a generalist or a specialist. A generalist seeks to meet all the customers' needs for this one product or service. Meanwhile, a specialist caters to one particular segment of the customer market. It may be low cost – low quality, high cost – high quality, or perhaps medium cost and quality.

Organizations that choose to compete as generalists should be wary of Michael Porter's warning about becoming 'stuck-in-the-middle' and subsequently 'dead-in-the-water'. While certain car companies have managed this generalist positioning successfully (for example, General Motors' making of everything from a low cost Saturn to a high cost Cadillac), other companies have been much less successful (for example, Continental Airlines' attempt to expand its airline service and become both a full- and limited-service carrier).

Specialist organizations choose to focus on a particular part or segment of the overall market. On the surface, the choice of where to focus involves deciding whether to be a cost leader or market differentiator. Undergirding this decision, however, is the organization's choice about being variety based, needs based, access based, or some combination of these three positions. These terms come from Michael Porter's *Harvard Business Review* article 'What is Strategy?' (1996).

Variety-based positioning involves providing a sharply focused product or service that suits a wide array of customers, but typically only meets a subset of their needs. For example, Jiffy Lube International specializes in low cost, fast service oil changes for automobiles. It does not, however, provide any of the other car repair or maintenance services needed by automobile owners. Nevertheless, Jiffy Lube's services are so efficient and cost effective that car owners are willing to subdivide their purchases. They purchase oil changes from Jiffy Lube and other car repair and maintenance services from perhaps their local service station.

Needs-based positioning seeks to provide a one-stop shopping experience that is capable of meeting the customer's homogeneous set of product or service needs. For example, IKEA tries to anticipate and provide for all the home furnishing needs of its customers. In addition to offering a full range of household furniture, it provides free strollers, supervised childcare, and playgrounds (for those shoppers arriving with children), as well as a cafeteria (for those shoppers who might be arriving straight from work).

Access-based positioning involves the provision of tailored approaches to reach different sets of customers with otherwise similar needs. Porter illustrates this third form of strategic positioning by describing Carmike Cinemas' operation of movie theatres in small towns, places that other movie theatre companies deem unprofitable and assiduously avoid. He describes how Carmike relies on a unique set of operating (including the use of low cost theatre complexes and less sophisticated projection technology than exists at big city theatres) and management practices (including centralized purchasing and low corporate overheads).

Once we understand that different organizations seek to implement different strategic positions, we might begin to question the relevance and appropriateness of using cost analyses that are indifferent to organizational strategy. Instead, we might wonder if certain types of cost analyses are more appropriate for different situations. In general, it is now commonly asserted that traditional cost analyses – such as standard costs – are appropriate for organizations that pursue a cost leader strategy. Meanwhile, traditional cost analyses, at least by themselves, are inappropriate measures for organizations that pursue differentiation strategies. This latter group of organizations needs to complement traditional cost analysis measures with long-term, non-financial performance measures.

Cost driver analysis

Traditionally costs have been portrayed as variable, fixed, step-fixed, and mixed. Meanwhile, production volumes and output levels are seen to cause or drive these costs.

SCM presents a new perspective on costs and their incurrence. Rather than seeing the production or service-rendering phase as the primary cause of cost incurrence, it suggests that decisions made during the design and development phases of a new product or service are the substantial cause of future costs. In particular, such factors as the size of the investment, the degree of vertical integration, the extent to which the new product or service offering is similar to previous or existing offerings, the types of process technologies planned, and the expected range and diversity of the new product or service lines – though only representing a fraction of the expenditures that will be made during the product or service's life cycle – largely determine the product or service's final cost. Daniel Riley calls these design phase decisions 'structural cost drivers'.

Notwithstanding the fact that decisions made during the design stages are the major determinants of the new product or service's final cost, there is still some opportunity for an organization to achieve cost reductions during the manufacture of products and rendering of services. While these cost reductions are small in comparison to the design phase cost savings, it is wrong and foolhardy to trivialize or downplay them. Often there is a very thin line separating successful and unsuccessful organizations. As a consequence, organizations need to ensure that all their activities are characterized by the highest standards of performance.

Post-design cost reductions are realized through the successful and expeditious execution of tasks. Some of the factors that determine the successful execution of tasks are workforce involvement, total quality management, capacity utilization, plant layout efficiency, product configuration, and exploitation of value chain opportunities. Daniel Riley calls these post-design cost factors 'executional cost drivers'.

There are two important points about structural and executional cost drivers to keep in mind. First, the basic thrust of the two cost drivers is quite different. Whereas a greater quantity of any one or combination of executional cost drivers is always better (e.g. it is always preferable to have more efficient plant layouts), the same is not true for structural cost drivers. More is not always better. There are economies of scale and scope, as well as diseconomies. Diverse product lines are not necessarily better or worse than limited product lines. The pioneering use of advanced, state-of-the-art technologies may be appropriate for one firm, while a strategy of observing and following may better suit a different firm. And finally, too much experience can have fatal outcomes. For example, Texas Instruments, back in the early 1980s, perfected the use of learning curve improvements and became the world's lowest cost producer of obsolete computer chips.

The second point to bear in mind about structural and executional cost drivers is the similar end objectives they share with target costing. Target costing's first stage, *genka kikaku*, or cost design reductions, can be linked to our discussion of structural cost drivers. Meanwhile, target costing's second stage, *genka kaizen*, or cost improvement, can be linked to our discussion of executional cost drivers.

As one final note on this topic of cost drivers, it is worth pointing out that Michael Porter has developed a set of 10 factors that drives the cost of value activities over time. Table 10.1 presents a list of Porter's 10 cost drivers.

Table 10.1 Porter's list of cost drivers

1. Economies or diseconomies of scale
2. Learning and spill-over
3. Pattern of capacity utilization
4. Value chain linkages
5. Inter-relationships and strategic alliances
6. Vertical integration
7. Timing (i.e. being a first mover or pursuing a follower strategy)
8. Discretionary policies
9. Geographic location
10. Institutional factors (political, legislative, cultural, etc.)

Executing SCM

There are seven steps associated with the execution of an SCM program. These seven steps are illustrated in Figure 10.2.

The proper identification of strategic business units (SBUs) represents a critical and often highly challenging first step. Pitfalls await the unwary. Sometimes organizations identify too many SBUs, with the end result being that some of the identified SBUs are artefacts of faulty thinking. On other occasions organizations identify too few SBUs, resulting in the loss of SBU integrity.

To aid in the identification of SBUs, the Arthur D. Little approach can be used. This approach analyses the organization's subunits from the following four perspectives: price, competitors, customer groups, and shared experience. In particular, subunits that experience spill-over effects from the pricing policies of other subunits, share competitors, share customer groups, and/or share similar organizational functions are more likely to be included as part of the same SBU.

The next step in executing SCM is the identification of the strategic problem or issue. The organization must be particularly careful about taking too narrow of an approach. For example, a commonly worded strategic issue such as 'How can we make major reductions in our manufacturing costs?' should be modified to 'How can we manage our manufacturing costs for both financial and competitive advantage?' Such a reorientation in wording is important because it suggests not just cost reduction efforts, but encourages revenue enhancement activities as well. Additionally, the revised wording implies that any cost-cutting measure should be carefully examined to ensure that it will not erode the organization's competitive position.

The third step in executing SCM is the development of a preliminary set of options. As just noted, the organization will wish to analyse ways in which it can best promote its competitive advantage. Accordingly, it will examine the issue through the lenses of value chain analysis, strategic positioning analysis, and cost driver analysis. It is at this stage of the strategic cost management process that the management accountant's skills are most needed.

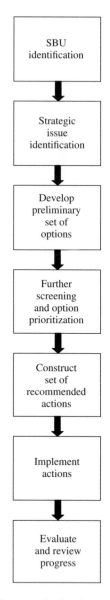

Figure 10.2 Steps to the implementation of SCM

The fourth and fifth steps in executing SCM are highly related. They involve performing a further screening and prioritization of the preliminary list of options and constructing a set of recommended actions. Here again, the management accountant is likely to play a prominent role.

In helping the organization to further screen and prioritize options, Tony Grundy's (1996) 'attractiveness/implementation grid' may prove helpful. The grid consists of two axes. One axis exhibits the option's cost/benefit attractiveness and ranges from low to high. Meanwhile, the other axis indicates the option's ease of implementation, and ranges from easy to difficult. The appeal of using the attractiveness/implementation difficulty grid is the ability to visually represent the various options in one succinct diagram. The prioritization of options can be done in one of two ways. One way involves looking for Pareto efficient opportunities, i.e. finding an option that is both more attractive and easier to implement than another option. The second way of prioritizing options is by computing a weighted attractiveness/difficulty score for the various options.

The sixth step in executing SCM involves the actual implementation of the programme itself. As with any major organizational initiative, especially those that involve a significant change or cultural reorientation, active senior management involvement and commitment is essential. Senior managers must seize every opportunity to champion and promote SCM's use. Of course, this support must go beyond mere lip service. Senior management must be willing to accept the significant investment in time that is required to generate and define issues, craft options, and debate and finalize recommended courses of action.

The seventh and final step in executing SCM involves the evaluation and review of the organization's SCM programme and the progress experienced to date. This step is critical for helping the organization to gauge its past performance and develop new ways for improving upon its use of SCM. In essence, the feedback will be used to promote organizational learning.

Summary

The increasingly competitive nature of the business environment has led many organizations to the realization that their management accounting systems are failing them. The internal, standard costing mentality that characterizes these traditional systems offers insufficient illumination for organizational decision making.

SCM stands out as a bold attempt to integrate the fields of management accounting, production, and strategic management. The ultimate purpose of SCM is to aid in the formulation of strategies, the communication of these strategies throughout the organization, the development and execution of tactics to implement the strategies, and the development and introduction of strategic controls.

The reliance SCM places on value chain analysis, competitive advantage analysis, and cost driver analysis helps to characterize it as a radical departure from traditional cost analyses. As such, SCM represents not only a major paradigm shift, but it also offers organizations an important vehicle for sustaining and promoting competitive advantage.

References

Dixon, R. and Smith, D. (1993). Strategic Management Accounting. *Omega Journal of Management Science*, **21**(6), 305–318.

Drucker, P. (1995). The Information Executives Truly Need. *Harvard Business Review*, **73**(1), 55–62.

Govindarajan, V. and Gupta, A.K. (1985). Linking Control Systems to Business Unit Strategy: Impact on Performance. *Accounting Organizations and Society*, **10**(1), 51–66.

Grundy, T. (1996). Cost is a Strategic Issue. *Long Range Planning*, **29**(1), 58–68.

Johnson, T. and Kaplan, R. (1987). *Relevance Lost: The Rise and Fall of Management Accounting*, Boston, MA: Harvard Business School Press.

Porter, M. (1985). *Competitive Advantage*, New York: The Free Press.

Porter, M. (1996). What is Strategy? *Harvard Business Review*, **74**(6), 61–78.

Riley, D. (1987). Competitive Cost Based Investment Strategies for Industrial Companies. *Manufacturing Issues*, Booz, Allen, Hamilton, New York.

Rucci, A., Kirn, S., Quinn, R. (1998). The Employee Customer – Profit Chain at Sears. *Harvard Business Review*, **76**(1), 82–97.

Shank, J. (1989). Strategic Cost Management: New Wine, or Just New Bottles? *Journal of Management Accounting Research*, **1**, 47–65.

Shank, J. and Govindarajan, V. (1993). *Strategic Cost Management: The New Tool for Competitive Advantage*, New York: The Free Press.

Wilson, R. (1997). *Strategic Cost Management*, Dartmouth Publishing Company.

11

Strategic investment decisions

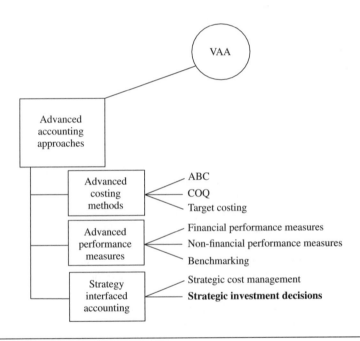

Chapter objectives

- Present the argument that is commonly used to condemn management accounting's approach toward the evaluation of strategic investment decisions.
- Discuss some of the literature that critiques this argument.
- Identify and discuss alternatives to the traditional evaluation approaches of strategic investments.

Strategic investment decision making involves the process of identifying, evaluating, and selecting among projects that are likely to have a significant impact on the organization's competitive advantage. More specifically, the impact will influence what the organization does (i.e. the set of product and service attributes that defines its offerings), where it does it (i.e. the structural characteristics that determine the scope and geographical dispersion of its operations), and/or how it does it (i.e. the set of operating processes and work practices it uses).

One of the more common strategic investment decisions faced by today's organizations is whether to and what types of advanced manufacturing technologies (AMT) to invest in.[1] AMT decisions often have wide-ranging effects and can simultaneously influence all three of the organizational processes noted above. For instance, AMT, due to its built-in flexibility, can enable an expansion of the organization's current product and service offerings. Additionally, AMT places a premium on worker knowledge. Accordingly, instead of siting operations in low-wage areas – that are commonly low skill as well – the organization will want to locate its operations in areas that are characterized by high educational attainment. And finally, AMT not only produces a further amount of automation, but it is also commonly accompanied by changes in workforce practices – such as greater worker involvement and commitment.

A classic case of cost-benefit analysis?

The benefits from adopting AMT are myriad. They include reduced labour costs (15–25 per cent), reduced inventories (20–50 per cent), reduced set-up times (20–60 per cent), reduced scrap and rework (15–75 per cent), and higher levels of machine utilization (10–20 per cent). Table 11.1 provides a listing of the AMT benefits and the factors that serve to make these benefits possible.

Individual organizations' experiences with AMT are quite striking. Yamazaki Machinery Company in Japan, for instance, reduced its number of machines from 68 to 18, its employees from 215 to 12, its required production floor space from 103,000 to 30,000 square feet, and its average processing time from 35 to 1.5 days after it introduced AMT. Meanwhile, one of General Electric's US plants reduced its throughput times from 16 days to 16 hours with its introduction of an AMT system.

Of course, these benefits do not come without a cost. AMT investments can be very expensive, ranging from several thousand dollars for a computer aided design (CAD) system to several billion dollars for a reengineered plant facility such as the one GM adopted for its Saturn automobile plant.

---

[1] AMT involves the use of electronically programmed machines, which are often linked in a network and controlled by a host computer. The goal of AMT is to enhance both quality and flexibility. The successful implementation of AMT can serve to bridge the divide between marketing, which wants to offer unlimited product diversity, and production, which wants to minimize diversity in order to maximize production efficiency.

Table 11.1 AMT benefits and factors that serve to make these benefits possible

AMT benefits	Facilitating factors
Reduced labour costs	A host computer centrally performs a set of tasks that was hitherto locally performed (including both direct labour such as machine operation and indirect labour such as scheduling work, supervising departments, etc.)
Reduced inventories	AMT reduces the number of operating processes needed and quickens throughput times
Reduced set-up times	Built-in flexibility is an inherent, defining trait of AMT
Reduced scrap and rework	AMT offers improved quality
Higher levels of machine utilization	Under AMT the host computer is able to maintain an around-the-clock vigilance over the organization's entire network of producing machines

In addition to the direct or out-of-pocket costs, there are also indirect or opportunity costs associated with AMT investment decisions. These opportunity costs arise from both making as well as not making investments in AMT. The former costs occur because money and people resources are committed and now cannot be used for other purposes. The latter costs (may) occur because the organization has missed an opportunity to exploit the potential gains that today's technological AMT achievement currently make possible or may make possible in the future. For example, organizations that made investments in computer numerically controlled (CNC) machines in the 1970s were able to quickly shift gears and exploit the technological breakthroughs that microprocessor-based technology made possible when it appeared in the 1980s. Meanwhile, firms that had failed to adopt the CNC technology faced steep learning curves and found themselves significantly behind the rest of the pack.

The task involved in making AMT investments, or any strategic investment for that matter, can be extremely challenging. On the one hand, there is the possibility of achieving substantial benefits from making these investments. On the other hand, there are extremely high price tags associated with making the investments or equally high or even higher costs associated with not making the investments. Accordingly, all the elements of a classic cost-benefit analysis are present.

As a result of the importance of getting the investment decision right, one would expect the evaluation and selection of potential projects to be aided by a well-defined set of investment appraisal criteria. Surprisingly this is not the case. As John Shank points out, the four steps involved in making strategic investments (i.e. identifying spending proposals, quantitative analysis of the incremental cash flows, the assessment of qualitative issues that cannot be fitted into the cash flow analysis, and the making of a yes or no decision) are poorly covered in textbooks and receive only marginally better coverage in the journals. As Shank (1996) says:

> Step one receives virtually no attention in the formal literature – proposals just appear, somehow. Step two gets nearly all the attention. Step three is a stepchild, always made to feel guilty because it can't fit into step two. Step four is assumed to flow logically out of step two. There is due consideration for the 'soft' issues in step three, but decisions, as described in textbooks, derive largely from the quantitative analysis.

Perhaps the poor coverage devoted to the process of strategic investment decisions is part of the reason why managers (especially Anglo–American managers) make investment decisions that are described by critics as lacking strategic sequence or cohesion. For instance, Hayes and Abernathy (in a *Harvard Business Review* article entitled 'Managing Our Way to Economic Decline') and Hayes and Garvin (in a *Harvard Business Review* article entitled 'Managing as if Tomorrow Mattered') chastise companies for increasingly relying upon quantitative analytical techniques that provide maximal attention to cash flows and minimal recognition to the strategic implications that such decisions can produce. As Hayes and Garvin so aptly phrase it, 'Investment decisions that discount the future may result in high present values, but bleak tomorrows.'

In addition to the academics' criticisms, practitioners from other countries, most notably Germany and Japan, have also derided their Anglo–American counterparts' strategic investment practices. One German chief executive, for instance, described American managers as mere financial engineers, who had lost any feel or intuition for the products they sell and markets they serve. Meanwhile, a Japanese senior manager criticized Anglo–American managers for failing to integrate technology appraisal with strategic formulation and control. According to this Japanese manager, 'Technology is too important to be excluded from corporate strategy' (Carr and Tomkins, 1996).

Before plunging headlong into a discussion about the merits of the alternative methods that have been offered as improved approaches to the appraisal of strategic investments, it is important to know what exactly it is about the present financial approaches that are found to be so objectionable. Without this knowledge, we are unlikely to appreciate how, if at all, the newly proposed methods represent an improvement to the identification and selection of strategic investments.

The shortcomings of traditional, financially focused approaches to strategic investment decisions

This section of the chapter discusses the many shortcomings that are commonly associated with the use of financially focused strategic investment appraisal techniques. Financially focused techniques include the payback method, accounting rate of return (ARR), return on investment (ROI), residual income (RI), and discounted cash flow (DCF). After discussing these weaknesses, we will sift through some of the recent research that examines managers' perceptions about the impact these supposedly flawed techniques have on strategic investment practices.

Critics of financially focused strategic investment techniques have condemned these techniques on a variety of grounds. The list of charges include the perspective taken, the benefits included/excluded, the time horizon used, the use of inflation adjustments, the calculation of terminal project values, and the computation of discount rates. Each of these issues will be discussed in turn.

The first problem associated with the use of financial techniques is the narrow perspective they take. Investment proposals are almost exclusively examined from the perspective of the investing department. As such, they often fail to recognize the reductions in indirect labour and inventories that materialize outside of the investing department. A good example is the introduction of computer-aided design/computer-aided manufacture (CAD/CAM) systems. A CAD/CAM proposal is typically initiated by the design department. Such an investment will benefit not only the design department's productivity, but manufacturing's as well. Yet often these cross-functional and cross-departmental benefits go unrecognized.

A second problem with the use of financial techniques is their inability to account for the non-financial benefits that frequently characterize strategic investments. In particular, such issues as increased manufacturing flexibility or being more efficient at providing information are seen as esoteric and are unable to be fitted into the financial calculus of traditional appraisal models. Unfortunately, such a disregard for the less easy to quantify characteristics of strategic investments can jeopardize an organization's survival, especially when its competitive advantage is based on such order-winning criteria as production flexibility or customer response and delivery speed.

A third problem with financial techniques is their short-term focus. Many strategic investments take many months, if not years, to become fully operational. A flexible manufacturing system (FMS), for example, requires that a number of interactive interfaces be aligned with one another before full performance of the system is achieved.

Financial appraisal methods uniformly display an impatient regard for long lead-times and snuff out such projects in their infancy. The payback method does this in a very explicit manner by requiring very short payback periods, typically 2–3 years. Meanwhile, ARR, ROI, and RI prematurely kill investment ideas in a more subtle fashion. Managers, who are evaluated under one of these latter three techniques, are unlikely to invest in projects that require long lead-times. Today's managers, who are never sure they will be around long enough to reap the benefits of long-term investments, would rather trade-off the long term to ensure their short-term survival.

DCF methods may also lead to a short-term decision horizon. DCF, in a similar way to the other financial methods, is generally unable to account for the added flexibility certain investments may provide. Take, for instance, the decision to replace dedicated manufacturing machines with an FMS. While an FMS offers the firm the possibility to change its production to match changes in the marketplace, and may therefore prove to be a cheaper system in the long run, DCF techniques have difficulty factoring in such a possibility. DCF further propounds a short-term focus by virtue of the capital rationing rules it promotes. For instance, the ranking of factory automation projects using projects' IRRs or profitability indices can result in piece-meal, standalone islands of non-integrated automation.

A fourth problem with financial techniques is the assumptions that underlie the status quo alternative against which strategic investments are commonly compared. It is commonly assumed that the current competitive position will remain unaltered if the strategic investment is not undertaken. But this assumption is not necessarily true. It is only true if the cost, quality, flexibility, and innovation features offered by one's competitors also remain unchanged. An unwillingness to invest today may jeopardize the organization's survival or simply postpone the need to make the investment. Peter Drucker (1995) very aptly points this out when he says, 'Cost accounting gives you information on the cost of doing, but not on the cost of not doing – which is increasingly the bigger cost.'

The assumption, therefore, that the baseline for comparison is a line that forms a right angle to the performance axis is often mistaken. Instead, it is generally better to view the baseline for comparison as a downward sloping line, going from upper left to lower right.

A fifth problem with financial techniques is the conservative terminal value that is commonly assigned to projects. Often when a substantial amount of the investment pertains to system design, database development, and software the terminal value assigned is zero. This seems highly capricious and foolhardy, especially since there is growing evidence suggesting that such investments often provide invaluable organizational learning, which can be subsequently applied to other projects.

A sixth problem with financial techniques is the often inconsistent treatment that is given to inflation. On the one hand, an allowance is made for the financing and opportunity costs associated with inflation. This allowance is implicit in the quick payback periods required for the payback method, somewhat explicit in the required rates of return for ARR, ROI, and RI; and very explicit in the discount factors that must be specified under DCF. On the other hand, seldom are allowances made for the increased cash flows that are likely to accrue (primarily through higher sales prices). Such an inconsistent approach to the treatment of inflation underestimates a project's likely return.

The seventh problem with financial techniques is the common use of excessive discount rates. For example, the findings from a 1990 study performed for the National Association of Accountants (USA) found that 36 per cent of manufacturers used discount factors of between 13 and 19 per cent, with over 30 per cent using a rate in excess of 19 per cent. These findings in the USA do not appear to be unusual. A study of UK practices conducted in 1987 found that the typical discount factor was between 13 and 15 per cent.

The use of discount rates in the mid-teens and above seems excessive when compared to the prevailing risk-free rate of return, i.e. the yields offered on AAA-rated government securities. The average risk-free rate over the past 10 years has been approximately 8 per cent. Meanwhile, the long-run average risk premium over government securities has been about 8 per cent. The combination of these two rates implies that a 100 per cent equity-financed company's required rate of return is 16 per cent. However, once debt is calculated into the cost of a firm's capital, the required rate of return decreases substantially. For example, if we assume that the firm's debt-equity ratio is 50 per cent, its cost of debt is 10 per cent, and its marginal tax rate is 35 per cent, then its after-tax cost of capital is 11.25 per cent ([0.5×16 per cent] + [$0.5 \times 0.65 \times 10$ per cent]). Consequently, the use of discount rates that are significantly above 11.25 per cent, at least for companies with similar debt and equity proportions as were assumed in the example, overestimates the cost of capital and discourages investment in projects with slow incoming cash flows. As a general rule of thumb, Robert Kaplan believes that the discount rate should be between 8–10 per cent.

In addition to the common practice of using too high a discount rate, firms are also guilty of not matching the various phases of a potential investment with the risk inherent in each phase. Instead, a single, unchanging discount factor is used. This is inappropriate. The project risk is highest during the pre-implementation and start-up phases, and decreases substantially once the project has been successfully commissioned and put on line.

In summary, there are a number of apparent flaws with financially focused strategic investment appraisal techniques. Yet, in spite of these flaws, financial techniques are the most touted appraisal method. The consequence of over-relying on financial techniques can lead to not only misguided investment decisions but also a perversion of senior managers' business imperative. Instead of investing in the company's long-term core business, senior managers become side-tracked and start investing for short-term cash flows. Simmonds (1981) points out this danger when he says:

> The emphasis . . . accounting and finance have placed on return on investment over the years has subtly transmuted into a widely and deeply held belief that return comes from the investment themselves. . . . The truth is much different. Sustained profit comes from the competitive market position. New production investment to expand sales must imply a change in competitive position, and it is this change that should be the focus of the investment review. Without it, the calculations must be nonsense.

Henry Mintzberg echoes Simmonds' comments. In a 1996 *Harvard Business Review* article, he admonishes firms for loosing touch with their businesses. He offers an example of just how disconnected some managers have become from their operating activities when he recounts how his book editor once quoted her boss as saying, 'We're in the business of filling the O.I. (operating income) bucket.' Mintzberg deplores this soulless practice of management, whereby 'sensible business behaviour has been distorted as people have been pushed to meet the numbers instead of the customers.'

Compounding the problems just mentioned (i.e. the many technical shortcomings and the common mistake of viewing strategic investments as one-off, unrelated events), there is a further problem associated with the use of financial appraisal techniques. In particular, managers who submit investment proposals frequently engage in fanciful calculations. Aware of the high hurdle rates that senior managers use to evaluate and select among strategic investment proposals, managers who submit investment proposals stretch assumptions to their utmost limit and sometimes beyond. For example, an MIT research project report entitled 'Management in the 1990s' provides a very telling quote about the extent of cheating that occurs.

> Everybody does cost/benefit analysis on projects. Most of them are fictional. The saddest part is that it is not just the benefits that are fictional, but the costs as well. They don't begin to assess what the real costs of the system are. You do cost/benefit analysis to get money. . . . [In essence] we cost-justify new systems on the basis of lies.

The general tenor of the MIT report is supported by the results of a UK field study by Carr and Tomkins that was published in 1996. According to these researchers, managers frequently base their financial calculations on 'very questionable assumptions and cheating sometimes occurs.' Carr and Tomkins reveal the nature of the cheating through the comments of one of the managers they interviewed:

> When we phrase the capital appropriation we sometimes have to phrase it in such a way that it looks as though it is a payback within two-and-a-half years, although realistically we know it will be nearer four. We work very much on the principle of 'let's see what we think they want to hear now,' and if we have to argue that in two-and-a-half years' time, then at least we will have the goods.
>
> That might make it difficult for the next time we want a proper Capital Appropriation but by that time, cynically, we would say to ourselves that maybe there will be a new guy in charge over there anyway.

At this point, the reader might well be shocked and understandably demoralized by the extensive failings of financially focused appraisal techniques. But before unleashing a chorus of condemnation on the financial techniques and the accountants who oversee them, it is worth noting some recent research findings that suggest a more sympathetic view be taken. Jones et al.'s (1993) research into UK investment practices, for instance, indicates that organizational managers (and especially management accountants) do not possess as rigid a view of the investment process as textbooks and academic critiques routinely portray. Instead managers 'have a more complex, more subtle and broader view of decision making . . . [and] there is a history of field research in the UK which goes back at least 30 years which is generally supportive of this view.'

Bill Lee's (1996) study of 21 UK companies echoes the conclusions of Jones. According to Lee, 'in all [21 company] instances, the companies were able to adapt their investment appraisals to reflect their proposed use of FMS.' Meanwhile, a US study by George Haley and Stephen Goldberg found that although reliance on the payback method stifled strategic investments, reliance on NPV did not. One must, however, be careful when interpreting Haley and Goldberg's NPV finding. In particular, because the firms they surveyed relied almost exclusively upon financial appraisal techniques, we can only conclude that the use of NPV is less likely to stifle strategic investment decisions than the use of other financial techniques (e.g. payback). We have no idea how NPV compares against the use of, for instance, Shank's strategic cost management framework.

We have reached the end of this critique of financially focused investment appraisal techniques. It is now time to turn our attention to a discussion of alternative techniques.

Alternative approaches to evaluating and selecting strategic investment proposals

There are two basic approaches that can be taken to developing alternative strategic investment appraisal techniques.[2] The first approach involves modifying the traditional, financial analysis framework. In particular, its various technical shortcomings (e.g. inflation inconsistencies, the use of inappropriately high discount factors, etc.) are corrected and its narrow focus is expanded to include commonly neglected benefits (e.g. improvements in flexibility, improvements in information quality and timeliness, etc.).

The second approach involves reliance on analytical frameworks that represent significant departures from the traditional approach. Among these different approaches are strategic cost management, the multiattribute decision model, value analysis, the analytical hierarchy method, the R&D method, and the uncertainty method. Each of these two broad approaches is discussed in more detail below.

The expanded financial analysis framework

Robert Kaplan has been the main champion of modifying the traditional financial framework. He feels that all of the criticized aspects of financial techniques are in truth a function of the user and not the technique itself. For example, the use of too high a discount rate is surely the mistake of the NPV user. Likewise the inconsistent treatment of inflation, the conservative valuation of terminal values, the assumption about the status quo alternative, and the narrow organizational unit focus are again all mistakes of the user. Even the difficulty of including non-financial

---

[2] While some authors, particularly Shank and Govindarajan, identify a third approach, which they call the minimalist approach, it is highly unlikely that such an approach actually exists. Furthermore, it is an insult to managers around the world. Suggesting, for instance, that General Motors, Westinghouse, General Electric, and RCA played 'technology roulette,' as they term it, is unfounded speculation. While it is true that these firms – based on the case instances uncovered by Shank and Govindarajan – may have engaged in incomplete strategic and/or financial analysis, it is hardly the same as saying that the behaviour of these managers was similar to a Monte Carlo game where you 'place your bet, spin the wheel, and hope.'

benefits is seen as a lack of financial analyst imagination rather than an inherent shortcoming of financially focused evaluation approaches.

In addition to Kaplan, there are other scholars with equally strong beliefs in the utility and robustness of financial appraisal techniques. Beyond simply exhorting practitioners to adopt a broader and deeper approach to the use of financial techniques, some writers have offered specific guidance on how this might be best accomplished. The work of Ramasesh is singled out and discussed here not for its novelty (for there are several other writers who have made reference to or alluded to similar processes), but for the thoroughness of its development – including the formalization of its procedures.

Ramasesh proposes a modified NPV approach that consists of four sequential stages. Each stage involves a deeper and more exacting refinement of the benefits associated with NPV. As such, not all investment proposals require that all four stages be undertaken. A subsequent stage of analysis is only needed in the event that the prior stage's NPV is negative.

In stage 1 of Ramasesh's model, the analyst corrects the NPV calculations for such commonly made mistakes as too high a discount factor, inconsistent treatment of inflation, etc. In stage 2, the analyst ascribes values to benefits that are typically deemed too uncertain, non-quantifiable, or 'soft' to allow their measurement. Such project attributes as enhanced flexibility or better information become the primary focus of analysis in this second stage. To aid in the measurement of these softer and more uncertain benefits, Ramasesh proposes the use of mathematical programming models. In stage 3, the analyst quantifies the learning curve benefits that will accrue when a future, related project is implemented. Finally, in stage 4, a 'residual strategic benefits qualitative analysis' is undertaken. In other words, all the factors that somehow defied measurement in the previous three steps are now qualitatively considered to determine whether their benefits can overcome what has hitherto been a negative NPV.

New-age evaluation methods

This section of the chapter describes a number of analytical techniques that are best viewed as a breed apart from the traditional financial model or its expanded-model cousin. Six different models will be discussed, including strategic cost management, the multiattribute decision model, value analysis, the analytical hierarchy method, the R&D method, and the uncertainty method.

Strategic cost management

Strategic cost management (SCM) represents John Shank's attempt to substantially broaden the traditional financial analysis with an explicit consideration of strategic issues. SCM consists of three components: value chain analysis; competitive advantage analysis; and cost driver analysis. Shank has shown, using various case studies to illustrate his points, how the use of SCM radically reorients the evaluation process and generally produces a different set of investment 'go versus don't 'go' signals than a traditional financial analysis does. Since SCM was discussed at length in the Chapter 10, no further mention of it is made here.

Multiattribute decision model

The multiattribute decision model (MADM) attempts to develop a general measure of utility, where utility is defined as the satisfaction of an individual's or set of individuals' preferences. A distinct advantage of this model is that it is able to assess an investment's impact even when some of the project's factors cannot be estimated in dollars.

To construct a MADM, a list of factors that are deemed important in judging an investment is made. For example, financial measures such as payback and NPV may appear, as well as such non-financial measures as reduced complexity, improved information, and enhanced company image. A weighting, which represents a factor's importance to the company, is then assigned to each factor and scaled so that the combined weightings equal 100.

Ratings are next assigned to the factors based on beliefs about the effect that the alternative courses of action (including the status quo) will have on each factor. These ratings are generally rather coarse and typically involve the assignment of a 0 if the expected outcome is decreased performance, a 1 if the expected outcome is unaffected performance, and a 2 if the expected outcome is improved performance. For example, a decision to stay with existing technology would receive a 1 for enhanced company image and a 1 for market share, while an upgraded IT system to facilitate customer service would likely receive a 2 for company image and (assuming its NPV was negative) a 0 for NPV. Note that a decision to remain with the status quo will not always result in an unchanged condition. Remember that this is only true if the actions of competitors remain unchanged.

When determining the rating to assign to financial factors, it may be best to work with bands. For instance, instead of assigning a 1 to NPVs that are exactly zero, it may be more appropriate to assign a 1 to NPVs between –$100,000 and +$100,000. This approach accommodates both the uncertainties of the estimates and assumptions that underlie financial calculations, as well as the growing trend for using sensitivity analysis with its inherent range of point values.

A further, though optional, step in using MADM is the determination of probabilities to associate with each of the assigned ratings. For example, if an upgraded IT system is believed to have an 80 per cent chance of enhancing customer service, then a likelihood factor of 0.8 will be assigned to its enhanced company image factor.

The final step of MADM involves the calculation of a total score for each course of action. This is performed by multiplying each factor weight by the cross product of its rating and likelihood to calculate the individual factor scores and then summing these factor scores to arrive at an aggregate score for each alternative. Table 11.2 includes an example that illustrates the use of MADM. For those readers who are interested in further details on how to apply MADM, they should refer to

Table 11.2 Strategic investment decision making using MADM

Factors	Existing strategic investment				Contemplated strategic investment			
	Factor weights	Ratings	Confidence	Scores	Factor weights	Ratings	Confidence	Scores
Quantitative								
Financial:*								
EVA	15 ×	2 ×	0.7 =	21	15 ×	0 ×	0.6 =	0
ROA	15 ×	2 ×	0.9 =	27	15 ×	0 ×	0.8 =	0
Quantitative								
Non-financial:*								
Market share	20 ×	1 ×	0.8 =	16	20 ×	2 ×	0.8 =	32
Product quality	15 ×	1 ×	1.0 =	15	15 ×	2 ×	0.9 =	27
Qualitative:*								
Company image	15 ×	1 ×	0.8 =	12	15 ×	2 ×	0.9 =	27
Improved information	10 ×	1 ×	1.0 =	10	10 ×	2 ×	0.8 =	16
Personnel development	10 ×	1 ×	1.0 =	10	10 ×	2 ×	0.9 =	18
Totals	100			111	100			120

* The factors listed in this example are chosen for illustrative purposes only. In actual practice, the factors will need to be a reflection of the specific organizational context.

Berliner and Brimson's book, which is listed among the references at the end of the chapter.

Value analysis and the analytical hierarchy method

There are two additional analytical techniques, called value analysis and the analytical hierarchy process that are very similar to MADM. In fact, it makes most sense to view these two further techniques as subsets of MADM. As will be described momentarily, value analysis and the analytical hierarchy process differ from MADM only in terms of the information source that is relied upon.

The value analysis method typically relies on a Delphi technique. The Delphi technique begins with the selection of a group of 'experts'. For example, if the proposed investment involved the forecast of benefits associated with the introduction of a new organization-wide IT system, then a representative group of managers from throughout the organization would be appropriate.

Each member of the Delphi group is asked to list the benefits that would accrue from the adoption of the proposed IT system. Although each member is separately asked his/her view, responses from the group as a whole – whereby no one individual's response can be detected – are fed back to all group members. This feedback mechanism helps each group member to ground his/her thinking in terms of the whole group. Additionally, the nature of the feedback mechanism ensures confidentiality and helps prevent groupthink, or the process whereby certain individuals – usually due to their rank or charisma – constrain and substantially influence the final group decision.

After a few iterations of collecting individual group member's perceptions and feeding back group level information (generally three rounds are sufficient), a group consensus is reached. This consensus then becomes the list of criteria for judging the proposed investment. If desired, the Delphi technique can also be used to determine the factor weightings, ratings, and the probabilities of performance achievement.

The analytical hierarchy process, which is also a subset of MADM, surveys a wide group of managers about their views of the factor weightings to use. Unlike the Delphi technique, which seeks resolution by iterative polling until consensus is reached, the analytical hierarchy process asks selected individuals to make pairwise comparisons about the factors' utilities. The comparisons are then analysed by a mathematical model to establish the relative weightings.

One of the advantages of using the analytical hierarchy process is its ability to check for consistent factor weightings. For example, if improved delivery times is judged to be twice as important as increased flexibility, which in turn is judged to be four times as important as enhanced company image, then improved delivery times should be judged eight times as important as enhanced company image. Should inconsistencies be detected in a person's responses, a follow-up interview should be conducted with the individual. (For more details on how to apply the analytical hierarchy process, refer to Saaty's book, which is listed among the references at the end of the chapter.)

Research and development method

The research and development (R&D) method views proposed investments less as capital investment candidates and more as applied research and development projects, which require further experimentation and testing before a decision can be made about their practicality and usefulness. Hence, this is where the name R&D method derives.

The R&D method is composed of two separate stages. The first stage seeks to study, simulate, and estimate the proposed investment's benefits. Based on an evaluation of these benefits, a decision is made to either continue proceeding with an assessment of the proposed investment or stop altogether.

The second stage of the R&D method seeks to determine if the project's total costs can be maintained below the level of expected benefits. Such a determination is often made by implementing the project in a particular segment or operation of the organization. If the results prove positive, the next step is to use the acquired cost/benefit data to assess the likely impact of fully adopting the proposed investment.

There are two distinct advantages gained from using the R&D method. First, the preliminary working model offers real data on the costs and benefits of adopting the new investment. Second, the working model provides senior managers, who might otherwise be sceptical of the project's benefits, with an opportunity to see and experience what they are buying.

Uncertainty method

The uncertainty method is particularly well suited to situations with highly uncertain probabilities. While it requires that the individual or group responsible for the investment decision recognize the likely monetary outcomes associated with the investment's success or failure, it does not require an estimate of the probability of success or failure.

There are two main steps to the application of the uncertainty method. First, the likely monetary effects from both the correct and incorrect decision to adopt the strategic investment must be determined. Second, the likely monetary effects from both the correct and incorrect decision not to adopt the investment must be determined. The inclusion of this latter pair of outcomes ensures that there is an explicit recognition of the difference between correctly deciding to do nothing and the mistake of failing to act.

The second step of the uncertainty model involves the selection of a mixture of optimism-speculation and pessimism-conservatism percentages for the correct and incorrect outcomes, respectively. These percentages are then multiplied by the monetary effects that were determined under Step 1. The decision, either to invest or not invest, is based on which option provides the highest positive value or the lowest negative value. Table 11.3 illustrates the uncertainty method. When viewing this table, assume the following facts:

Table 11.3 Strategic investment decision making using the uncertainty method

Should we adopt the new strategic investment?	What happens if our decision is:		20% of the best estimate	80% of the worst estimate	Expected value
	Correct	**Not correct**			
Yes	$6 million profit	$3 million loss	$1.2	–$2.4	–$1.2
No	No profit impact	$2 million opportunity cost	$0	–$1.6	–$1.6

1 the cost of the investment is $3 million;
2 an expected profit of $6 million is associated with correctly anticipating the need for the investment;
3 an opportunity cost of $2 million is associated with not making the investment when in hindsight the company should have done so.

Summary

The importance of making sound strategic investment decisions cannot be underestimated. Correct decisions serve to enhance an organization's competitive advantage, while poor decisions erode it.

This chapter began with a critique of the traditional, financially focused approaches to strategic investment decision making. Two facts are apparent from this critique. First, there are many critics of the traditional approach. Second, in spite of these critics and the criticisms they have raised, a number of people remain committed to the utility of using financially focused evaluation criteria.

Following the critique, the chapter proceeded to discuss some of the newer methods for evaluating strategic investment decisions. Included in this discussion were the expanded financial analysis framework, strategic cost management, the multiattribute decision model, value analysis, the analytical hierarchy method, the R&D method, and the uncertainty method.

References

Berliner, C. and Brimson, J. (1988). *Cost Management for Today's Advanced Manufacturing*, Boston , MA: Harvard Business School Press.

Bruggeman, W. and Slagmulder, R. (1995). The Impact of Technological Change on Management Accounting. *Management Accounting Research*, **6**, 241–252.

Carr, C. and Tomkins, C. (1996). Strategic Investment Decisions: The Importance of SCM (A Comparative Analysis of 51 Case Studies in UK, US, and German Companies. *Management Accounting Research*, **7**, 199–217.

Carr, C. and Tomkins, C. (1998). Context, Culture and the Role of the Finance Function in Strategic Decisions: A Comparative Analysis of Britain, Germany, the USA and Japan. *Management Accounting Research*, **9**(2), 213–239.

Drucker, P. (1995). The Information Executives Truly Need. *Harvard Business Review*, **73**(1), 54–62.

Hayes, R. and Abernathy, J. (1980). Managing Our Way to Economic Decline. *Harvard Business Review*, July/August, 66–77.

Hayes, R. and Garvin, D. (1982). Managing as if Tomorrow Mattered. *Harvard Business Review*, May/June, 71–79.

Jones, T., Currie, W. and Dugdale, D. (1993). Accounting and Technology in Britain and Japan: Learning from Field Research. *Management Accounting Research*, **4**(2), 109–137.

Lee, B. (1996). The Justification and Monitoring of Advanced Manufacturing Technology: An Empirical Study of 21 Installations of Flexible Manufacturing Systems. *Management Accounting Research*, **7**, 95–118.

Luehrman, T. (1998). Strategy as a Portfolio of Options. *Harvard Business Review*, **76**(5), 89–101.

Mintzberg, H. (1996). Ten Ideas Designed to Rile Everyone Who Cares About Management. *Harvard Business Review*, **74**(4), 61–67.

Saaty, T. (1982). *Decision Making for Leaders*, Lifetime Learning Publications.

Shank, J. (1996). Analysing Technology Investments – From NPV to Strategic Cost Management. *Management Accounting Research*, **7**, 185–197.

Sharpe, P. and Kellin, T. (1998). How Smithkline Beecham Makes Better Resource-Allocation Decisions. *Harvard Business Review*, **76**(2), 45–57.

Simmonds, K. (1981). The Fundamentals of Strategic Management Accounting, Paper presented to the Institute of Cost and Management Accountants, Technical Symposium, Pembroke College, Oxford, 6–8 January.

Slagmulder, R. (1997). Using Management Control Systems to Achieve Alignment Between Strategic Investment Decisions and Strategy. *Management Accounting Research,* **8**, 103–139.

Tomkins, C. (1991). *Corporate Resource Allocation: Financial, Strategic & Organizational Perspectives*, Oxford: Basil Blackwell.

Van Cauwenbergh, A., Durnick, E., Martens, R., Laveren, E. and Bogaert, I. (1996). On the Role and Function of Formal Analysis in Strategic Investment Decision Processes: Results from an Empirical Study in Belgium. *Management Accounting Research*, **7**, 169–184.

12

Strategic dimensions to transfer pricing and outsourcing

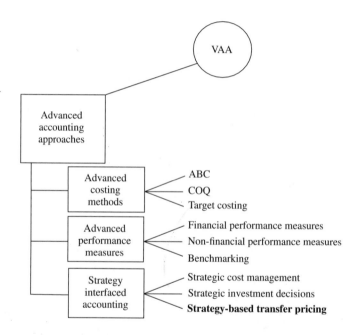

Chapter objectives

- Show how transfer pricing can promote or erode competitive advantage.
- Identify the strategic dimensions to transfer pricing.
- Present a model that illustrates how transfer pricing can be matched with organizational strategy.
- Discuss the strategic transfer pricing model's implications for practising managers.

Transfer pricing is often seen as little more than a subset of the cost allocation decision. In particular, the organization must somehow allocate the cost of work performed by sister divisions or departments. This work can be in the form of product costs or service costs. An example of the former is the assignment of upstream manufacturing costs to downstream production centres or the marketing division. Meanwhile, an example of using transfer pricing for services is the assignment of an organization's computer services department costs to the various departments that use this service.

To view transfer pricing as merely an operational costing problem, as is almost always the case, overlooks the significant effect that transfer pricing can have on promoting or eroding an organization's competitive advantage. This chapter is devoted to an investigation of the link between transfer pricing and organizational strategy. More specifically, it intends to show how to choose a transfer pricing method that will harmonize with the organization's chosen strategic orientation and thereby enhance its competitive advantage. Although this chapter focuses on the setting of transfer prices by manufacturers, the advice given is equally applicable to service organizations.

The importance of transfer pricing

The determination and setting of transfer prices can have significant strategic implications. Unfortunately, many organizations fail to understand this fact. They marginalize the importance of transfer pricing and often see the process in narrowly prescribed cost/benefit terms. This neglect can undermine the organization's strategy and erode its competitiveness.

As an example of the strategic implications of transfer pricing, James Welch and Ranganath Nayak (1992) recount the misguided sourcing decisions of US radio manufacturers during the 1940s. Intent on cutting costs, these manufacturers sought to replace the radio components made in-house with less costly Japanese components. Although successful in the short run, this decision triggered the end of the US dominance of the transistor radio market. The Japanese suppliers, after literally being handed the transistor technology, eventually integrated forward and usurped the US manufacturers' markets both abroad and at home. The lesson to be learned, say Welch and Nayak, is that a market-based transfer pricing system is an especially foolhardy approach when a firm's competitive advantage hinges on its process technology.

In spite of Welch and Nayak's calls for caution when determining transfer prices, market-based prices are typically perceived as the quintessential transfer price. Such prominent scholars as David Solomons, Robert Anthony, Robert Kaplan, and Anthony Atkinson strongly advocate the use of market-based prices, and unanimously agree that they should be used whenever a competitive market exists. Their advice appears to have been accepted by the business world. The results of a survey conducted by Roger Tang (1992) shows that market-based transfer prices are a very popular method. In particular, a survey of the US *Fortune* 500 industrials indicated that they use market-based pricing for 37 per cent of their domestic product transfers and 46 per cent of their international product transfers. But is it wise to recommend and so overwhelmingly use market-based transfer pricing, especially in light of the strategic concerns raised by Welch and Nayak?

Strategic dimensions of transfer pricing

The strategic dimensions of transfer pricing have been long overlooked in favour of transfer pricing approaches that promote economic and mathematical programming models. Only more recently has attention been turned to the strategic issues involved in the transfer pricing and sourcing decisions made by companies. In particular, three key strategic dimensions that have emerged in the literature are the transferred good's position along the product life-cycle continuum, the significance of the process technology used to manufacture the product, and the diversification strategy the firm employs for its divisions. Each of these dimensions is discussed in turn below.

Product life-cycle considerations

A product's position along the product life-cycle continuum has important implications for the setting of transfer prices. These implications can occur at two levels. At the first and more practical level, the clarity of a reference price, and therefore the use of market prices, changes as the product passes from its introduction stage through to its growth, maturity, and decline phases. Newly introduced products are associated with markets that are characterized as 'limited', or less able to provide relevant market prices. Meanwhile, established products trade in markets that are defined as 'available', or capable of providing relevant market prices.

Barry Spicer (1988) echoes the above comments when he proposes that the nature of the product (ranging from standardized to idiosyncratic) will influence the type of transfer pricing method adopted. Highly standardized products will be amenable to market-based transfer prices, while idiosyncratic products will require cost-based transfer prices.

The life-cycle stage of a product can influence the setting of transfer prices at a second and more strategic level. In particular, the impact of learning curve effects on a firm's cost to manufacture products should be included in the transfer price. Setting too high a transfer price during the introduction or growth stages of a product's life cycle is likely to promote the early entry of competitors. As a consequence, low transfer prices, which are typically provided from cost-based transfer pricing methods, are encouraged for products and services that are in their early life-cycle stages.

By contrast, competition will be at its peak for products that have attained maturity. Preventing competition through the use of transfer pricing is not a viable option. Instead the firm should ensure that profit margins are being maintained. The use of market-based prices is more likely to accomplish this goal. In particular, it might help identify where cost reductions can be made.

Process technology and competitive advantage

Welch and Nayak find that firms frequently neglect the implications that transfer prices have on sourcing decisions. These authors are especially troubled by situations whereby the organization divulges important process technology to low wage producers, who are presently capable of supplying the product components at a lower cost. Welch and Nayak castigate such sourcing decisions, and note the danger that such approaches have for transforming suppliers or licensees into competitors.

As previously noted, Welsh and Nayak point to the US radio manufacturers' miscalculated surrender of their process technology as a prime example of a penny wise and pound foolish approach. In their opinion, transfer pricing methods that fail to recognize the competitive advantage that superior process technologies can provide, and instead concentrate on short-term cost minimization, can severely undermine the firm's ability to compete.

Diversification strategy

The organization's diversification strategy can also influence the determination of transfer prices. The link, however, is not direct. According to Robert Eccles (1983), organizational strategy helps to determine the organization's structure, which in turn helps to determine the appropriate transfer pricing method to adopt.

Eccles posits four organizational types: collective, competitive, co-operative, and collaborative. These organizational types are distinguished from one another according to their emphasis on independence (or diversification) and interdependence (or integration). Collective firms exhibit low independence and low interdependence. Competitive firms display high independence and low interdependence. Co-operative firms are characterized by low independence and high interdependence. And finally, collaborative firms exhibit both high independence and high interdependence.

Transfer pricing, says Eccles, is an issue for all organizational types except the collective form, whose structure is sufficiently simple to avoid the transfer pricing issue altogether. Eccles believes that co-operatively operating divisions should use cost-based pricing, collaborative divisions should use mandated market-based pricing, and competitive divisions should be provided free rein to formulate their own pricing policies. According to Eccles, competitively operating divisions will generally find market-based pricing most appropriate.

One final consideration to keep in mind when examining the link between strategic diversification and transfer pricing is the advice of Paul Lawrence and Jay Lorsch (1967). According to Lawrence and Lorsch, organizational effectiveness is the result of correctly matching the firm's structure to its environment. Stable or predictable environments suggest the use of centralized structures. When stable conditions prevail, senior managers' experience and knowledge should be the basis for decision making. Employee consultation or delegation is both unnecessary and wasteful. Uncertain or turbulent environments, by contrast, require the use of differentiated or decentralized structures. Being unable to anticipate events, senior managers will need to harness the learning capabilities of their employees. Here the costs of decentralization are more than recompensed by the benefits such a structure offers. However, due to the increased complexity and potential for unco-ordinated (and even conflicting) organizational behaviour, firms that decentralize will find that they need to include some kind of co-ordinating mechanism. The process whereby organizations achieve this co-ordination is called integration.

Tying Lawrence and Lorsch's ideas back to the link that Eccles has made between organizational structure and transfer pricing, we can see that highly complex organizations (i.e. collaborative firms) will require an integrating mechanism. One such mechanism, as pointed out by David Watson and John Baumler (1975) is the use of a negotiated transfer pricing system. Such a transfer pricing system, by virtue of the face-to-face interactions it promotes, offers a valuable dose of integration. Consequently, it would appear that negotiated transfer prices are more in harmony with Eccles' belief about the dangers of 'suppressing or alleviating conflict beyond a certain point' than his suggested solution of market prices.

Selecting transfer prices that support organizational strategy

Three main observations can be drawn from the above discussion. First, transfer prices for newly introduced products should tend toward cost-based transfer prices, while transfer prices for more established products should tend toward market prices. Second, when competitive advantage is primarily a function of the firm's superior process technology, then transfer prices should be used that encourage the sustainability of this competitive advantage. Generally, this will involve using cost-based transfer pricing. Third, different strategic diversifications are supported by different transfer pricing methods. Competitive strategies call for market-based prices, co-operative strategies for cost-based prices, and collaborative strategies for negotiated prices. Combining these three observations leads to the tree diagram shown in Figure 12.1. Definitions for the various transfer pricing methods are provided in Table 12.1.

As noted in Figure 12.1, practical considerations associated with the limited and available market characteristics of new and established products, respectively, mean that transfer prices associated with new products will be either cost-based or the result of negotiation. In other words, with limited markets, there is no readily available market price to reference. Meanwhile, transfer prices for established products have the potential to assume the full range of transfer pricing methods. In reality, however, the feasible set of transfer pricing methods is more limited. For instance, it may not be beneficial to use cost-based transfer prices for products with a well-established market. Such markets are generally characterized by significant competition, and therefore the idea of preventing competition – by using low, cost-

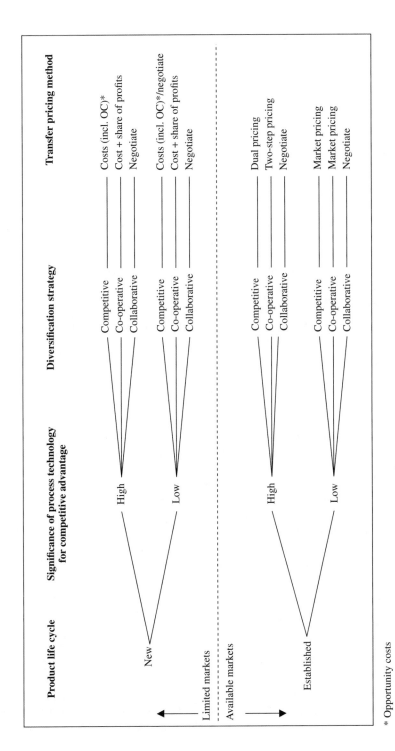

Figure 12.1 A strategic transfer pricing model

* Opportunity costs

Table 12.1 A glossary of transfer pricing terms

Cost basis	The actual or standard cost to produce a good is used as the basis for determining a transfer price.
Dual pricing	The selling division records the internal sale at the current market price, while the buying division records the purchase at either the selling division's actual or standard cost to produce the good.
Market pricing	The internal transfer price equals the price that outside companies would charge for producing an identical product.
Negotiated pricing	The buying and selling division mutually agree on the internal transfer price.
Two-step pricing	The transfer price is the sum of two separate charges. The first is equal to the standard variable cost to produce the good. The second charge is based on the percentage of the selling division's production capacity that is reserved for the buying division's purchasing requirements.

based transfer prices – is not viable. In fact, under such circumstances, the use of cost-based transfer prices is likely to do more harm than good. Using transfer prices based on cost may encourage an attitude of complacency. The selling division, realizing that its costs will automatically be borne by units further downstream, may perceive no advantage to eliminating inefficiencies in its operations. As a consequence, market-based transfer prices are usually better suited to products with well-established markets.

In summary, practical considerations associated with a transferred good's position along its product life cycle strongly influence whether the transfer price will tend toward cost- or market-based. Since a new product lacks a market-determined price, some form of cost-based or negotiated transfer price will represent the only viable choice. While established products are amenable to a full range of transfer pricing methods, strategic considerations may limit the set of appropriate alternatives to market-based transfer prices. It is for this reason that a dotted 'boundary' line in Figure 12.1 runs between the product life-cycle stages termed new and established. Finally, it should be pointed out that firms with multiple product lines will need to apply Figure 12.1's strategic transfer pricing model to each of its product lines. As a consequence, different transfer pricing methods are likely to be associated with different product lines.

Using organizational strategy to determine preferred transfer pricing methods

We will now discuss Figure 12.1 in greater detail, examining each branch of the tree diagram. Branch 1 shows a situation where the product is new, the process technology contributes significantly to the organization's competitive advantage, and the divisions operate in a competitive fashion. Both the newness of the product and the importance of the underlying process technology suggest that a cost-based price be used. By contrast, the organization's choice of a competitive diversification strategy would ordinarily mean that a market-based price would be preferred. Practical considerations, however, do not permit the use of market prices. In particular, there is no readily available market price to reference. It is, however, imperative that the established transfer price ensures that the supplying division does not suffer a disadvantage from making and supplying the product. Accordingly, the transfer price should include all costs involved in making and supplying the product, including any opportunity costs. Opportunity costs are the profits that are forgone by adopting one alternative over another, e.g. supplying a sister division with product versus using the plant capacity for some other purpose.

Branch 2 highlights a situation where the product is new, the process technology contributes significantly to the organization's competitive advantage, and the divisions operate in a co-operative fashion. The newness of the product and the importance of the underlying process technology again point to using a cost-based transfer price. The organization's choice of a co-operative diversification strategy also suggests the use of a cost-based approach. In fact, the co-operating nature of the transacting divisions makes it essential that the transfer price clearly communicates the build-up of costs. It is imperative that the division that ultimately sells the product to an outside customer is aware of the actual costs to manufacture the product. The final division in the chain of co-operating divisions needs to ensure that a fair return is made on the combined total of all the divisions' *actual* costs and not some inflated figure that might be determined using a non-cost-based transfer pricing method. Consequently, the preferred transfer price is cost plus an eventual sharing of the profit that ultimately results from selling the product to an outside customer.

Branch 3 represents a situation where the product is new, the process technology contributes significantly to the organization's competitive advantage, and the divisions operate in a collaborative manner. While the newness of the product and the importance of the underlying process technology point to using a cost-based transfer price, it is essential that collaborative organizations, which are represented by maximum structural complexity, adopt some form of integrating mechanism. A negotiated transfer pricing system can serve this purpose, and accordingly is recommended as the preferred transfer pricing method.

Branch 4 shows a situation where the product is new, the process technology contributes only marginally to the organization's competitive advantage, and the divisions operate in a competitive fashion. While the competitive diversification strategy and the low significance of the process technology for competitive advantage would suggest the use of a market-based transfer price, new products are generally characterized by a desire to protect current market share by adopting cost-based transfer prices. Ultimately, practical considerations will prevail. In particular, the fact that there is no readily available market price to reference will require the use of either a cost-based or negotiated transfer price. The benefits of a negotiated transfer price is the ability for the supplying division to establish a transfer price that potentially allows it to receive a fairer return on its capital. There are, however, additional costs of time and administration associated with using a negotiated transfer pricing system. As a consequence, the divisions may wish to base the transfer price on costs, including any opportunity costs. Remember that due to the organization's competitive diversification strategy it is important that the supplying division is not disadvantaged by virtue of supplying the product to its sister.

Branch 5 depicts a situation where the product is new, the process technology contributes only marginally to the organization's competitive advantage, and the divisions operate in a co-operative fashion. On the one hand, the insignificant nature of the process technology for competitive advantage points to the use of a market-based transfer price. On the other hand, both the desire to protect the new product from early competition and the organization's chosen diversification strategy suggest the use of a cost-based transfer price. Once again, practical considerations related to the lack of a readily available market price will mandate the use of either a negotiated or a cost-based transfer price. Most organizations will find that a cost-based transfer price is best suited to this set of circumstances. It is critical that the division that ultimately sells the product to an outside customer is aware of the actual costs to manufacture the product. Consequently, the preferred transfer price is costs plus an eventual sharing of the profit that ultimately results from selling the product to an outside customer.

Branch 6 highlights a situation where the product is new, the process technology contributes only marginally to the organization's competitive advantage, and the divisions operate in a collaborative fashion. While the insignificant nature of the process technology suggests a market-based transfer pricing method, the newness of the product and the organization's chosen diversification strategy point to the use of a cost-based or negotiated transfer price. Once again, however, the practical considerations related to the newness of the product will prevent the use of market-based prices. The transfer price can either be based on costs or negotiation. Due to the organization's complex structure and the associated need for an integrating mechanism, it is recommended that a negotiated transfer price be used.

Branch 7 reveals a situation where the product is established, the process technology contributes significantly to the organization's competitive advantage, and the divisions operate in a competitive fashion. The established nature of the product and the competitive nature of the transacting divisions suggest the use of a market-based transfer price. Meanwhile, the importance of the process technology for competitive advantage points to the use a cost-based transfer price. Under this situation the use of dual pricing is most appropriate. Dual pricing is a hybrid of cost- and market-based transfer pricing. In particular, the downstream or purchasing division receives the product at cost, while the upstream or selling division is credited with the transfer at the market price. Such an approach encourages the selling division to continue supplying the product – for it is receiving a market price – while at the same time it discourages the buying division from looking elsewhere to source its needs – for it is receiving the product at cost.

Branch 8 portrays a situation where the product is established, the process technology contributes significantly to the organization's competitive advantage, and the divisions operate in a co-operative fashion. The established nature of the product suggests the use of a market-based transfer price. Mitigating against using a market-based price are the co-operative nature of the diversification strategy and the important nature of the process technology for competitive advantage. As a consequence, a two-step transfer pricing method is recommended. Under two-step transfer pricing the buying division commits to purchasing a specific amount of product from the selling division. Accordingly, the transfer price includes the variable costs to manufacture the product, as well as a cost related to the plant capacity of the selling division that has been reserved for the buying division. Two-step pricing promotes planning and equity. Planning is promoted by requiring the buying division to forecast accurately its product requirements, which it should be capable of doing now that the product has attained maturity and customer demand has stabilized. Equity is promoted by shifting the risks of outside customer acceptance of the product to the division that directly interacts with this final customer.

Branch 9 shows a situation where the product is established, the process technology contributes significantly to the organization's competitive advantage, and the divisions operate in a collaborative fashion. The established nature of the product suggests a market-based price, while the importance of the process technology for competitive advantage points to a cost-based price. Once again, however, the collaborative nature of the interacting divisions suggests that a negotiated transfer pricing system, with its ability to promote organizational integration, be used.

Branch 10 depicts a situation where the product is established, the process technology contributes only marginally to the organization's competitive advantage, and the divisions operate in a competitive fashion. In other words, all the conditions point to the use of a market-based transfer price. Market pricing provides a price that is equitable to both parties. Additionally, it helps senior management to assess the relative contributions made by each division and determine which divisions to grow or discontinue.

Branch 11 portrays a situation where the product is established, the process technology contributes only marginally to the organization's competitive advantage, and the divisions operate in a co-operative fashion. The established nature of the product and the insignificant nature of the process technology for competitive advantage both suggest the use of a market-based transfer price. Meanwhile, the organization's co-operative diversification strategy points to a cost-based transfer price. It would appear that in this particular situation the co-operatively based structure is an anachronism. At an earlier point in time, when the product was in a beginning stage of its life cycle and/or the process technology served as a competitive weapon, the structure was appropriate. Now, however, the divisions must prove their individual worth or face closure. Upstream divisions must show that they can produce at a price that is competitive with outside companies. Downstream divisions must show that they can create further customer value, and do so in a cost-beneficial manner. A market-based transfer pricing system is best suited to promoting these objectives.

Branch 12 highlights a situation where the product is established, the process technology contributes only marginally to the organization's competitive advantage, and the divisions operate in a collaborative fashion. Once again, the complex structural nature of the organization serves to override other considerations, and the integrating benefits that come from using a negotiated transfer pricing system will predominate. Accordingly, a negotiated transfer price is recommended here.

Implications of the transfer pricing model for managers

Figure 12.1 is intended to connect a set of strategic considerations with preferred transfer pricing methods. The choice of a tree diagram is meant to facilitate a manager's ability to link his/her company's strategic characteristics with suitable transfer pricing methods. Hopefully the tree diagram will provide managers with insights into a set of key strategic issues that has been largely ignored in the past.

It must be pointed out that Figure 12.1 should be used more as a guide than followed in a mechanistic way. This is especially true for situations in which the product is new and/or the significance of process technology for competitive advantage is high. As an example, transfer prices for new products computed using today's actual costs, versus tomorrow's improved costs, are more likely to encourage the early entrance of competitors. Consequently, senior management may find they need to play a more active role in the setting of transfer prices.

One seemingly objective way in which senior managers could subtly nurture the internal sourcing of products is through the definition of cost-based transfer prices. In particular, senior managers might choose to define cost as variable costs. Fixed costs, such as amortization of intangibles and general overheads, could be excluded.

A minor tinkering with the definition of 'costs', however, will not always be sufficient. On certain occasions senior managers will find they need to be less concerned with demonstrating the accounting defensibility of their transfer pricing choices and more concerned with the strategic consequences of the sourcing decisions. Under these circumstances, senior managers may need to step in and mandate transfer prices.

Of course, senior manager intervention into the transfer pricing decision is likely to have implications for the process of evaluating subordinate managers. As Earl Spiller (1988) has very passionately argued, it is unfair to hold managers responsible for uncontrollable factors, such as mandated costs. Thus, as a superior's intervention into the setting of transfer prices increases and the subordinate's influence decreases, the manager will find that he/she must move away from a bottom-line or budget-constrained mentality. In particular, traditional accounting performance measures that have not been adjusted for controllable items, as is typical with such measures as return on capital employed and other profitability ratios, should be avoided. In their place, senior managers may wish to use specially tailored non-financial measures that can be developed from Robert Kaplan and David Norton's balanced scorecard.

Tax implications, at least for multinationals, represent another important consideration that senior management will need to keep in mind when applying the transfer pricing methods proposed in Figure 12.1. Strategically determined transfer prices, as suggested by the model, may run counter to the firm's wish to minimize taxes (i.e. shift profits to low tax countries) and/or the taxing authorities prescriptive rules on transfer price determination (e.g. IRS Code Section 482). While there is nothing to prevent a firm from using different transfer pricing methods for tax versus internal management decision making, the presence of multiple transfer prices could, in the event of a tax audit, complicate the firm's ability to demonstrate to the taxing authorities the reasonableness of its transfer pricing method. Consequently, firms may find they need to make a conscious choice of where to locate themselves along the continuum between 'sticking to the knitting' and using their financial finesse to optimize profits by minimizing taxes.

Summary

This chapter presented the need to consider organizational strategy when setting transfer prices. Three strategic dimensions were explored: the product life cycle; the firm's process technology; and the firm's diversification strategy. The chapter then proceeded to connect these three strategic dimensions with preferred transfer pricing methods. A tree diagram was constructed to illustrate the connections between the strategic characteristics and specific transfer pricing methods. The final section of the chapter explored the implications of the strategic transfer pricing model for practising managers.

References

Adler, R. (1996). Transfer Pricing for World-Class Manufacturing. *Long Range Planning*, **29**(1), 69–75.

Catts-Baril, W., Gatti J. and Grinnell, D. (1988). Transfer Pricing in a Dynamic Environment. *Management Accounting*, **69**, 30–33.

Eccles, R. (1983). Control with Fairness in Transfer Pricing. *Harvard Business Review*, **61**, 111–123.

Lawrence, P. and Lorsch, J. (1967). *Organization and Environment*, Homewood, IL: Irwin.

Shih, M. (1996). Optimal Transfer Pricing Method and Fixed Cost Allocation. *Abacus*, **32**(2), 178–195.

Spicer, B. (1988). Toward an Organizational Theory of the Transfer Pricing Process. *Accounting, Organizations and Society*, **13**(3), 303–322.

Spiller, E. (1988). Return on Investment: A Need for Special Purpose Information. *Accounting Horizons*, June, 1–9.

Tang, R. (1992). Transfer pricing in the 1990s. *Management Accounting*, **73**(8), 22–26.

Watson, D. and Baumler, J. (1975). Transfer Pricing: A Behavioral Context. *The Accounting Review*, **40**(3), 466–474.

Welch, J. and Nayak, R. (1992). Strategic Sourcing: A Progressive Approach to the Make-or-Buy Decision. *Academy of Management Executive*, 23–31.

13

A destiny for management accounting

Chapter objectives

■ Identify and discuss important evolutionary landmarks in the development of management accounting.

■ Present a blueprint for enhancing the role of the management accountant.

During the past decade, various accountants have philosophized on the past and future direction of management accounting. As one example, Robert Elliot sees today's unfolding revolution in information technology as fundamentally changing the way businesses operate. These changed operations are in turn having a flow-through effect on the type of accounting information that senior managers require to effectively run their businesses. Far from being trivial in nature, these accounting changes will be significant and sweeping. The changes that have occurred to date are but a minor harbinger of what is yet to come. When this revolution in accounting information is through running its course, says Elliot, it will be every bit as major and far-reaching as the changes that accompanied society's movement from the agricultural to the industrial era.

Elliot's ideas harmonize well with the thesis of this book. In particular, it is mutually agreed that the transition from mass producers to lean producers, from local market competition to global market competition, from manufacturing assembly lines to information superhighways, and from an emphasis on leveraging plant and equipment to an emphasis on leveraging intellectual capital will require substantially changed accounting systems. One of the changes that is likely to occur (and some would argue has already begun occurring) is a shift in accounting's focus 'from tangibles to intangibles, from products to customers, from events to real-time dials on the processes, and from mapping the hierarchy to enabling the network' (Elliot, 1991).

An important item that is missing from Elliot's argument, however, is a description of how the role of the management accountant has been steadily evolving *throughout* time. An identification of these smaller, but still significant, evolutionary landmarks is helpful in two ways. First, the reader is in a better position to judge the extent and direction of change that has occurred to date. Second, the reader is better able to appreciate the magnitude of the task that lies ahead.

This chapter provides a richer discussion of the context behind the mandate for changing the role of management accounting than is commonly offered. Following this initial discussion, the chapter proceeds to offer a set of prescriptions for management accounting change. These prescriptions are tied into the major themes of this book.

The evolving nature of management accounting

In early times the role of the accountant was similar to an historian. As D.R. Scott, Thomas Johnson, and Robert Kaplan have all noted, early accountants were primarily responsible for cataloguing historical events (e.g. the return of a Venetian ship from India) into Fra Pacioli's double entry accounting system. Many of today's run-of-the-mill management accounting activities, such as standard costing and interim reporting, were unknown. The accountant's historian role persisted until the early 1800s.

The advent of the Industrial Revolution, with the accompanying paradigmatic shifts in the production and distribution of goods, ushered in a new set of roles and responsibilities for the accounting function. The substantially larger organizations that began appearing in the early nineteenth century (e.g. railroads and textile mills) presented management with a novel set of administrative complexities and challenges. To help senior management plan, co-ordinate, and report on the activities of these large manufacturing firms, the accountant's role changed; he/she progressed from being purely an historian to being a combination of an historian and budgeteer. The accountant of the nineteenth century was very successful at devising highly comprehensive and sophisticated budgeting systems, the main purpose of which was the promotion of efficient operations.

During the mid to late nineteenth century accounting underwent another major shift. Although the large US railroads' development of a performance measure based on the cost per rail-mile travelled may have triggered this evolution, it was Andrew Carnegie's steel company that solidified the change in accounting's role. In particular, the accountants added to their role of historian and budgeteer a third perspective, that of coster. A good example of the accountant's new role is provided by Alfred Chandler's (1977) discussion of Carnegie's cost system in which:

> . . . department[s] listed the amount and cost of materials and labor used on each order as it passed through a subunit. Such information [was used to prepare] monthly statements and, in time, even the daily ones providing data on the costs of ore, limestone, coal, coke, pig iron (when it was not produced at the plant), spiegel, molds, refractories, repairs, fuel, and labor for each ton of rails produced.

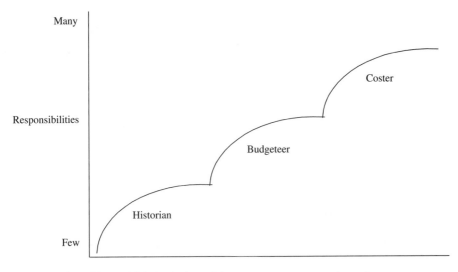

Figure 13.1 Evolution of the management accounting role

Table 13.1 Management accounting responsibilities and evolutionary stages

| | Distinctive competence | | |
Evolutionary stage	Complying with statutory requirements	Promoting efficient operations	Exploiting market opportunities
Historian	Dominant	Non-existent	Non-existent
Budgeteer	Assumed	Dominant	Non-existent
Coster	Assumed	Assumed	Dominant

Not only do many the features of Carnegie's cost system prevail today, but the accounting mindset and approach it nurtures remains dominant. Even the recent activity-based costing (ABC) contribution of Robin Cooper and Robert Kaplan can be argued to represent an extension of this 'coster' approach. For as we have seen, ABC, especially when combined with Mike Walker's activity-based costing attributes (ABCII) system, is a particularly powerful tool for understanding how product lines, as well as unique product features, can be best promoted to enhance contribution margins and produce competitively priced products and services.

Figure 13.1 illustrates the evolution in management accounting's role. Meanwhile, Table 13.1 highlights the set of activities and responsibilities that has accompanied these various roles. When viewing Table 13.1, note that the role assumed by the management accountant has grown with each successive evolutionary wave. The management accountant continues doing what he/she did in the past, as well as takes on a further set of duties as mandated by the latest evolution.

Where to from here?

The majority of management accountants have yet to advance beyond the triad of historical, budgeting, and costing functions. Such a state of affairs retards the organization's progression to a world class enterprise and jeopardizes its survival. The management accountant must break away from what has hitherto been a largely historically based, internally focused approach to accounting information.

It is surprisingly all too common for management accountants to assume a reactive, and even at times passive organizational role. Of course, with each passing day, the non-sustainability of such an approach is becoming increasingly evident. The marketplace is characterized by intensifying competition. All organizational activities are coming under closer scrutiny and being held to a stricter level of accountability. The mantra of value added and non-value added is being heard again and again. It is long overdue that management accountants shed their old habits and, like their other organizational brethren, start assisting the organization with its twin goals of waste elimination and continuous improvement. John Escover (1994) captures the essence of this imperative when he says:

> Worth (value) to the organization is measured in two ways: the ability to provide services that enhance the value-added process, and the ability of a group to justify its existence. As long as justification is allowed, organizations will struggle to survive.

While the need for management accounting change may be obvious, the path to take forward has engendered considerable debate. Some writers suggest that management accounting must become more firmly linked to the organization's strategy (Hiromoto, 1991; Shank, 1989). Meanwhile, other writers advocate redesigning the organization's structure and making greater use of teams. Included in this latter approach is Al Pipkin's conception of the '21st Century Controller' as the 'chief business intelligence officer', who supplies information to the 'President's Strategy Circle', and Robert Elliot's (1991) suggestion that organizations tear down their traditional 'stovepiped' functional groupings and create structures that focus on product/service offerings.

A careful listening to the respective arguments on each side of the debate reveals that the best way forward is not the result of choosing one of the alternatives, but a hybrid approach that embraces the two alternatives and combines them into one. In other words, management accountants need to change both what they do and the manner in which they do it. In particular, they must strike out on a new path and seek to establish themselves as the information linchpin of market-focused, forward-looking data that promises *both* feedback and feedforward control.

In trying to help management accountants improve what they do, this book has promoted the use of a number of advanced management accounting techniques. These techniques were divided into three major groupings: advanced costing methods, advanced performance measures, and strategy-interfaced accounting approaches. It is important that today's management accountant learns about and starts earnestly adopting these techniques. Each technique has some benefit to offer the organization. Additionally, due to their complementary nature, when used in combination these techniques provide a beneficial synergy that greatly exceeds what a tabulation of the individual parts might otherwise suggest.

Some readers may believe (and rightfully so) that this book has focused on the identification and description of advanced management accounting techniques. Accordingly these readers may argue that, by virtue of its silence, this book has not offered support for the need to change the structure under which management accountants operate. The answer to this concern is that the adoption of the advanced management accounting techniques described herein will automatically set in motion a revolutionary change to the way in which management accountants conduct and execute their responsibilities. In particular, they will find themselves becoming increasingly integrated into group/team structures that cut a broad swath across the organizational spectrum. Accordingly, the adoption of the advanced management accounting techniques will transform management accountants not only metaphysically (i.e. helping them to become less reactive and more proactive) but also physically (i.e. by requiring them to leave the corporate glass tower and begin assuming an ongoing, facilitative presence on the production floor).

Beyond listing and describing a set of advanced management accounting techniques that can be used to enhance organizational performance, this book also revealed the manner in which these techniques are connected and interrelated with the philosophies of JIT and TQM. In particular, advanced management accounting techniques neatly fall under the umbrella of value-added accounting (VAA). VAA, like JIT and TQM, serves as an energizing organizational philosophy and is committed to continuous improvement and waste elimination. VAA rallies organizational activity around the idea of promoting improvements in the collection, analysis, and communication of relevant and timely management information.

The benefits from adopting the advanced management accounting techniques mentioned in this book can only be earned through hard and persistent work. These benefits do not glide down from the corporate heavens and softly fall into one's lap. Rather than being a matter of 'ask and you shall receive', management accountants will find that these benefits are only available after a long and arduous odyssey of organizational self-discovery.

It is important that we do not lose heart and become dismayed or overwhelmed by the challenges associated with the use of advanced management accounting techniques. Our many years of inaction and neglect have served to impoverish our function and put in jeopardy our organizational future. According to many of our organizational colleagues, we may still be best in class, but only when it comes to producing objectively measured, carefully dissected, and precisely reported information that no one wants or uses. Other critics accuse us of being past our 'use by date'.

Like the traveller in Robert Frost's poem 'The Road Not Taken', today's management accountant seems to be at an important junction. Hopefully, like the traveller in Frost's poem, tomorrow's management accountant will be able to say:

Two roads diverged in a wood, and I,
I took the one less traveled by,
And that has made all the difference.

References

Adler, R and Everett, A. (1996). On the Existence of Accounting Strategies and Their Links to Manufacturing and Competitive Strategy. *Proceedings of the Decision Sciences Institute's Annual Meeting*, **1**, 133–135.

Chandler, A. (1977). *The Visible Hand: The Managerial Revolution in American Business.* Cambridge, MA: Harvard University Press.

Cooper, R. and Kaplan, R. (1991). Profit Priorities from Activity-Based Costing. *Harvard Business Review*, **69**(3), 130–137.

Elliot, R. (1991). The Third Wave Breaks on the Shores of Accounting. *Accounting Horizons*, **6**(2), 61–85.

Escover, J. (1994). Focus: Value. *Business Horizons*, July–August, 47–50.

Hiromoto, T. (1991). Restoring the Relevance of Management Accounting. *Journal of Management Accounting Research*, **3**(3), 1–15.

Johnson, T. and Kaplan, R. (1987). *Relevance Lost*, Cambridge, MA: Harvard Business School Press.

Pipkin, A. (1989). The 21st Century Controller. *Management Accounting*, February, 21–25.

Sakurai, M. (1996). *Integrated Cost Management: A Company-Wide Prescription for Higher Profits and Lower Costs*, Portland, OR: Productivity Press.

Scott, D. (1931). *The Cultural Significance of Accounts*. New York: Henry Holt.

Shank, J. (1989). Strategic Cost Management: New Wine, Or Just New Bottles? *Journal of Management Accounting Research*, **1**, 47–65.

Walker, M. (1991). ABC Using Product Attributes. *Management Accounting*, October, 34–35.

List of abbreviations

AAA	Advanced Accounting Approaches
ABC	Activity-Based Costing
ABM	Activity-Based Management
AHP	Analytical Hierarchy Process
AMT	Advanced Manufacturing Technology
ARR	Accounting Rate of Return
BCG	Boston Consulting Group
BSC	Balanced Scorecard
CAD	Computer-Aided Design
CAM	Computer-Aided Manufacturing
CIM	Computer Integrated Manufacturing
CNC	Computer Numerically Controlled
COQ	Cost of Quality
DCF	Discounted Cash Flow
ECLA	Economic Conformance Level Approach
EVA	Economic Value Added
FMS	Flexible Manufacturing Systems
JIT	Just-in-Time
MADM	Multiattribute Decision Model
MRP	Material Requisition Planning
MRPII	Manufacturing Resources Planning
MVA	Market Value Added
PDCA	Plan, Do, Check, Action
QFD	Quality Function Deployment
QLF	Quality Loss Function
SBU	Strategic Business Unit
SCM	Strategic Cost Management
SPC	Statistical Process Control
SVA	Shareholder Value Analysis
RI	Residual Income
ROA	Return on Assets

ROI	Return on Investment
TC	Target Costing
TQM	Total Quality Management
VAA	Value Added Accounting
WCO	World Class Organization

Glossary

Activity-based costing (ABC) A two-stage costing process that first traces costs to business activities and second assigns these business activity costs to products/services. ABC is meant to overcome the many problems associated with traditional costing systems, which primarily cost products/services using volume-based drivers.

Advanced accounting approaches (AAA) A set of business practices and methods that is intended to support an organization's value-added accounting philosophy. AAA comprises advanced costing methods, advanced performance measures, and strategy interfaced accounting.

Advanced manufacturing technology AMT involves the use of electronically programmed machines, which are often linked in a network and controlled by a host computer. The goal of AMT is to enhance both quality and flexibility. The successful implementation of AMT can serve to bridge the divide between marketing, which wants to offer unlimited product diversity, and production, which wants to minimize diversity in order to maximize production efficiency.

Balanced scorecard A strategically driven performance measurement system that consists of financial, customer, internal business, and innovation and learning measures. Ideally it is used to enlighten and focus decision making on the relatively few, but highly significant, critical performance indicators that influence current and future success.

Benchmarking A process involving the comparison of a company's performance in key success areas with the world's best companies. The comparisons are used to highlight company performance deficiencies and often lead to changes in process, technology, and work practices as a way to bridge the performance gap and improve organizational competitiveness.

Competitive position monitoring   The process of collecting information about competitors' sales, market share, volume, unit costs, and return on sales for the purpose of gleaning insight into their enacted strategies.

Competitor cost analysis   An attempt to analyse competitors' cost structures. The ultimate goal is to estimate competitors' unit costs.

Competitor financial statement performance appraisal   A type of competitive position monitoring that involves the analysis of a competitor's published financial statements.

Cost of capital   The return that a company must earn on its total capital in order to pay interest on its debt obligations and provide an acceptable return to its shareholders.

Cost of quality reporting system   Provides the organization with information about its prevention, appraisal, and failure costs. This information helps employees to prioritize quality problems and may offer clues about how such problems can be overcome.

Cost modelling   A technique for analysing product costs, generally involving the use of computer simulation. This technique forms an integral part of target cost management.

Cross skilling   This training concept stands in sharp contrast to specialization. Cross skilling promotes and actively encourages employees to master multiple task proficiencies. Cross skilling helps the organization achieve more balanced and smoothly running production systems.

Demand forecasting   The process of anticipating customer requirements to ensure that there will be sufficient, but not excessive, quantities of inventory on hand to provide a smooth and uninterrupted flow to and through the production process.

Economic value added (EVA)   A measure of corporate performance that links strategic management (the deployment of capital) with the financial markets (the provision of capital). It is computed as the difference between an operating unit's profit and an imputed interest charge.

Employee empowerment   The process of supplying employees with autonomy over how they structure, organize, and execute their work. Certain supporting mechanisms are required to successfully implement programmes of employee empowerment, including quality circles, cross skilling, and process-complete departments.

Fishbone chart   A visual aid that is used to help identify, explore, and display the possible causes of a problem. This technique is also sometimes referred to as a cause and effect diagram.

Flexible manufacturing systems   A general approach for enhancing the ability of an organization to respond to varying customer requirements by using machinery that is capable of producing a variety of models of a good or service, with quick changeover time and low changeover cost.

Genka kaizen   A set of organizational processes that seeks to produce continuous cost improvement during the life of a product's production. Some of the organizational practices include quality circles, employee empowerment, and downward ratcheting cost standards.

Genka kikaku   A set of organizational processes that is directed at managing the costs of products and services during their design. Some of the processes include cost modelling, value engineering, and cost driver analysis.

Just-in-time (JIT)   A philosophical business orientation with a twin objective of continuous improvement and waste elimination. JIT seeks to achieve this twin objective through a series of production and inventory control initiatives. JIT was designed and perfected at Toyota by Taiichi Ohno.

Kaizen   The Japanese word for improvement. It is synonymous with the concept of continuous quality improvement.

Kanban   A communication tool in the just-in-time production and inventory control system. A kanban is a card system that regulates the flow of inventory through the production system. There are two main types of kanbans: production-ordering kanbans and withdrawal kanbans. The kanban system was developed at Toyota by Taiichi Ohno and is a good example of what the Japanese call visible management.

Manufacturing resources planning (MRPII)   A manufacturing control system whose purpose is to ensure that the necessary materials, labour, and equipment are available in the needed amounts and at the prescribed times so as to properly execute production tasks. MRPII typically involves the use of complex computer software to track component lists (commonly termed 'bill of materials') and calculate the necessary quantities and duration lengths of necessary resources.

Market value added (MVA)   A measure of the value a company has created in excess of its committed resources. In theory, it should equal the net present value of all past and present capital investment projects.

Pareto analysis   A technique for helping managers to zero in on business problems. The '80–20' rule that embodies Pareto analysis suggests that 80 per cent of an organization's outcomes are attributable to 20 per cent of its actions.

Performance pyramid   A performance measurement framework that includes linkages between firm strategy and operations. In particular, the firm's strategy is translated down the organizational hierarchy – ultimately to the very work centres themselves – in the form of strategic objectives. Meanwhile measures of the performance achieved filter back up the organization and serve as the basis for senior management's fine-tuning of either the presentation or substance of strategic objectives.

Process-complete departments   Reorganizing and empowering departments so that they are capable of performing all the cross-functional steps or tasks required to meet customer needs. Under this approach, employees come to see customer problems not from a truncated functional perspective, but instead in their natural and holistic form.

Quality assurance   The process of ensuring the delivery of satisfactory, reliable, and cost-effective products/services.

Quality circles   A small group of employees, often representing a diverse cross-section of functional areas, committed to the goal of discovering ways to improve organizational activities.

Quality monitoring   The process of formulating quality targets and assessing the organization's achievement of these targets. Quality monitoring is supported through the use of statistical process control, Pareto analysis, and fishbone charts.

Queuing theory   A production technique that seeks to minimize waiting times by ensuring an equilibrium between arrivals (be they customers, product, or processes) and servers (be they human or mechanical).

Statistical process control (SPC)   A statistical technique that offers early warning signals about the potential for a quality control problem. SPC was developed by W.E. Deming.

Strategic cost management   A relatively new field of management accounting that integrates management accounting and strategic management. Its use involves the collection of cost information both internal and external to the organization, especially as it pertains to Porter's five-competitive forces model, for the purpose of fine-tuning and, when necessary, evolving the organization's strategy.

Strategic pricing   The formulation of product and service prices based on an analysis of such strategic factors as competitor price reaction, price elasticity, market growth, economies of scale, and experience.

Target cost management   The systematic process of planning product and service offerings, determining their sales prices, establishing highly challenging target costs, and motivating employees to be ever vigilant for opportunities that can lead to cost reductions.

Total quality management (TQM)   A philosophical business orientation with a twin objective of continuous improvement and waste elimination. TQM comprises a set of business activities that seeks to create an organizational culture encouraging pride in one's work and an urgency to continuously improve upon the set of product/service attributes a customer receives.

Value-added accounting (VAA)   A philosophical, information-based business orientation with a twin objective of continuous improvement and waste elimination. VAA involves the production of operational and strategic information that aids senior manager decision making and provides the information infrastructure to support an organization's implementation of JIT and TQM.

Value engineering   A systematic, interfunctional process involving the examination of factors that affect the cost of a product. The goal of value engineering is to achieve the established product standards for quality, functionality, and target cost.

Vendor certification   The process of ensuring that suppliers meet stringent requirements for delivery reliability and product reliability. Suppliers who can meet the highly demanding requirements set out for the supply of products are awarded exclusive supplying rights. As a result, vendor certification leads to the development of long-term and trusting bonds with a single or very limited number of suppliers.

Vendor proximity   A feature of just-in-time that advocates the nearness of suppliers. This physical closeness facilitates the frequent deliveries required under just-in-time.

Visible management   A business practice that seeks to provide workers with clearly visible cues that will help to enhance productivity and quality. The kanban system is an example of visible management.

Name index

Abernathy, J., 83, 96, 148, 160
Adler, R., 26, 95, 96, 173, 180
Albright, T., 55, 61
Altany, D., 122
Anthony, R., 163
Atkinson, A., 96, 163
Austin, W., 45

Baumler, J., 166, 174
Berliner, C., 157, 160
Bhimani, A., 37, 45
Bogaert, I., 161
Bolwijn, P., 15, 47
Boone, W., 30
Brignall, T., 107, 111
Brimson, J., 157, 160
Bromwich, M., 17
Bruggeman, W., 160
Bruns, W., 111

Camp, R., 113, 114, 116, 122, 127
Carnegie, A., 176, 177
Carr, C., 148, 152, 160
Carr, L., 61
Catts-Baril, W., 173
Chan, Y., 110
Chandler, A., 180
Chew, W., 63, 77
Chrysler, W., 116
Clausing, D., 61
Cooper, R., 63, 71, 72, 73, 74, 76, 77, 177, 180
Cooray, S., 77

Crosby, P., 3, 13, 48, 49, 51, 53, 54, 55, 60, 61
Cross, K., 101, 107, 108, 109, 111
Cucuzza, T., 45
Currie, W., 160

Daniel, S., 55
Dean, J., 14, 15
Deming, W., 3, 13, 24, 44, 48, 49, 50, 51, 53, 54, 55, 58, 60, 61, 186
Dimonte, R., 40
Dixon, J., 111, 132
Dixon, R., 144
Drucker, P., 45, 102, 111, 135, 144, 150, 160
Dugdale, D., 160
DuPont, P., 100
Durnick, E., 161

Eccles, R., 165, 173
Elliot, R., 175, 180
Elsayed, E., 61
Erlang, 22
Escover, J., xii, 178, 180
Everett, A., 26, 54, 180

Feigenbaum, A., 47, 48, 61
Fitzgerald, L., 111
Flood, R., 15
Flynn, B., 15
Foster, G., 30
Frost, R., xii, 179
Fukuda, J., 77

Garvin, D., 148, 160
Gatti J., 173
Gibb, J., 116, 127
Goldberg, S., 152
Gooselin, M., 45
Govindarajan, V., 25, 133, 144, 153
Grinnell, D., 173
Grundy, T., 132, 144
Gupta, A., 144
Gurd, B., 111

Haley, G., 152, 153
Hall, R., 61, 102, 103, 104
Hayes, R., 83, 96, 148, 160
Hiromoto, T., 178, 180
Hsiang, T., 61

Innes, J., 45
Ishikawa, K., 48, 61
Ito, Y., 55, 61
Iwabuchi, Y., 77

Jaikumar, R., 83, 96
Johnson, T., 132, 144, 176, 180
Johnston, R., 111
Jones, T., 152, 160
Juran, J., 3, 13, 47, 48, 49, 50, 51, 53, 54,
    55, 59, 60, 61

Kaplan, R., 4, 13, 25, 34, 45, 101, 105,
    106, 107, 108, 110, 111, 132, 144,
    151, 153, 154, 163, 173, 176, 177,
    180
Kato, Y., 73, 77
Keen, P., xi, 16
Khandwalla, P., 44
Knapp, E., xi, 16
Kumpe, T., 15, 47

Laveren, E., 161
Laverty, K., 4
Lawrence, P., 165, 166, 173
Lee, B., 152, 160
Lemak, D., 45
Locke, E., 118
Lorsch, J., 165, 166, 173
Lynch, R., 101, 107, 108, 109, 111
Lynn, B., 15, 110, 111

McClelland, L., 95, 96
McNair, C., 99, 111
Macneil, J., 127
Malmi, T., 45
Martens, R., 161
Mosconi, W., 99
Miles, L., 64
Miller, J., 8, 34
Mills, R., 95, 96, 97
Mitchell, F., 45
Monden, Y., 77
Montgomery, J., 45

Nanni, J., 111
Nayak, R., 163, 164, 165, 174
Ness, J., 45
Nishimura, A., 77
Norkiewicz, A., 37, 45
Norman, R., 133
Norton, D., 101, 105, 106

Ohinata, Y., 127
Ohno, T., 185
Okano, H., 77

Pacioli, F., 176
Pare, T., 97
Partovi, F., 123, 127
Peters, T., 99, 111
Pickering, M., 40
Pigott, D., 45
Pipkin, A., 180
Porter, M., 42, 139, 140, 144
Print, C., 95, 97
Pryor, L., 122

Ramasesh, R., 154
Ramirez, R., 133
Rappaport, A., 95, 96, 97
Reed, R., 45
Reitsperger, W., 55
Riley, D., 140, 144
Rimmer, M., 127
Roth, H., 61
Rutledge, J., 97

Saaty, T., 127, 161
Sakakibara, S., 15

Sakurai, M., 180
Schiederjans, M., 15
Schildbach, T., 45
Schonberger, R., 9, 15
Schroeder, R., 15
Scott, D., 90, 176, 180
Shank, J., 25, 55, 61, 134, 135, 136, 144,
    147, 148, 153, 154, 161, 178, 180
Sheridan, T., 134
Shewart, W., 50
Shih, M., 173
Shimizu, N., 77
Shingo, S., 53, 61
Silvestro, R., 111
Simmonds, K., 151, 161
Simmons, R., 113, 114, 120, 128
Simons, R., 4
Slagmulder, R., 160, 161
Sloan, A., 61, 100
Smith, D., 132, 144
Snell, S., 14, 15
Solomons, D., 97, 163
Southwick, A., 111
Spendolini, M., 116, 122, 128
Spicer, B., 164, 173

Spiller, E., 172, 173
Stern, J., 89, 95, 96, 97
Stewart, G., 96, 97, 104
Stewart, T., 100, 111
Sweeney, M., 116

Taguchi, G., 48, 49, 51, 52, 53, 54, 55, 60,
    61, 70
Tani, T., 66, 77
Testi, J., 127
Thorne, H., 111
Tomkins, C., 148, 152, 160, 161
Tully, S., 97

Van Cauwenbergh, A., 161
Vollman, T., 111

Walker, M., 3, 41, 44, 45, 180
Watson, D., 166, 174
Weinstein, W., 97
Welch, J., 163, 164, 165, 174
Wilson, R., 144

Yoshikawa, T., 71, 77

Company index

3M, 48

Airways Corporation, 90, 106
Alcoa, 113, 121, 122
American Express, 126
American Hospital Supply, 126
Apple Computers, 106
AT&T, 90, 113, 121, 126
Australian Centre for Best Practices, 116

Bank of Montreal, 106
Bell Labs, 50
Benchmarking Centre, 116
Benchmarking Competency Centre, 116
BHP, 116
Bic, 7
Bluebird Foods, 113, 114
Briggs & Stratton, 90

Carmike Cinemas, 139
Chrysler Motors, 116
CIGNA Corporation, 106
Coca-Cola, 90
Continental Airlines, 138
Corning, 113
Credit Suisse, 12
Cummins Engine, 68, 126

Daihatsu, 68
Deere and Company, 126
Dover Corporation, 12
Du Pont, 113

Eastman Kodak, 113
Ericsson Australia Limited, 106

Fay, Richwhite & Co., 90
Fletcher Challenge, 90
Florida Power and Light, 126
Ford Motor Company, 126
Fuji-Xerox, 126

General Electric, 64, 146, 153
General Motors, 64, 113, 153
GTE, 113

Harley-Davidson, 7, 12
Hershey Foods, 126
Hewlett-Packard, 12, 126
Honda, 57, 58

IBM, 16, 47
ICI Australia, 106
IKEA, 7, 8, 133, 136, 137, 139
International Benchmarking Clearinghouse, 116
International Organization for Standardization, 56

Jiffy Lube International, 139

Komatsu, 126
Kreigsmann Research, 113

L. L. Bean Inc., 126

McDonalds, 12
Mary Kay Cosmetics, 125
Mazda, 51
Milliken, 113, 126
Motorola, 7, 113

National Association of Accountants, 150
NCR, 90
New Zealand Dairy Industry, 90
New Zealand Post, 106
NYNEX, 113

Olympus, 68, 70
Ormon, 47

Penfold Wineries, 110
Procter and Gamble, 126

Quaker Oats, 90

RCA, 153
Rockwater, 106

Sanford, 90
Schrader Bellows, 40

Scott Paper, 90
Scoville Industries, 30
Skandia Assurance and Financial Services,
    104
Skellerup Group, 90

Telecom New Zealand, 106, 116
Texas Instruments, 126, 140
Toyota, 48, 64, 75, 77, 116, 126,
    185
Trans Power, 90
TransAmerica, 90

US Department of Defence, 47, 48

Vanguard, 7, 8

Western Electric, 47, 48
Westinghouse, 153
Whirlpool, 90
Wrightson, 90

Xerox, 12, 48, 113, 121, 126

Yamazaki Machinery Company, 146

Subject index

Activity-based costing, 3, 25, 29–45, 118, 127, 134, 177, 180, 181, 183
  activity overhead rates, 39
  appropriate conditions, 42–3
  arguments against its use, 43–4
  cost drivers, 36, 38, 45
  cost level analysis, 35–7
  cost pools, 38
  defined, 37
  steps to implementation, 37–9
Advanced accounting approaches, 21, 25, 150, 181, 183
Advanced costing methods, 3, 25, 178
Advanced manufacturing technology, 7, 14, 15, 20, 23, 146, 160, 181, 183
Advanced performance measures, 25, 178, 183
Analytical hierarchy method, 153, 154, 157, 160
Analytical hierarchy process, 123, 157, 181
Autonomous work groups, 24

Balanced scorecard, 25, 101, 105–7, 108, 173, 181, 183
Baldrige Award, *see* Malcolm Baldrige National Award for Quality
Benchmarking, 3, 112–28, 183
  defined, 114
  internal versus external, 123
  limitations, 125–7
  management, 119
  operational, 119
  performance gap, 114–15

  process, 119
  product, 118
  stages of, 121–6
  strategic, 119
Best in Class, 48, 114, 117, 118, 123, 127, 179
Boston Consulting Group, 67, 181
Business risk, 84–5
  determination of, 84–5
  financing approach, 84
  operating approach, 84

Cause and effect diagrams, 25, 185
Competitive advantage analysis, 135, 137, 143, 154
Competitor surveillance, 125
Computer aided design, 23, 146, 149, 181
Computer aided manufacturing, 23, 149, 181
Computer numerical control, 14, 23, 63, 147, 181
Concurrent engineering, 70, *see also* Simultaneous engineering
Continuous improvement programmes, 10
Co-productive activities, 137
Core competencies, 33, 102
Cost commitment, 65, 69
Cost decompositions, 71, 72
Cost driver analysis, 4, 71, 135, 139–41, 143, 154, 185
Cost drivers, 31–8, 45, 71, 72, 134, 139–40, 141, 183
  activity-based, 36, 38, 45
  executional, 71, 134, 140

structural, 134, 140
volume-based, 31–7, 134, 139–40,
    183
Cost modelling, 25, 71, 72, 184, 185
Cost of capital, 83, 84–5, 86, 87, 88, 89,
    90, 91, 94, 96, 151, 184
    defined, 84–5, 184
    financing approach, 84
    operating approach, 84
Cost of quality, 3, 25, 46–61, 63, 68, 71,
    72, 75, 76, 100, 134, 140, 141, 165,
    181
    approaches, 49–54
    categorization of costs, 55–7
    defined, 55
    historical roots, 47–58
    quality loss function, 52, 181
    reporting systems, 56–60, 184
    robust designs, 56–60
Cost reduction, 63, 65, 68, 71, 72, 75, 76,
    100, 140, 141, 165, 187, see also
    Genka kaizen
Cross skilling, 23, 24, 184

Dantotsu, 116, see also Benchmarking
Delphi, 110, 157
Demand forecasting, 20, 184
Design for manufacturability, 70
Diversification strategy, 164, 165–6, 167,
    169 170, 171, 173
DuPont formula, 82

Economic conformance level approach, 50,
    59, 60, 181
Economic value added, xii, 3, 25, 81, 82,
    89–96, 181, 184
Employee empowerment, 10, 14, 23–4, 63,
    107, 184, 185
Expanded financial analysis method,
    153–4, 160, see also Strategic
    investment analysis

Financial accounting, 1, 2, 32, 74, 93
Financial performance measures, 3, 81–97,
    98, 99, 100, 101, 102, 106, 107, 139
    economic value added, xii, 3, 25, 81, 82,
    89–96, 181, 184
    residual income, 83–6, 94–6

return on investment, 82–3, 94–6
    shareholder value added, 82, 86–9, 94–6
Fishbone charts, 21, 25, 185, 186
Flexible manufacturing systems, 14, 23,
    160, 181, 185
Function decompositions, 71, 72

Genka kaizen, 3, 62, 66, 75, 76, 140, 185
Genka kikaku, 3, 76, 140, 185

Industrial Revolution, 176
Information Revolution, 2, 17
Intellectual capital, 18, 100, 104, 175
International Labour Organization, 18
International Organization for
    Standardization, 56

Just in time, xi, xii, 7, 9, 10–13, 14, 15,
    16, 17, 19, 20, 21, 22, 23, 26, 44, 65,
    133, 179, 181, 185

Kaizen, 75, 185
Kanban, 15, 22, 63, 187
Knowledge workers, 17
Kousuu management, 71

Lean organizations, 4, 64, 76
Learning organizations, 17, 107
Life cycle costing, 3, 134

Malcolm Baldrige National Award for
    Quality, xi, 16, 103
Manufacturing resources planning, 21, 181,
    185
Market value added, 96, 181, 185
Multiattribute decision model, 153, 154,
    155–7, 160, 181

Non-financial performance measures,
    98–111, 139
    balanced scorecard, 105–7
    Drucker's views, 102
    Hall's four dimensions, 102–4
    performance pyramid, 107–9

Obsolete cost systems, 32–3
Opportunity cost, 83, 85, 104, 147, 150,
    159, 160, 167, 169, 170

Pareto analysis, 14, 24, 186
Pareto efficiency, 135, 143
Performance measures, 3, 25, 30,
    81–97, 98–111, 113, 172, 178,
    see also Financial performance
    measures; Non-financial performance
    measures
Performance pyramid, 101, 107–9, 186
Poka-yoke, 53, 61
Process complete departments, 23, 24, 184,
    186
Product costing, 30, 31–2, 33, 35, 36, 38,
    132
  cost allocation bases, 30, 31–2
  creating cost pools, 31, 35, 38
  penetrating beyond gross margin
    analysis, 30, 32
  use of IT, 31
Product life cycle, 67, 120, 134, 164, 165,
    168, 173
Product planning, 41, 56, 58, 64, 65, 66–8,
    69, 70, 120

Quadratic loss function, 60, 181, *see also*
    Cost of quality
Quality circles, 14, 23, 24, 184, 185, 186
Quality function deployment, 70, 181
Quality loss function, 52, 54, 60, 181
Quality monitoring, 20, 24, 186
Queuing theory, 22

Research and development method, 153,
    154, 158, 160
Residual income, 3, 81, 83–6, 94–6, 149,
    181
Resource grid, 137–8
Return on assets, 93, 181
Return on investment, 3, 81, 82–3, 94–6,
    149, 151, 173, 182
Reverse engineering, 116, 118

Sales margin ratio, 82
Shareholder value analysis, 3, 25, 81, 82,
    86–9, 94–6, 181
  free cash flows, 87
  value drivers, 86–7
Shusa, 69, 74
Simultaneous engineering, 70, 71

Standard costs, 75, 139
Statistical process control, 14, 15, 20, 24,
    50, 54, 181, 186
Strategic business unit, 47, 120, 141, 142,
    181
  Arthur D. Little approach, 141
Strategic cost management, 131–44, 153,
    154–5, 160, 161, 180, 181, 186
  competitive advantage analysis, 4, 135,
    137–9, 143, 154
  cost driver analysis, 4, 135, 139–41,
    143, 154
  defined, 186
  value chain analysis, 4, 135–7, 143, 154
Strategic investment analysis, 145–61
  analytical hierarchy method, 153–4, 160
  defined, 146
  expanded financial analysis method,
    153–4, 160
  multiattribute decision model, 153, 154,
    155–7, 160, 181
  research and development method, 153,
    154, 158, 160
  strategic cost management, 131–44, 153,
    154–5, 160
  traditional financial evaluation
    techniques, 148–53, 160
  uncertainty method, 153, 154, 158–60
  value analysis method, 153, 154, 157,
    160
Strategic management accounting, 144
Strategy interfaced accounting, 25, 176,
    178

Taguchi design method, 70
Target cost management, 62–77, 187
  allowable cost, 69–70, 71, 73–4
  barriers to implementation, 76
  breaching the allowable cost, 73–4
  cost gap, 70
  defined, 63
  five stages of, 66–75
  shusa, 69, 74
Total preventive maintenance, 63
Total quality management, xi, xii, 2, 3, 9,
    10–11, 13–14, 15, 16, 17, 19, 20, 21,
    23, 24, 26, 44, 60, 65, 117, 118, 140,
    170, 179, 182, 187

Transfer pricing, 4, 162–74
  available markets, 166–8
  defined, 163
  diversification strategy considerations,
    165–6
  limited markets, 166–8
  matching with strategy, 164–7
  methods, 168
  process technology considerations, 165
  product life cycle considerations, 164–5
  strategic importance, 163
Turnover ratio, 82

Uncertainty method, 153, 154, 158–60

Value added accounting, 16, 17–19, 20, 21,
    24, 25, 26, 179, 182, 187
  defined, 17–19
Value analysis method, 153, 154, 157, 160
Value chain analysis, 4, 135, 136, 141, 143,
    154
  contrasted with value added approach, 135

Value drivers, 86, 87
Value engineering, 68, 70–1, 72, 74, 185,
    187
  cost reduction databases, 68, 71
  cost tables, 68, 71
  defined, 68, 187
  first look, 70, 72
  function tables, 68, 71
  zero look, 68, 70, 71
Vendor certification, 21, 22, 187
Vendor proximity, 21, 22, 187
Visible management, 187

Weighted average cost of capital, 83, 84,
    85
Worker autonomy, *see* Employee
    empowerment
World class organization, 2, 3, 7–15, 16,
    19, 20, 25, 26, 182

Zero defects, 50, 51, 52, 54